BCCC
a31111000229748n

Beggar to King

Beggar to King

ALL THE OCCUPATIONS OF BIBLICAL TIMES

by Walter Duckat

1968
DOUBLEDAY & COMPANY, INC.
GARDEN CITY, NEW YORK

LIBRARY OF CONGRESS CATALOG CARD NUMBER 67–19112

PRINTED IN THE UNITED STATES OF AMERICA
FIRST EDITION

TO

Esther for her prodigious efforts

AND TO

Gila and Hillel, my major preoccupations

Contents

Introduction

A study of the occupations in the Bible is a fascinating enterprise that I first undertook years ago in preparing an article for *Occupations* (now the *Personnel and Guidance Journal*). I was astounded to learn of the wide range of occupations mentioned or implied in Scriptures. Unfortunately, other activities intervened and prevented me from developing the theme further, so I was pleased at the opportunity to resume my investigation of the subject.

Normally, the Bible is viewed as an inspired religious and literary document that has guided and comforted many generations of Jews and Christians. Its language has influenced such titans of literature as Shakespeare, Milton, Browning, and others. Immortal artists, such as da Vinci, Raphael, Rembrandt, and Blake have illustrated Biblical characters and events. Handel, Bach, and Mendelssohn are among the many who have written music based on Biblical themes. Every jot and tittle of the Bible has been scrutinized by thousands of scholars. Yet, curiously, although the people of the Bible spent most of their waking time in the effort to earn their daily bread, little attention has been given to this aspect.

Understandably, the authors of the Bible were mainly concerned with religious and ethical themes. Consequently, their references to work and occupations were usually brief and incidental. Also, written sources generally describe the lives of members of the upper classes and speak little of the average person. Moreover, there are a number of occupations which undoubtedly existed in Bible times that are not expressly mentioned in the Bible, probably because they were so familiar that the Biblical authors saw no reason for mentioning them. Most of our knowledge of these and other occupations comes from other sources, mainly archaeological findings.

A study of how the people of the Bible and of earlier times spent most of their waking hours, namely, an account of their jobs during the period spanned by the Old and the New Testaments, may be a most illuminating, tridimensional single source of information about them.

In all societies, a man's occupation plays a central role in his life and influences other aspects of his life. The function of occupations in the evolution of civilization is far more significant than is commonly known. As Ann Roe indicates (*Psychology of Occupations,* Preface, p. 6), "the role of the occupation in the life of the individual has much broader psychological importance than has been generally appreciated."

We may define occupations in the Bible as those activities in which persons spent most of their time, whether for economic return or not. A careful analysis of the occupations in the Bible reveals that about two hundred different occupations are either mentioned or implied. Some were several thousand years old before Biblical characters walked the earth. Among these early occupations are farming, wine production (viticulture), pottery, basketry, weaving, wood carving. The oldest and earliest distinct occupations have universally been such occupations as magician, soothsayer, prophet, medicine man, singer, mason, carpenter, and smith (who produced both weapons and jewelry).

Since life cannot be maintained without work, early in the history of mankind, much before Biblical times, a division of labor occurred. Men usually assumed the heaviest and most dangerous tasks, while women pursued domestic chores including child rearing. Other factors that determined occupation were age, skill, geography, family, and caste. Special skills were often handed down secretly within the family, such as the secret formulas of apothecaries who blended incense used in all temples of antiquity. Even musical compositions were zealously guarded and consequently are now lost to us. In more modern times, a number of cheeses are produced by families who have guarded their formulas with great secrecy over many years.

The life of the Hebrews as portrayed in the Bible was comparable to the perhaps-more-familiar medieval village. The unit was a group of farm families, a small community, which grew its own food and produced virtually all of its necessities and even a few comforts. They baked their own bread, produced their own fruit and wine and oil, and made their own clothing and household effects. The men were usually the farmers, while both men and women tended the sheep. The men sheared, washed, and carded the wool. The women ground the meal, baked and cooked, tended the children, and spun and wove clothing. From woolen cloth they made not only clothing but also coverings, carpets, hangings, and draperies. Such homemade products are still common in much of the Near East.

Many of the legislative portions of the Bible implicitly suggest that it is dealing with an agricultural society. The father and his sons, his slaves, and his women performed all the essential chores: plowing, sowing, reaping, feeding and watering the herds, and shearing the sheep. The soil was the primary source of sustenance and wealth. Farming was one of the oldest and most respected of occupations, to which a person usually longed to return if he were forced to abandon it. Biblical man also made and used tools to make tents, to build huts, boats and later to design more commodious homes. Specialists soon began to make furniture, household equipment, earthenware, musical instruments for entertainment, and other luxuries. Embroidery and dyeing were home activities that eventually became specialized crafts whose products were exported to distant lands. Excavations reveal that dyeing was done in wholesale quantities and employed a considerable number of persons.

A sequel to the specialization of labor was that eventually families employed in the same craft formed clans that later grew into guilds. Members of these guilds tended to live in their own districts and to band together for common social, economic, and cultural benefits. There were guilds not only of skilled craftsmen, but also of prophets, seers, and merchants. There are also believed to have existed guilds of potters and perfumers. In the Talmud (Meg. 26a) there is reference to a guild arrangement in the huge basilica synagogue of Alexandria where separate sections were assigned to goldsmiths, silversmiths, workers in bronze, textile workers, and blacksmiths. Each group aided its own poor and unemployed. There was a fraternity or union of butchers that instituted an arrangement whereby each member might have at least one day of work in periods of economic depression. Punishment was meted out to any member of the group who disobeyed this arrangement (Tos. B.M. 11:25). Similar groups existed among bakers.

The Biblical merchant was more commonly a non-Jewish Canaanite, Edomite, Midianite, Syrian of Damascus, Egyptian, or Asiatic Greek. He most commonly hailed from the city of Tyre, the great mart of Biblical times, where surrounding nations, among them the Israelites, gravitated. Compared with other nations of antiquity, the Jews became a merchant people late. They were antedated by the Mesopotamian merchants who as early as 3000 B.C. were businessmen experienced in drawing up contracts and often engaged in litigation. By 2500 B.C. these merchants had formed trading companies and were exporting to foreign countries. Business was well established when the earliest written documents were recorded on clay tablets, placed in clay jars for protection, and filed for reference in office vaults. Many laws regulated a wide range of business transactions and market prices. Rulers became richer by monopolizing certain business activities such as trading in olive oil and grain and exporting and importing luxury items. Many kings were thus heavily engaged in business, letting contracts to the trader. Bars stamped with the guarantee of some temple or its deity served as money prior to the minting of coins. Those who lacked cash could offer promissory notes. Lively business correspondence was carried on between foreign representatives of "dry goods" firms and their home offices in Ashur. They included inquiries about samples of Cappadocian cloth, as well as reminders to take enough food for the donkeys and to provide military protection for the caravan. According to W. F. Albright, recent archaeological and documentary evidence indicates that during the nineteenth and eighteenth centuries B.C., Abraham and his clan were active in leading caravans in Syria and Palestine. These were donkey caravans consisting of as many as six hundred donkeys each.

Virtually all temples in antiquity served not only as places of worship, but as centers of commerce. Several thousands of years before Homer, when Atidum the merchant needed more office space, he agreed to rent a location from Ribatum, priestess of Shamash, for one and one-sixth shekels of silver a year, to pay a certain portion down and the remainder in installments. Priestesses also ran real-estate offices near their temple. Since the gods were believed to offer safety, those who came from far and near brought gold, silver, and other products to trade. They deposited their gold and other valuables at these ancient temples where careful records of their accounts were kept by the priests. Money changing and loans also occurred at these temples. Priests served both as caretakers and judges when disputes broke out. The Babylonian Shamash was one of the market gods. Among the Hebrews, too, priests served as judges when adjudication of disputes became necessary. The Jerusalem temple was also a financial center.

These ancient temples, which usually served as state treasuries, were raided to pay tribute or were filled with captured booty. If a monarch neglected the temple, its revenue would decline and the temple would sink into disrepair (2 Ki. 12:4–15). Solomon's Temple suffered the fate of being raided by Shishak of Egypt during the reign of Rehoboam (1 Ki. 14:26). Some kings, such as Hezekiah, who had beautified the Temple (2 Ki. 18:15), appropriated funds from its treasury to win allies (1 Ki. 15:18) or to pay tribute to pay off invaders (2 Ki. 16:8).

In later Biblical times the fashion center of the world was Alexandria. She proudly set the tastes of the times, both determining the styles as well as selling the luxury goods of the period. From her garment center, usually run by Jews, came embroidered robes of Chinese silk and other luxury items.

There is scarcely a phase of business that is not adumbrated in the Bible: finance, accounting, banking, agriculture, mining, export and import, inflation, exploitation, price gouging, dishonest merchandising. The Bible's emphasis on honest weights and measures indicates that dishonest merchants troubled the Biblical man as they do our present society.

Other contemporary subjects mentioned or implied in the Bible are alcoholism, apprenticeships, police service, contracting, labor recruiting, attitudes toward the disabled person and toward the older worker. The status of the housewife sheds interesting light on the role of women in the economy of the Bible. (The attitudes of the people of the Bible toward these various groups of workers, as well as the general socio-economic aspects of work and labor in ancient Israel, are dealt with in some detail in the four Appendixes on Commerce and Trade, Finances, Attitudes toward the Worker, and Labor Organization that conclude this book. It is hoped that the reader will study these for general background information applying to all, or at least most, of the specific job descriptions that are in the core of this book.)

Many curiosa are uncovered in the occupations of the barber and of the beauty practitioners as well as of musicians. Those interested in the evolution of the military and of the merchant marine will find interesting historical material. The evolution of teachers and the seemingly perennial role of prostitutes are among many other aspects of occupations treated.

The predecessors of our professional workers are also mentioned or implied: the physician, priest, lawyer, accountant, engineer, teacher, librarian, architect, musician, nurse, diplomat, judge, counselor, and writer.

One noteworthy distinction between Biblical times and our own is regarding the choice of an occupation. Unlike today where the father may be a laborer and his son a distinguished scientist or industrial tycoon, in Biblical times children naturally followed in the footsteps of their father. The entire idea of selecting an occupation on the basis of one's interests, abilities, or personality, which constitutes the approach of the modern vocational guidance movement, was unknown. Probably the only time when the son diverged from his father's occupation was when the latter became impoverished, a situation which commonly led to his and his son's enslavement. Additional exceptions were those who voluntarily joined the army or who were drafted, as well as those who, in their efforts to improve their economic status, chose to become colonists.

Closely related to the modern idea of vocational choice is the belief that a person who deliberately selects his career on the basis of pertinent factors is more likely to achieve vocational satisfaction than one who drifts into an occupation. We have no clear evidence as to what extent job satisfaction was present in Biblical times. Probably here, too, the working person rarely had the time, the sophistication, or the inclination to pause to examine his emotional response to his work. These are characteristically the by-products of modernity and of our preoccupation with our psyche.

In all societies, certain occupations are held in high esteem while others may be depreciated. This is also true in the Bible. One specific reference to this is the comment that to the Egyptians "shepherds were an abomination" (Gen. 46:34). Another refers disdainfully to merchants (Hos. 12:8). We also know that publicans are habitually linked in the Gospels with sinners. Basically, occupations that required leadership qualities or that were related to religion and the occult enjoyed a higher status. Others esteemed were higher governmental officials and military officers, as well as judges. Also, the more difficult, the more abstruse, the greater the autonomy—the greater the prestige and status of the occupation.

The occupational role of the Biblical woman throws interesting light on ancient times and on the variations that existed between the status of the Jewish woman and that of other peoples of antiquity. She clearly enjoyed a higher status than that of most women of the distant past. Though she worked hard rearing the children, grinding corn, baking, cooking, and engaging in other domestic arts to provide for the needs of her family, she could also rise to high position as prophetess, or as adviser to her husband and to others. Women were also midwives, weavers, production workers, professional mourners, harlots, singers. They engaged in business or in varied domestic arts. The Jewish housewife usually did not engage in the arduous chores related to agriculture, nor are women known to have been miners in Biblical times. There were, however, shepherdesses. While the Jewish woman did not enjoy complete equality with her husband, she was not entirely at his mercy, and she enjoyed some legal protection against cruelty and otherwise intolerable behavior of her spouse.

In short, a close examination of the Bible reveals or suggests a wealth of information that makes the Biblical text become more alive as we consider the persons who sought to earn their daily bread in so many different ways.

II

How work is viewed in any society casts important light on the prevailing thinking, social structure, and values of that people. Primitive peoples, especially warlike tribes, often shun labor. Essential tasks are performed by their women or by foreigners captured and enslaved in feuds and in wars.

Slavery flourished as a social institution both in Asiatic and in European antiquity under democratic as well as totalitarian societies. Impressive buildings built by Asiatic monarchs or by Egyptian despots were created through the toil of numerous slaves. Similarly, in later times the factories of Roman magnates, the silver mines in Spain, or fleets of Roman galleys functioned on slave labor. In the Greek city-states, which left us an imperishable cultural legacy, the entire structure rested on the bent backs of exploited slave labor. According to Mommsen (*The History of Rome*, III, 308), "It is very possible that compared with the suffering of Roman slaves, the sum of all Negro sufferings is but a drop."

Contempt for labor prevailed in ancient Greece where even a citizen who was a laborer was held in contempt (Plato, *Republic*, 6, 54; *Laws*, 5, 7, 8; Aristotle, *Politics*, 3, 4, 13, etc.). While the gods of all nations of antiquity, such as the Olympians, are described as spending their lives in either debauchery or pleasures, or, like the Hindu gods, passively in everlasting repose, God of the Bible is the Master Worker who is Maker and Sovereign of the world (Gen. 1; Isa. 40). Man, created in God's image, was placed in the Garden of Eden "to till it and keep it"

(Gen. 2:15). Although work was initially considered as a punishment for man's sin, it was also a way of lifting him to a higher level.

The Hebrews were virtually the only ancient people who preponderantly viewed work as dignifying rather than demeaning. Ancient China and Japan were other exceptions in their esteem for the peasant. In the Bible, especially in the Old Testament, work is regarded approvingly. God Himself is described as a manual worker (Isa. 40) and the originator and teacher of agricultural skills (Isa. 28:26–29; Jubilees 3:15, 35).

Unlike other peoples of antiquity who despised both slaves and workers, humble workers attained exalted positions in Israel. Isaac was a farmer and a shepherd; Jacob was a shepherd. From their humble positions as plowman and shepherd respectively, Saul and David rose to occupy the throne. Elisha, the plowman, was a successor to Elijah, the prophet. Amos was a part-time shepherd and part-time dresser of sycamore trees. Moses was a shepherd when he was summoned to lead his people. Gideon had been a wheat thresher before he became a distinguished general. In Chronicles, potters and linen makers are listed as members of the aristocracy. In Nehemiah, goldsmiths and perfumers are found among the wealthy who contribute to the repair of the city gates.

Great sages of the Talmud pursued humble vocations. Akiba was a shepherd; Hillel, a dayworker; Hanina and Oshaya were cobblers; Papa, a brewer; Johanan, a sandal maker; Isaac, a blacksmith; while others were tailors, potters, waiters. And, of course, Jesus the carpenter selected his first disciples from among fishermen.

In the Bible, the Hebrews condemn idleness. Man is urged to learn industry from the ant (Pro. 6:6–11) and the bee. The Sabbath was given to man to bless labor (Gen. 2:3) and was designed to attest to the dignity of labor.

A slightly different view, however, is found in Psalms 127:2 where extreme absorption in work is mildly criticized and in Proverbs 10:22 where the thought is expressed that the joys of life result more from divine favor than from human efforts.

Adam's agricultural difficulties are attributed to divine punishment for his sin.

The Talmud elaborates on the theme of the dignity of labor expressed in the Bible. Not only is God depicted as the first farmer, but He is also credited with originating all trades (Mid. Gen. 24:7). Those who might excuse themselves from work because of their lineage are rebuked with, "Thy Maker worked before you were born" (Midrash Sefer Ha-Aggadah, VIII, 40).

Praise of work is frequently expressed in the Talmud. "Greater is the merit of industry than idle piety for it says, 'If thou eat of the labor of thy hands, happy shalt thou be and it shall be well with thee'" (Ps. 128:2). "Love work" (Pirke Aboth 1:10). "Labor dignifies man" (Ned. 49b). "No work, however offensive, is as degrading as idleness. Let no one say, 'I am the scion of a noble family and ought not to lower myself by labor'" (B.B. 110a).

Even in Eden, Adam was not permitted to eat before he earned his bread by work. "Live on the Sabbath as on a weekday and be not dependent on others," says Akiba (Shab. 118a). The manna in the wilderness was given only upon the condition that Israel would engage in some labor. "God," declares the Midrash (Gen. R. 24:7), "taught Abraham to do all kinds of work."

Additional views include:

"No stigma is attached to working for a living."

"Great is work for it honors him that performs it."

"Choose life" (Dt. 30:19) was interpreted to mean an occupation.

"Flay a carcass in the street and say not, 'I am a great man!'" (It is beneath my dignity.)

Almost contemporary in thought are the following:

"He who does not teach his son a trade is as if he teaches him robbery" (Tos. Kid. 1:11).

"Seven years a famine may last but it will not enter the door of the artisan" (Sanh. 29a).

There were a few negative opinions expressed toward work, such as Ben Sira (*Ecclesiasticus*) (second century B.C.) who declared, "Conversation with animals and the noise of the hammer and the anvil are not conducive to wisdom" (38:24–33), but for the most part, this criticism was directed against work that consumed time that might have been spent in the study of the Torah (Ber. 35b).

Christianity also condemned idleness even when the lazy sought to condone their idleness in the name of religion (1 Thess. 4:11; 1 Tim. 5:13). Jesus worked as a carpenter, and Paul and the apostles pursued such humble vocations as tent-maker and fisherman (Acts 18:3). An influential view was, "If any would not work, neither should he eat" (2 Thess. 3:10). Conversely, "the laborer is worthy of his hire" (Lk. 10:7) would be quoted by proponents of the workingman. The opinion was also expressed that idolatry results when work becomes an end in itself (Lk. 12:16–22). Work as a means of exploitation and oppression was also condemned (Jas. 5:4). The Bible also advocates that work should be performed for the sake of God, and those who did so were regarded as thrice blessed. The one who works is himself blessed by his reception of divine grace to perform his labors for the glory of God. The beneficiary of his work gains, and God, too, is glorified (Rom. 14:7–8; Eph. 6:5–9). Man is thus viewed as becoming a steward of God's riches (1 Cor. 4:1) and a servant of his neighbor (Gal. 5:13; 1 Pet. 4:10).

Luther may have derived his profoundly influential concept of work from the Jews. To him, work was both punitive and educational. He urged that all who could work should, and he condemned idleness, beggary, and the contemplative life as well as moneylending at interest. Like the Hebrews (until the Exile) he held commerce in low esteem. Work, however, was one way to serve God, and the best way to serve Him was to do most perfectly one's vocation. Luther held that each vocation had equal spiritual dignity.

Freud and other mental therapists have emphasized that both love and work are essential to mental health. This modern emphasis on work as not only necessary for sustenance but as a therapeutic factor is additional evidence of the perennial relevance of the Biblical message.

Abbreviations

BIBLICAL

Acts	Acts	Jer.	Jeremiah
Am.	Amos	Jg.	Judges
Cant.	Canticles (Song of Solomon)	Jl.	Joel
		Jn.	John
Chr.	Chronicles	Jon.	Jonah
Col.	Epistle to Colossians	Jos.	Joshua
Cor.	Corinthians	Jud.	Judith
Dan.	Daniel	Ki.	Kings
Dt.	Deuteronomy	Lam.	Lamentations
Eccl.	Ecclesiastes	Lev.	Leviticus
Ecclus.	Ecclesiasticus (Ben Sira, Sirach)	Lk.	Luke
		Mac.	Maccabees
Eph.	Epistle to Ephesians	Mal.	Malachi
Esd.	Esdras	Matt.	Matthew
Est.	Esther	Mic.	Micah
Ex.	Exodus	Mk.	Mark
Ez.	Ezra	Nah.	Nahum
Ezek.	Ezekiel	Neh.	Nehemiah
Gal.	Galatians	N.T.	New Testament
Gen.	Genesis	Num.	Numbers
Hab.	Habakkuk	O.T.	Old Testament
Hag.	Haggai	Pet.	Peter
Heb.	Hebrews	Phil.	Philemon
Hos.	Hosea	Pro.	Proverbs
Isa.	Isaiah	Ps.	Psalms
Jas.	James	Rev.	Revelation

Rom.	Romans
Ru.	Ruth
Sam.	Samuel
Thess.	Thessalonians
Tim.	Timothy
Tit.	Epistle to Titus
Zec.	Zechariah
Zeph.	Zephaniah

POST-BIBLICAL

Ab.	Aboth
Ab. Zar.	Abodah Zarah
Ar.	Arakin
B.B.	Baba Batra
Bek.	Bekorot
Ber.	Berakot
Bez.	Bezah
Bik.	Bikkurim
B.K.	Baba Kama
B.M.	Baba Metsiah
Dem.	Demai
Eduy.	Eduyyot
Er.	Erubim
Gen. R.	Genesis Rabbah
Git.	Gitin
Hor.	Horayot
Hul.	Hulin
Kel.	Kelim
Ker.	Kerithot
Ket.	Ketubot
Kid.	Kiddushin
M.	Mishnah
Ma'as.	Ma'asrot
Mak.	Makkot
Maksh.	Makshirin
Meg.	Megillah
Men.	Menahot
Mid.	Midot
Midr.	Midrash
Mik.	Mikwaot
Mish.	Mishnah
M.K.	Moed Katan
Ned.	Nedarim
Neg.	Negaim
Nid.	Niddah
Pes.	Pesahim
Rab.	Rabbah
R.H.	Rosh Hashonah
Sanh.	Sanhedrin
Shab.	Shabbat
Sheb.	Shebuot
Shek.	Shekalim
Sot.	Sotah
Suk.	Sukkah
Ta'an.	Ta'anit
Toh.	Toharot
Tos.	Tosefta
Tos. Git.	Tosefta Gitin
Tos. Kid.	Tosefta Kiddushin
Vay. Rab.	Vayikrah Rabba
Yeb.	Yebamot
Yer.	Yerushalmi
Yer. R.H.	Yerushalmi Rosh Hashonah
Yer. Shek.	Yerushalmi Shekalim

OTHER ABBREVIATIONS

BASOR (Bulletin American Society Oriental Research)

Josephus (Joseph.)
- Ant. Antiquities
- B.J. Bello Judaico (Jewish Wars)
- Vita Vita (Autobiography)

Maimonides
Yad Kele ha Mikdash
Yad Lulav
Yad Malveh
Yad Sanhedrin

Pliny
- Ep. Epistles

Beggar to King

Accountant and *Accounting*

Primitive accounting started soon after man learned to engage in business, since even the simplest commercial transactions required some sort of record. The system of double entry, basic in completing financial statements, was employed in Phoenician, Greek, and Roman times.

The levying and collection of taxes in the Babylonian Empire required proof of individual obligations and payment. Clay tablets, stone, and wooden devices were used to record payments for services in temples. The development of papyrus and the pen in Egypt further aided the progress of accounting procedures.

There were undoubtedly fiscal experts in Israel serving the kings and keeping the financial records of the Temple in Jerusalem. Allusions to such experts may be found in 1 Chronicles 27:24; Ecclesiastes 7:27; 1 Kings 4:6, 27.

See *Appraiser, Banker, Census Taker, Money-Changer, Paymaster, Quartermaster, Tax Collector,* APPENDIX I.

Actor and the *Theater*

As early as the fifth century B.C. there were theaters in Greece built on the natural contours of the area. Their purpose was to present dramatic performances in honor of Dionysus as well as to serve as a meeting place for the citizens of the community (Acts 19:29–41). In 1 Corinthians 4:9 and Hebrews 10:33, references are made to the theater. The apostle Paul quotes from Menander's comedy *Thais*, in 1 Corinthians 15:33. The remains of the theater at Ephesus are believed to reveal accommodation for as many as twenty-four thousand spectators.

Probably the best-preserved theater was at Epidaurus in the Peloponnesus; it dates from the fourth century B.C. and may have accommodated about fourteen thousand people. It was semicircular with a circular orchestra or chorus space in the center and a raised wooden stage for the actors. Herod the Great built theaters in Caesarea (2 Mac. 4:14), Damascus, Geder, Kanatha, Scythopolis, and Philadelphia. According to Josephus (Ant. 15.8.1) he also built a theater and amphitheater in Jerusalem and introduced Greek actors at his court in Jerusalem, thereby scandalizing the Jews. Josephus also speaks of Aliturus, an actor of farces, who enjoyed the favor of Nero (Vita 3).

Professional persons in the theater were playwrights and actors. Professional actors were known during the time of Aristotle (384 B.C.) and earlier. In Greece, actors were privileged and honored members of society, but in Rome they were held in low esteem. Later, they were honored by governments and entertained by kings and queens or reviled and banished. The actors in Greece performed with stately gesture and movement and with beautiful diction, although they usually wore masks from behind which they declaimed before a huge outdoors audience.

In later times the pre-Maccabean Hellenistic party introduced gymnasia into Jerusalem (2 Mac. 4:12), to the dismay of the pious elements. Religious Jews were appalled by the brutality of throwing men as food to wild beasts, as well as by the idolatrous images erected in the theater (Ant. 15.8.1). Once they rioted only to be suppressed with much bloodshed.

Other members of the Herodian family were also fond of the theater. There were theaters in Palestinian cities with Hellenistic populations. The Jewish community in Alexandria, Egypt, produced a dramatic poet called Ezekiel who wrote a play on

Exodus. Nevertheless, because the theater was morally offensive as well as being the scene where many Jews suffered martyrdom, pious Jews viewed it unfavorably. Rabbinical statements regarding the theater include: "In four ways the Roman Empire eats up the wealth of the nations: with taxes, with baths, with theaters and with imposts" (Ab. Rabbi Nathan 28). "The feet of man will take him as he desires, either into the house of God and the synagogue or into the theater and the circus" (Gen. R. 65:3).

Notwithstanding these strictures, Jews attended the theater and the circuses even on the Sabbath, providing public affairs were to be discussed (Ket. 5a). Because of their large audience capacity, theaters were often used for gatherings (Josephus, B.J. 7.3.3). Some sages viewed the theater tolerantly: "We must thank the heathens that they let mimes appear in the theater and circuses, and thereby provide innocent recreation for themselves; otherwise they would be constantly getting into great quarrels as soon as they had any thing to do with one another" (Gen. R. 80:1). Rabbi Nathan held that there were valid reasons for visiting the circus such as the possibility of rescuing Jews who might be gored by bulls or of testifying to the death of a Jewish gladiator so that his widow might be free to rewed.

In time, however, rabbinical opposition to the theater and circuses increased so that Jews were forbidden to attend them. Not only had thousands of Jews under the rule of Vespasian and Titus been slain in theaters, but Jews were also flagrantly mocked and jeered in the circuses and theaters. The Midrash on Psalms 69:13 reads: "The heathen are meant who sit in the theaters and circuses, after they have feasted and become drunk, they sit and scoff at Israel, saying to one another, 'Let us beware that we do not resemble the Jews who have nothing to eat but locust beans.'"

In early times, actors were mimes dealing with themes from humble life and offering character studies with clever mimicry. When they later changed the themes to subjects from classic literature, the pantomime evolved. The Romans relished the grace of the actors, their lavish costumes, their masks, versatile impersonations, and hand movements.

During the early Christian centuries, however, the rabbis viewed every place of amusement "as a seat of the scornful" (Ps. 1:1) and commented: "He who frequents the stadia and the circuses and sees the magicians, the tumblers, the buccones, the maccus, the moriones, the scurrae and the ludi saeculares—this is sitting in the seat of the scornful" (Tos. Ab. Zar. 26). Devastating earthquakes "result from the theater and circus" (Yer. Ber. 13c). A special prayer was prepared expressing thanks that Israel did not participate in the (pagan) circus: "I give thanks to Thee, O Lord, and God of my fathers, that Thou hast placed my portion among those who sit in the house of learning and the house of prayer and did not cast my lot among those who frequent theaters and circuses" (Yer. Ber. 7d; B.B. 28b).

Christianity, too, condemned the pagan theater (1 Cor. 15:32), since Christians as well as Jews were slain in the theaters. The church Father Tertullian declared that the theater was a place of sexual immorality.

Centuries before Christ there was a guild of actors and musicians known as the "Dionysian Artists" who banded together for common interests. As for the income of actors, stars earned enormous fortunes. Aesopus, the tragedian, left twenty million sesterces (a sesterce was worth about five cents); and Roscius, the comedian, earned 500,000 sesterces a year. The average actor, of course, earned a far more modest income.

See *Dancer.*

Ambassador

"Malach," which means messenger, is a term used to describe an ambassador sent to other nations on special occasions such as to make alliances (Jos. 9:4), to congratulate (1 Ki. 5:1; 2 Sam. 8:10), or to protest against wrongs (Jg. 11:12). After Israel established diplomatic relations with Syria, Babylonia, and other countries, ambassadors became more common, although they negotiated treaties only occasionally (2 Ki. 18:17, 19:8). One example of the violation of diplomatic immunity is cited (2 Sam. 10:4) wherein David's emissaries to Hanun had half their beards shaven and "their garments cut off in the middle even to their buttocks and [he] sent them away." For this affront to his ambassadors, David went to war against Hanun and defeated him.

Ambassadors in Biblical times were undoubtedly worldly persons who had won the confidence of their monarchs by their sagacity and loyalty, and they probably possessed superior education and ability.

See *Counselor.*

Apothecary

Apothecaries are mentioned in Exodus 30:25 as compounders of the incense and the holy anointing oils used in religious ceremonies. They also blended extracts and medicinal herbs as well as prepared perfumes, unguents, and cosmetics. It is likely that the apothecary may have also served as a beautician to royalty and to the wealthy, and, consequently, enjoyed a higher standard of living than the average person. Moreover, his close relationship with prominent persons probably gave him considerable influence and prestige. Since apothecaries were often priests, their art was considered mysterious and was highly esteemed.

The preparation of beauty aids was one of the main roles of the apothecary. How ancient this activity is may be deduced from the fact that in the eighteenth century B.C., the great palace at Mari on the middle Euphrates had its own perfumery to provide a large supply of different ointments for court officials and soldiers as well as perfumes that were used for personal hygiene, for rituals, or for royal banquets and festivals.

Archaeologists have unearthed at Beth-shan a little stone mill for grinding eye paint. This mill dates from about 1500 B.C. In other ancient Israel towns many domestic bowls have been found which were probably scent bottles. There is an exquisite thirteenth-century-B.C. ivory ointment flask from Lachish. In Egypt, and to some extent in Palestine, elegant ladies used elaborate ivory cosmetic spoons decorated with beautiful lotuses, maidens, and ducks. Many small boxes and tubes contained eye paint, which was applied with a little spatula of wood or bronze.

In ancient times, ground minerals, vegetable oils and extracts, and animal fats provided the materials used for cosmetics and perfumes. The Egyptians are believed to have initiated the use of such ointments after they found that they both cleansed and cooled the body. The use then spread to neighboring countries. A basic substance for medicinal or cosmetic purposes was olive oil, one of Palestine's main products. In its pure form, it was extensively used as an ointment, as was balsam (Est. 2:12; Cant. 4:10).

The perfumes and ointments of Bible lands (Eccl. 7:1, 9:8; Matt. 6:17) were compounded by perfumers, apothecaries, confectioners (Ex. 30:35), private individuals, or temple priests.

Perfume manufacturers in Biblical times usually obtained perfume in three different ways: first, they soaked flowers in fat; second and most commonly, they dipped the flowers into hot fats or oils at 150 degrees Fahrenheit; or third, they compressed flowers in a bag.

To obtain oil of myrrh and other gum resins, the substance was heated in a greasy-type "fixative" oil or fat and water to prevent the evaporation of the scent. In this way, the perfume essence was transferred to the greasy oil or fat which was then strained off as liquid perfume. An Egyptian tomb painting of the fifteenth century B.C. depicts persons engaged in pouring and stirring a mixture, probably cosmetics, in heated pans.

Most of the ingredients used by apothecaries were imported from Arabia though some were grown in Egypt. Sesame oil was a very popular raw material for aromatics, as were olive oil, myrrh, frankincense, and spikenard.

Cooking and the preparation of perfumes were allied arts

which may explain why in 1 Samuel 8:13 perfumers, confectioners, cooks, and bakers are grouped together.

Moses is credited with the formula for the holy anointing oil used in sprinkling the Tabernacle, its priests, and its appointments. Ointments were also employed by prophets to anoint new kings (2 Ki. 9:3) as well as to anoint the sick (Jas. 5:14; Isa. 1:6; Mk. 6:13) and the dead (Lk. 23:56; Mk. 14:8). Shepherds used olive oil ointment to soothe the bruised faces of sheep, and soldiers were supplied by the king with olive oil to anoint themselves (2 Chr. 28:15). The rich, of course, used expensive ointments (Am. 6:6).

Even the humble classes of the Biblical East applied oil to cleanse and soothe their sun-dried skin. At banquets, small containers of perfumed ointments were perched on the forehead, and as they melted, the ingredients perfumed the face (Ps. 92:10, 133:2). During Jesus' time as a sign of hospitality, guests at banquets were anointed with oil (Lk. 7:46). There is also the familiar flask of precious ointment or spikenard with which the repentant woman anointed Christ's head (Lk. 7:37; Mk. 14:3).

Women, of course, used unguents and cosmetics extensively. They painted their toenails and fingernails, hands, feet, and hair with henna juice that left the orange stain mentioned in Canticles 1:14 and 4:13. Excavations have unearthed containers that doubtless had cosmetics for coloring the face as well as ivory and metal kohl sticks and unguent spoons. Both men and women applied rouge and paint to their faces and, like Jezebel, traced heavy black lines under their eyes to make them appear larger (2 Ki. 9:30). Ezekiel charged the Israelites, "You enlarge your eyes with eye paint" (23:40). Job's third daughter was called Keren-happuch, "horn of eye paint" or source of beauty.

Hairdressings and restoratives were widely used throughout the ancient Near East. Josephus states that Herod the Great dyed his hair (B.J. 24:7). In Egypt, there were skilled hairdressers who served the titled classes and who used a variety of perfumes and tonics. Semitic men were proud of their luxurious beards and took excellent care of their hair.

The Jewish attitude toward the use of cosmetics, as expressed in the Bible and the Talmud, is basically favorable though disapproving of excessive use. While Jeremiah 4:30 and Ezekiel 23:41 deplore its excessive use, the Talmud (200–500 A.D.) suggests that women should beautify themselves for their husbands. Yerushalmi Berakot 50a declares that a woman grows ugly if she fails to use cosmetics. One Talmudic passage favors the use of eye cosmetics. Shabbat 94b mentions a heavy salve whose description suggests a mud pack. The Mishnah urges that each husband give his wife ten gold dinars for her toilette box (Ket. 64b). Rabbi Akiba declared that a woman must not fail to beautify herself for her husband, even when she is physically indisposed (Ket. 6b).

So highly did the Jews appreciate fragrance that burning of incense was permitted in the Temple even on the Sabbath. The Talmud (Shab. 62a) mentions women placing myrrh and balsam oils in their shoes so that the fragrance would be emitted while they walked. They also wore balls of perfume suspended from necklaces.

See *Embalmer, Hairdresser, Perfumer, Spice Dealer.*

Appraiser

Although there is no reference to an appraiser in the Bible we can conjecture that he functioned in Biblical times and probably earlier. Since taxes were imposed upon residents during even the earliest civilizations, men were needed to determine the value of property, livestock, and valuables so that the maximum revenue might be collected. Appraisers may have combined their duties with tax collecting.

In Scriptures, there are references to "estimations" (Lev. 27:4; 2 Ki. 12:4) and to "taxation" (2 Ki. 23:35; Lk. 2:1, 3, 5) which may relate to the activities of an appraiser.

See *Accountant, Tax Collector, Weigher.*

Apprentice

Each generation is faced with the problem of transmitting its skills to the generation that follows. Biblical man perceived that the young learned best by doing and apprenticeship training was designed to achieve this. How this operated in Biblical times is noteworthy.

Apprentices were known from the earliest historical times and apprenticeships are mentioned in the code of Hammurabi (*ca.* 1800 B.C.) as lasting up to six years. Apprentices usually came from outside the family group. From about 626 B.C. (Neo-Babylonian period), young slaves were sent by their owners to learn trades. During their apprenticeship, they learned dyeing, fulling, gem cutting, leatherwork, and weaving. They were fed, clothed, and housed by their employer.

Apprenticeship is often mentioned in Talmudic literature. The master was called *rav* and the apprentice, *talmid* or *shulya.* The terms of apprenticeship were agreed upon between the master and the parents of the boy and were usually for a period of five years (Midr. Ekha Rab. 3:6). Children usually followed the vocation of their fathers, but occasionally some rebelled and followed other careers. Sometimes Jewish boys were apprenticed to Samaritans or pagan masters. It appears that apprentices usually got along well with their masters. During the period of their apprenticeship, the apprentice both observed and practiced his craft under the tutelage of his master until he mastered it.

During the fifth century B.C., stonemasons and sculptors had apprentices who worked under their tutelage for several years. In all likelihood, this was true of other occupations as well. In Rome, during the early Christian era, most ironworkers, coppersmiths, goldsmiths, and blacksmiths worked with one or two apprentices.

See APPENDIX III, APPENDIX IV.

Architect and *Architecture*

The first Biblical reference to an architect is Bezalel, described in Exodus 36–38 as the architect of the Tabernacle as well as teacher of the arts (35:34) and as a divinely inspired craftsman. Though there are many indications of architecture in Biblical times, the ancient Hebrews appear to have derived much of their knowledge from Asiatics, Egyptians, Greeks, Mesopotamians, Phoenicians, and Romans.

Many architectural works created in Biblical times have been excavated. They include castles (Gen. 25:16), among them David's (1 Chr. 27:25) and Jehoshaphat's (2 Chr. 17:12), and the castles of the Midianites, which Moses commanded Israel to burn (Num. 31:10). Also unearthed have been forums (Acts 28:15), the markets of Tyre mentioned in Ezekiel (27:13, 27) and gates, many of which were casemated (Acts 3:10), a term describing a system of thick outer walls and thick inner walls linked by cross walls.

Digs have also cast light on ancient inns, which were usually bare shelters for travelers and their beasts, though sometimes they were palaces for governors, monarchs, and high priests. Many such palaces were discovered at Samaria.

Ancient architects created a variety of structures to serve various needs. Perhaps most important were the temples which were usually the costliest, most expressive, and most enduring buildings in the community. Other public buildings were stadia for athletic, dramatic, and musical events; public gatherings; and also banks, museums, and libraries. Architects also built synagogues, theaters (Acts 19:29), tombs, sepulchers, and aqueducts as well as domestic structures for the private citizen and his family.

The *architekton* mentioned in 1 Corinthians 3:10 was not the trained architect of our day who designs blueprints of the structures to follow. He was comparable to the master mason of the medieval cathedral who developed his plan as the structure developed in accordance with the material he used.

There was no formal town planning in Palestine before the Hellenistic period. Buildings had to be accommodated within the cramped space afforded by narrow streets and protective walls. Towns were usually laid out near water and strategic sites to protect their residents in time of danger. Thus, they were built on a hill or on a ruin mound (Jos. 11:13). Generally, the citadel occupied the higher portion and constituted the inner defense, which included the main public buildings and, at Jerusalem, the Temple (1 Chr. 29:1, 19; Neh. 1:1).

Under the affluent, united monarchy, the mason-architect developed a characteristic Israelite fortification consisting of a huge structure of unhewn stones. At Beth-shemesh and Debir, an outer five-foot-thick wall and an inner one three feet thick joined by cross walls represents the casemate fortification. Saul had a similar structure built in his fortress capital, Gibeah.

Solomon's architect used carefully cut stones in the walls of Gezer and Megiddo, two store or supply cities, and at Hazor (1 Ki. 9:15). The same architect built identical gatehouses set in casemate walls, three chambers on each side with square towers in the sixty-six-foot-long external walls.

At Tell Beit Mirsim, the gate tower had a courtyard near which were six paved rooms with built-in cupboards, washbasins and other conveniences for official travelers. At Megiddo and Hazor, there were large pillared buildings with paved courtyards. These buildings may have been public chancelleries. Excavations of similar buildings have been made at Eglon, Gezer, and Taanach.

The early architects commonly used rough stone for the lower sections, which were aligned and bonded by carefully dressed cornerstones supporting courses of wood interspersed with mud-brick. In other buildings at Beth-shan, Megiddo, and Samaria, large stones, marginally drafted and with embossed centers, were laid regularly without the use of mortar, all of which revealed significant architectural progress.

Solomon's Temple, which was built by Hiram of Tyre about 960 B.C. and based on a Syrophoenician pattern, used white limestone trimmed at the quarries (1 Ki. 5:17). Its architectural details are given in 1 Kings 6. Solomon's Temple was similar to the layout of temples found at Tell Tainat (Syria, ninth century B.C.) and Hazor.

As for the architecture of private homes, an eighteenth-century-B.C. villa was unearthed near Shechem; it had a single entrance leading to an open courtyard near which were rooms used by servants and for storage. This layout was common throughout the ancient Near East. At Hazor, steps led to the second floor where the owners lived and thence to the flat roof which was used for relaxation during the summer and for drying stores (Jos. 2:6). Most of the homes had roofs thatched with straw and mud and held up by twelve- to fifteen-foot wooden beams. Periodic rolling with a heavy stone kept the roof watertight. Larger buildings are believed to have been supported by the arch and vaulting processes known since about 3000 B.C. (Jg. 16:26–29).

For safety, there was usually a parapet around the flat roof (Dt. 22:8). From the twelfth century B.C. on, most homes had their own cisterns in the courtyard to collect rain water from the roof. From the tenth century B.C. on, it became popular to erect one or two rows of stone or wooden pillars along the axis of the main rooms.

The homes of the poor are believed to have been similar to those in primitive Syrian or Turkish villages today. They were either one or two rooms (Lk. 11:7). The structures were frail and easily penetrated by thieves (Matt. 6:19).

Large buildings were planned and constructed under the close supervision of master builders who would first survey the site with a measuring line consisting of a rope, cord (2 Sam. 8:2; Zec. 2:1), or twisted linen thread (Ezek. 40) marked in cubits (1 Ki. 7:15, 23). During Hellenistic times, a reed rod marked in furlongs was also used (Rev. 11:1, 21:15). The progress of the building was checked by the architect, who used a plumb line or cord weighted with lead or tin (Am. 7:7–8), a stone, or any other heavy object (2 Ki. 21:13) to test any vertical structure.

In New Testament times, a splendid illustration of architecture was Herod's Temple, which he built to demonstrate his splendor and to woo the good will of the populace. Construction began about 20 B.C. and was finally completed about eighty-four years later. Mark 13:1, 2 refers to the magnificent impression it made. Unfortunately, the Temple was destroyed by the Romans during the siege of 70 A.D. This Temple was a triple structure; the lower court formed a splendid terrace. In its center was an inner court raised on a platform, and the sanctuary rose from this and crowned the entire site. The outer court was surrounded by cloisters and porticoes. In the open area, animals were sold for sacrificial offerings (Jn. 2:13–17).

At Capernaum an ancient floor was unearthed beneath a fourth-century synagogue which may be the remains of the building in which Jesus preached (Lk. 7:5).

In Biblical times there were specialists in building aqueducts. The construction was usually done by slaves under the skilled supervision of artisans. The ancient aqueduct builder was unfamiliar with the high-pressure pipeline. He used an inverted siphon furnished with blowholes, multiple pipelines of lead, and other devices to reduce pressure. Though the flow of water was never retarded, tree roots often disrupted flow.

Tunneled conduits for springs feeding open pools were well known in the ancient world. The best-known example was Hezekiah's aqueduct at Jerusalem, built about 725 B.C., which fed the pool of Siloam (Isa. 36:2). It brought Jerusalem's water supply from the spring Gihon outside the walls to a safer pool beyond the reach of Sennacherib's (705–681 B.C.) approaching Assyrians. He is believed to have ordered the construction of the oldest Babylonian aqueduct yet discovered. It carried water thirty miles to Nineveh's gardens. There were also aqueducts in Tyre, Jericho, and Caesarea. There is a reference to a "conduit of the upper pool" (2 Ki. 18:17), which was an underground watercourse to Jerusalem from beyond the Damascus gate.

One of the best surviving aqueducts is that of Claudius, believed to have been known to Paul as he traveled to Rome along the Appian Way.

Pontius Pilate, appointed procurator of Judea in 26 A.D., apparently enraged the Jews because he allegedly diverted money from the Temple treasury to build an aqueduct to convey water to the city from a spring twenty-five miles away. When tens of thousands of Jews demonstrated against the project, Pilate sent his troops against them and slew many of the crowd (Lk. 13:1).

We have no information regarding the training of the ancient architect. Probably, some form of apprenticeship existed. Architects were often master masons who planned, supervised, and worked along with the other masons in the actual construction.

See *Bricklayer, Carpenter, Furniture Designer, Marble Setter, Mason, Stoneworker, Surveyor.*

Armor-Bearer

In early Biblical times, the armor-bearer was a personal attendant of a warrior chieftain. He was probably selected for his bravery, loyalty, and skill in warfare. He not only accompanied his master in battle, but fought alongside him. Besides carrying his master's weapons, he probably kept them in good condition.

Jonathan's armor-bearer is reported to have slain all those wounded by his chief (1 Sam. 14:13). When Abimelech and Saul were defeated in battle, they ordered their armor-bearers to kill them so as to escape capture by their enemies (Jg. 9:54; 1 Sam. 31:4; 1 Chr. 10:4, 5).

David was selected as an armor-bearer by King Saul (1 Sam. 16:21). Joab is also recorded as having had an armor-bearer (2 Sam. 18:15, 23:37; 1 Chr. 11:39). Armor-bearers are believed to have functioned throughout Biblical times.

See *Armorer, Metalworker, Runner, Smith, Tanner, Toolmaker.*

Armorer

Early in his history, man expressed his aggressive impulses by using the commonest available implement, stones (1 Sam.

17:49). Later, he used slingballs of flint and stone, many of which have been excavated. Still later, he employed flint knives. During the time of the judges, armorers produced double-edged knives (Jg. 3:16–22). In the tenth century B.C., the Philistines used daggers whose handles were inlaid with ivory. The Hittites also made daggers, which were their favorite weapons.

Skilled weaponmakers also made spears with wooden shafts and with tops of barbed bronze or iron (1 Sam. 17:7). Jonathan and his men used swords, javelins, lighter and shorter spears of unknown materials (1 Sam. 20:33). Joshua also used swords as well as the armorer's bows and arrows. The bows were either a single or double curb, and were generally made with seasoned wood or from horn, frequently mounted with bronze (Ps. 18:34). Bowstrings were usually made of ox gut, and the arrows of reed and light wood were topped with metal. They were extensively used in Israel's battles (1 Sam. 20:20 ff.). Armorers also produced battle-axes used by Babylonians, Assyrians, and Elamites.

Typical weapons of Biblical times were excavated from a tomb of the Hebrew monarchy period. They included a broad-bladed dagger; a curved scimitar of Babylonian type; slingballs; a stone-headed mace; leaf-shaped, bronze arrow tips and darts. At Gerar, which the archaeologist Sir Flinders Petrie discovered, there was a sword factory which produced many swords.

In ancient times, virtually all peoples used shields to defend themselves in battle. The Israelites employed two kinds: a large shield called the "buckler" was made to protect the entire body and was carried by the heavily armed infantry (2 Chr. 14:8). Goliath had a special shield-bearer (1 Sam. 17:7).

The second type was a small shield, the "magen," also translated "buckler," which was carried by archers such as the Benjamites in King Asa's army (2 Chr. 14:8). It was usually made of wood or wickerwork overlaid with leather (Ezek. 39:9), which was oiled before battle either to preserve it or to make it shine (Isa. 21:5).

In ancient times, the helmet or "kova" was apparently worn only by kings or important leaders. King Saul provided David with his personal bronze helmet (1 Sam. 17:38). These helmets may have resembled the Hittite helmets engraved on the walls of Karnak in Egypt that look like skullcaps. At the request of King Uzziah, his armorers made for Hebrew soldiers helmets which are believed to have been of leather. Later, bronze helmets were also supplied to the soldiers (1 Mac. 6:35).

Armorers made body armor of both leather and bronze. Leaders wore bronze while the rank and file wore leather. Goliath's armor was made of bronze scales (1 Sam. 17:5) and he also wore over his leg between his ankle and knee a protective covering which may have been a boot but is translated as "greaves" (1 Sam. 17:6).

Armor scales were discovered at Ras Shamra (Ugarit), Boghazköy and Alalakh, which indicates that such armor was common in the fifteenth century B.C. Many such plates have been found at Nuzi. There was also armor for chariots and horses discovered in Assyrian cities. This armor was always rectangular and was bound either vertically or horizontally to the horse's harness by a cord. There was also armor to protect elephants (1 Mac. 6:37).

The most frequently used weapon which the armorer produced was the straight-blade sword made of iron (1 Sam. 13:19). Occasionally, it was double-edged (Ps. 149:6). Daggers like those excavated at Lachish and Megiddo dating from the seventeenth century B.C. were also commonly used.

See *Armor-Bearer, Bodyguard, Captain, Charioteer, Executioner, Harness Maker, Saddle Maker, Soldier.*

Artist and *Artwork*

During its long history, Palestine was inhabited by many peoples whose diverse cultures make it difficult to distinguish their art from native Jewish art. Ancient art of the Near East was a commingling of Egyptian, Mesopotamian, Phoenician, Syrian, and Hellenistic influences. Frequent migrations of the Hebrews may have thwarted their creative capacities. Many scholars also believe that the second commandment's prohibition against making graven images was a powerful inhibiting factor to Jewish artistic expression. In any event, Jewish artistic expression in the plastic arts does not equal the enormous literary and religious creativity represented primarily in the Bible. Nevertheless, the Hebrews were not lacking in artistic skill or appreciation.

We do not know when various practitioners of the arts began their vocations. Probably, it came with the rise of the large communities which led to the specialization of labor. The following is a brief sketch of artistic growth in Biblical lands.

The earliest Palestinian art dates back to about 8000 B.C. when the cave dwellers of Mt. Carmel and of the hilly country east of the plain of Sharon carved and engraved their bone artifacts. Surviving are the handle of a sickle shaft illustrating a young fawn in full relief and a slab of gray limestone with touches of red ocher revealing the profile of a gazelle. There are also, incised on rock, attempts at portraying the human figure.

In the pre-pottery levels of neolithic Jericho dating about 6000 B.C. there survive a number of human masks of lime marl touched with red paint, with sea shells representing eye globes. The masks were discovered together with animal figurines and plastic illustrations of human genitals which may have had magical or ritual importance.

In Canaanite art drawn before the settlement of the Israelites in the thirteenth century B.C., we find a mixture of Anatolian, Aegean, Egyptian, and Mesopotamian influences. In Ugaritic art of the fifteenth and fourteenth centuries B.C., there are images on a limestone stele of the thunder-god of Ugarit who stands holding a mace in his right hand while his left hand strikes down with a spear. He wears a tight loincloth and his head, body, and legs are in right profile.

Sculpture

The ancient sculptor usually worked in clay, wax, plaster, or some other soft material, building up his creation from a central nucleus, shaping and molding his three-dimensional work from the inside out. The figure was later hardened by baking. According to experts, the sculpture of Canaanite Palestine that has survived is typically imitative of foreign models, especially those of the Egyptians. Surviving from Hazor (about 1000 B.C.) are a roughly engraved stele with a pair of raised arms, altars, and the skillfully wrought feet of a statue. There was a guild of ossuary workers at Jerusalem who left several chests engraved with six-pointed stars, flowers, rosettes, and architectural designs. Many crudely executed clay figures have also survived. Unearthed from about the same time have been two goblets of highly glazed work from Tell abu Huwam near Haifa. They depict a woman's head adorned with ear and nose rings.

Carving

Carvers in ivory and bone produced furniture, figurines, and other objects as early as the thirty-fourth century B.C. The carving, mainly in panels, was incised, sculptured in the round, or cut as openwork or relief. One ivory plaque from Lachish (thirteenth century B.C.) depicts bulls and lions fighting while an eagle or vulture hovers above, a common theme in the seal engraving of Mesopotamia. Recurrent patterns are the lotus and cherub. There is also a collection of sculpture and engraved inlays from Megiddo dating from the early twelfth century B.C., and these reveal a wide variety of decorative themes. Some of the ivories are inlaid with gold, glass, lapis lazuli, and colored stone. These inlays once adorned the palace and furniture of the Canaanite kings who ruled the fortress of Megiddo before the Hebrew kings. Among other interesting items excavated are a decorated ivory casket embellished with animals in high relief as well as combs, mirrors, game boards, and spoon handles. Hebrew carvers were skilled in woodwork. Thus, the cherubs which were in the compartment known as the Holy of Holies were carved out of olivewood. Bezaleel and his aide Aholiab supervised the wood carving in the Tabernacle, which contained pillars and curved capitals (Ex. 35:33, 36:38) and a horned altar recessed to take a grating (Ex. 38:2–4), as well as other artwork. Solomon's Temple was roofed with pine with appliquéd palmette and guilloche borders (2 Chr. 3:5) paneled in cedar (1 Ki. 6:15–16). The walls and doors were sculptured in bas-relief with carvings of lotus birds, fleurs-de-lis forming a triple flower, palm designs, and cherubs. The olivewood doors had similar designs and intaglio work (1 Ki. 18:32–35) all overlaid with gold. Beautifully carved furniture and wooden objects such as boxes and spoons were found in the Ammonite tombs at Jericho.

The decorations of early Galilean synagogues at Kefr Bir'im and Tell Hum (Capernaum) about the third century A.D. were richly carved with vegetable ornaments, a six-pointed Star of David, the Torah shrine, the wheeled chariot of 1 Chronicles 28:18, and figurines of Eros and sea horses. Human and animal figures are frequently seen in the mosaic pavements of Palestinian synagogues of the fourth and fifth centuries.

Wall frescoes, executed in a technical style akin to the Roman and Alexandrian paintings, adorned the synagogue of Dura-Europus on the Euphrates (third century) and portrayed such Biblical subjects as Moses, the anointing of David, Elijah on Mt. Carmel, and Mordecai honored by Ahasuerus.

Metalwork

Although little metalwork of the Hebrews has survived, it is believed that they were expert in the craft. One illustration is the miniature bronze stand, about 1000 B.C., from Megiddo that is in openwork style showing the invocation of a seated god. Another example is the bronze "sea of Solomon's Temple"—a huge basin from which the priests drew water for the ablutions. It was estimated to have weighed about twenty-five tons and was made of cast bronze three inches thick with a bowl fifteen feet in diameter, seventeen and one-half feet high with a petaled rim. It rested on the backs of twelve oxen separately cast and arranged in four supporting triads (1 Ki. 7:23–26), and contained about ten thousand gallons of water. It is considered an unusual artistic achievement.

The Hebrews also possessed considerable skill in overlaying with metal plate. It is believed that the ephod, an apronlike garment worn under the breastplate of the high priest, was overlaid with gold or silver foil. The calves of gold at Dan and Bethel are said to have been overlaid rather than made of solid metal (1 Ki. 12:28). The walls and even the floors of the Temple were overlaid with gold leaf.

A considerable number of cylindrical scarab and stamp seals have been dug up in Palestine. They reflect typical Phoenician motifs such as ivories with engravings, and, more abundantly, winged disks and winged scarabs. The human figure, too, was often engraved up to the period of the monarchy. Judah seals reveal few pictorial representations, possibly because of growing religious aversion to the portrayal of the human figure. Nevertheless, the Hebrews appear to have excelled in seal engraving (Ex. 28:11–23).

Painting

The earliest known wall paintings were found in the ruins of Teleilat el Ghassul, a village of mud-brick houses of the chalcolithic period (*ca.* 3500 B.C.) situated in the lower eastern portion of the Jordan Valley. The artist employed the alfresco technique, using mineral pigments, red and yellow ocher, black, white, and dark red to form geometric patterns and such pictures as an eight-ray star and a realistically drawn bird. The Egyptians and the Ammonites often painted scenes on plastered walls, which the Hebrews may have also imitated, though none survive.

There is no painting mentioned in Solomon's Temple, but the Mishnah asserts that in the second Temple a red line was painted halfway up around the altar of burnt offering to direct the sprinkling of the blood. In Jeremiah 22:14 we read that Jehoiakim beautified his palace by painting it with vermilion. When denouncing idolatry in Jerusalem, Ezekiel (8:10) referred to animals and idols portrayed or carved on the wall of a secret place in the Temple. In Ezekiel 23:14 there is a reference to a bas-relief of Chaldeans "portrayed in vermilion." The Medes and Babylonians who attacked Nineveh bore reddened shields (Nah. 2:3) which were either painted or dyed.

While pottery painting is not mentioned in the Bible, we

know that it was nonetheless extensively practiced in the Near East. During the early bronze period in Palestine, painting in designs and figures was common. About 1500 B.C. there were already friezes, and geometric patterns and pictures of fish painted on pottery.

In the Wisdom of Solomon (13:14) an image made and smeared with vermilion is mentioned as well as an idol spotted with various colors (15:4). Additional references to painting are found in 2 Maccabees 2:29 where painting a house with figures is mentioned and in 4 Maccabees 17:7 where the absence of a painting depicting the martyrdom of some pious Jews is decried. The latter adds that such a painting would have been a sin. During the third century A.D. some Galilean synagogues and the synagogue of Dura-Europus were painted with figures.

In New Testament times, art in the Near East was mainly imitative and commercialized, and no known great works have been found from this period. Surprisingly, there is little reference to art in the New Testament. While Paul stood on the hill of Areopagus, from where he could view the full beauty of the Acropolis and its immortal works of art, he was unimpressed because he believed that they symbolized the evils of idolatry (Acts 17:24, 29). Pausanias refers to a thronelike altar to Zeus on the Pergamenian acropolis, a portion of which still survives. John, who opposed idolatry, described the Christian Pergamum as living where "the Satan seat is," referring to the thronelike altar of Zeus (Rev. 2:13).

See *Architect, Furniture Designer, Glassmaker, Ivory Carver, Jeweler, Metalworker, Mirror Maker, Potter, Publisher, Seal Maker, Stoneworker.*

Assayer

There were assayers in antiquity who tested ores and alloys and analyzed the results to determine the value of the precious metals. They used furnaces, beakers, and crucibles to separate the precious metals from dross materials. This was achieved either by a liquid process such as solution or flotation, or by a dry process such as using heat to form slags of borax or lead. The assayer would then weigh the residue on balances to find out the proportion of pure gold, silver, or other metal.

The work of the assayer is usually alluded to in the Bible in a figurative, moral sense (Ps. 66:10; Isa. 48:10; Pro. 17:3, 25:4; Zec. 13:9; Mal. 3:3; Jer. 6:28–30; Ezek. 22:17–22).

See *Metalworker, Miner, Mining Engineer, Refiner.*

Athlete and *Athletics*

Professional athletes, in our modern sense of persons who earn their living from their athletic prowess, do not seem to have been known in Biblical times. However, in later times among the Greeks and Romans, athletes enjoyed prestige and certain emoluments that also gave them economic benefits.

The Biblical expression "let the young men . . . arise and play before us" (2 Sam. 2:14) suggests that there were friendly tournaments. There is also a specific reference to discus throwing (2 Mac. 4:9–17) and to a game held every fifth year at Tyre, probably in imitation of the Olympic games. Under Herod the Great, there were wrestling and chariot racing with very valuable prizes awarded to the winners (Josephus, *Ant.* 15.8.1).

Athletic contests were especially important in the lives of the Greeks and Romans. Since Paul makes many references to athletic contests, especially in 1 Corinthians 9:24–27, he probably viewed them at Corinth. He seemed most familiar with the game of Ephesus (2 Tim. 4:7). The contests of Olympia included boxing (Eph. 4:27), chariot races, foot races (Rom. 9:16; Gal. 2:2; Acts 20:24), and wrestling (Eph. 6:12) for men and youths.

The prize always included a crown of leaves. The victor was

also given a palm branch. When he returned to his city, he was given many privileges and immunities, and his victory was often celebrated in verse. His statue might be placed in the sacred grove of Elis and he was regarded as a celebrity.

The athlete probably spent much of his leisure time practicing his sport.

See *Charioteer, Wrestler.*

Baker, Baking, and *Bread*

The occupation of baking was already well established in the time of the Pharaohs. An Egyptian papyrus mentions thirty different kinds of bread. The tomb of Rameses III in the twelfth century B.C. depicts a royal baking scene. A chief baker who had been imprisoned by a Pharaoh was a fellow prisoner of Joseph (Gen. 41:10). Generally, however, girls or women did the baking for their families. Women slaves also worked as bakers for royal or wealthy families. In Canaanite Palestine, feudal landlords drafted girls to serve as their cooks and bakers.

In some periods, it seems to have been regarded as demeaning for a woman to be a baker (1 Sam. 8:13), though later in Talmudic times women sold their products in the market place without loss of dignity (Hallah 2:7; Ber. 58b).

In Biblical times, bread was usually made from either wheat flour or barley meal, though sometimes spelt and millet were used. The poor used barley because it was cheaper (Jg. 7:13; 2 Ki. 4:42; Jn. 6:9, 13), while the wealthier classes preferred wheat bread. During periods of economic depression or of inadequate harvests, seeds from peas, beans, etc., were mixed with flour to increase the production of bread.

Dough was prepared by pouring flour into boiling water or boiling water into flour and then kneading into the desired consistency. During the nomadic period, the Hebrews, like the modern Bedouins, did not add leaven before kneading (Gen. 18:6). When they settled in Canaan, they customarily retained a small piece of the previous day's dough and crumbled it into the water before mixing it with flour to act as a yeast. After it was thoroughly mixed, the dough was placed on boards, and then stretched, rolled, and molded into the desired shapes. This was mainly done by hand, but sometimes a shaper was used. The size and weight of the baker's loaves were always uniform (Mish. B.M. 11.1).

In Biblical times, baking was done in three ways. The simplest was to build a fire over a large, flat stone, remove the ashes, place a flat piece of dough on the hot stone, and cover it with ashes. The ashes were removed and replaced when the cake had to be turned (Isa. 44:19; 1 Ki. 19:6).

A second method was to bake the cake on a griddle (Lev. 2:5, 6:20–21; 1 Chr. 23:29; Ezek. 4:3) that at various times was made either of clay or of iron. The fire was made in a pit and the dough placed on the griddle and baked into flat cakes (1 Chr. 9:31).

The last and most popular method was to use an oven that probably looked like a large overturned earthenware jar. The fire was prepared the night before. The baker usually watched his oven at night, so that it did not become "flaming fire by morning" (Hos. 7:6–8). The ashes were raked out the next morning. The cakes were baked on the stones lining the bottom of the oven. Another type of oven was earthenware, cylinder-shaped, in which a fire was lit and the dough was applied to the hot walls either inside or outside.

In Biblical times, village bakers used public ovens. The children of the village would bring flat, round loaves of dough on trays from their homes to this outdoor oven. Bread was baked daily. The round loaves could be bent into the shape of a spoon for scooping up gravies and juices.

The ovens in the Temple were of metal. The priests kneaded the dough for sacrifices with lukewarm water, taking great care to avoid fermentation. The two loaves used at Pentecost were both kneaded and baked separately. They were four-cornered, seven hand-breadths long, four hand-breadths wide, with corner pieces or horns four finger-lengths (Men. 11.1 ff.). There were twelve distinct meal offerings made in the Temple. Flour was made from the wheat crushed with the pestle, and the grains were finely ground. It was then strained through a sieve, mixed with water, and kneaded thoroughly.

In any of the before-mentioned methods, the final appearance of most bread was thin flat-shaped disks about eighteen inches in diameter (Jg. 7:13). Some breads were perforated, others were heart-shaped, and still others, such as the special Temple Bread of the Presence or "Show Bread," may have looked like modern bread. In fact, long, thick loaves of burnt bread were discovered at Gezer (Jerusalem).

The Talmud, which provides more information regarding baking than about any other skilled vocation, gives exact details about the preparation of the "Show Bread" (Ex. 25:30), which was twelve baked cakes made of fine flour, set in two rows, six to a row; upon each row of cakes frankincense was placed for a memorial. It was the priest's duty each Sabbath to place fresh or hot bread on the table (1 Sam. 21:6). The old cakes were eaten by Aaron and his sons.

The preparation of the "Show Bread" required special skill. Each loaf was kneaded singly but every two loaves were baked together. Golden molds were used in the preparation. The dough was kneaded in the first, baked in the second, and, in order to retain its shape, placed in the third directly after it was taken from the stove (Men. 11.1.94a). So complicated was the process of preparing this bread that only one family, the Garmus, was considered sufficiently qualified to do it. Because of their unusual skill, they charged high fees for their services (Yoma 38a).

The Hebrew meal offerings consisted of flour alone or of various kinds of unleavened cakes of fine flour mixed with oil, or of unleavened wafers spread with oil (Lev. 2:4). These had to be seasoned with salt (Lev. 2:13).

From earliest times, bread served a number of purposes. As a basic food, it became known as the "staff of life." The Hebrew word *lehem*, meaning bread, is often translated *food*. During the final siege of Jerusalem, the total absence of bread was regarded as the height of deprivation (2 Ki. 25:3; Job 15:23; Ru. 2:14). Ben Sirach (Ecclus. 29:21) declared that the essentials of life were "water and bread, a house, and clothing to cover one's nakedness."

Bread was the main fare of the average person who, along with soldiers (1 Sam. 16:20), usually consumed three loaves a day (Lk. 11:5–6). A prisoner, however, was allotted only one loaf daily (Jer. 37:21).

In Biblical Jerusalem, there was a bakers' street (Jer. 37:21) where there were probably a number of small baking establishments. It was from one such bakery that Jeremiah's daily bread supply came while he was incarcerated.

In Talmudic times, there were large communal bakeries, where dough previously prepared at home was baked. To avoid disputes, each family had a distinctive mark on its bread, such as a pebble pressed on the loaves (Tebul Yom. 1:3). In large cities, bakers did not sell their bread directly to the consumer but rather to distributors (Dem. 5:4; Ab. Zar. 35b). The housewife, on the other hand, continued to do her own baking for the entire week, which she did on Fridays (Ta'an. 24b).

Bread was given as a gift (1 Sam 9:7); giving it to the hungry was considered meritorious (Isa. 58:7; Ezek. 18:7), while denying it to the hungry was considered inhuman (Job 22:7). Whenever Rabbi Huna broke bread for his meal, he first opened his door and said, "Let every one in need come and eat" (Ta'an. 20b).

The rabbis of the Talmud introduced a special blessing to be recited before eating bread, which is still recited: "Blessed art Thou, O Lord Our God, King of the Universe, who bringest forth bread from the earth" (Ber. 6:1; Ps. 14:4).

Simeon ben Yohai, a Talmudic sage, declared, "A loaf of bread and a rod were handed down from heaven tied together as if to say 'if you observe the Law, there will be a loaf of bread for you to eat; if not, there will be a rod for you to be punished with'" (Ber. 29b). The rabbis also urged that bread be handled respectfully, not hung up in a basket (Pes. 111b) or thrown across the table, or used to support any other object (Ber. 50b). An interesting comment on how advanced baking had become is found in Midrashic literature (during the first centuries), which states that pastry bakers in Caesarea produced one hundred varieties of egg pastries.

In New Testament times, Palestinian bread looked like stones, which explains the temptation of Jesus, "command that these stones be made bread" (Matt. 4:3). In Christian symbolism, Jesus identified himself as "the bread of life" (Jn. 6:48–51) and Paul spoke metaphorically of "a little leaven" leavening the whole lump" (1 Cor. 5:6, 8).

See *Brewer, Cook, Housewife.*

Banker and *Banking*

There are records of loans issued by the temples of Babylon as early as 2000 B.C. Money stored in temples was considered safe since temples were considered sacred and under the protection of the gods. There were also some companies such as the Egibi bank which flourished in the sixth century B.C. and which engaged in some banking functions related to the buying and selling of merchandise.

During the period covered by the Old Testament, some banking activities were conducted by merchants, traders, and landowners. The occupation of banker, in the sense of someone providing protection for money and valuables, making loans, and offering commercial credit, does not seem to have existed in ancient Israel.

In Biblical times, when most Jews lived in an agrarian society, there were limited opportunities for obtaining credit. Jews were forbidden to lend money on interest to their coreligionists (Ex. 22:25), although they were permitted to charge interest to non-Israelites (Dt. 23:20).

During the postexilic period when Jews entered commercial relations in large numbers and came into frequent contact with foreigners, credit expanded. During the first exile, there was considerable commercial activity. With this development, the objection to lending money on interest seems to have been ignored.

By the fourth century B.C., however, financial activities were conducted in the temples by public bodies and by private firms in Greece. Private firms accepted deposits, made loans, tested and changed coins, and negotiated credit transactions between cities. This system was later adopted by Hellenistic Egypt where banking was a monopoly. There was a state bank in Alexandria, and banks in villages lent money to private individuals. They served as branches of the state bank, receiving money, taxes, and making payments on treasury accounts similar to the state banks in Greek cities. In the New Testament there is a reference to an Alexandrian Jew who was treasurer for Candace, Queen of Ethiopia (Acts 8:27).

Before temples served as places for depositing valuables, the ancients either buried their valuables (Jos. 7:21) or deposited them with neighbors (Ex. 22:7). The national wealth, however, was kept at the temple and the palace (1 Ki. 14:26). Later, private property was also deposited for safety in temples (2 Mac. 3:6, 10 f.). Money-changers, by exchanging currency, performed one of the functions of banking (Matt. 25:27; Lk. 19:23).

See *Accountant, Money-Changer, Money Lender, Pawnbroker, Priest, Steward, Treasurer,* APPENDIX II.

Banner Maker

Banner makers produced the flags or standards which were carried at the head of a military troop to indicate the line of march or rallying point. Sometimes, it was a streamer attached to a lance (Isa. 13:2; Ps. 20:5; Cant. 6:4; Num. 2:2). Banners usually bore some insignia such as an animal or bird which represented the distinctive emblem of the group carrying it.

Barber

Barbering is a craft that was established during early Egyptian times. We know that the upper-class Egyptian cut his hair and had his beard carefully shaved save for a small tuft under his chin to which he attached an artificial beard on state and religious occasions. In Genesis 41:14 Joseph is described as having been shaven before he was brought before Pharaoh.

Mutilating another person's beard by cutting it or shaving it was a grave affront (2 Sam. 10:4). During periods of mourning, however, it was common to disfigure one's own beard (Isa. 15:2; Jer. 48:37) except for the priest (Lev. 21:5). The mandatory shaving of lepers seems to have been a means of informing the public of the presence of the disease (Lev. 14:8–9).

Ultrapious Jews to this day prefer to wear beards, following the view that "God gave man a beard to distinguish him from woman and it is wrong to oppose nature" (Bahya Abravanel's interpretation of Lev. 19:27). Moreover, according to the Talmud, the adornment of a man's face is his beard (Shab. 152a).

The tools of the ancient barber were razors, combs, and shears, some of which survive in various museums throughout the world, especially in those housing Egyptian artifacts. We do not know what the barber charged for his services, but it was probably modest.

See *Hairdresser.*

Basket Weaver and *Basketwork*

This is one of the oldest and almost universal human crafts, which early became an occupation, usually pursued by women.

Despite the perishability of the vegetable fibers from which baskets are made, early examples have been preserved in arid sands, dry caves, and other suitable environments.

In Biblical times, baskets were made, as they still are today, by hand. Vegetable fibers such as canes, grasses, roots, or twigs are interlaced or coiled or sewed. Baskets were made then and even today without the use of a loom or frame.

All basketry is either plaited, woven, or coiled. Plaited basketry is made by the crossing of two or more sets of elements called warp and weft. When the warps cannot be differentiated by rigidity or direction, both elements may be called wefts. The main varieties of plaited work are check, which includes wattlework, twilled, turned, and hexagonal work.

Coiled work, the sewing of a spiral foundation of cane, twigs, or grass, includes simple oversewn coil, the furcate coil, the skep coil, figure-eight, "lazy squaw," crossed figure eight and cycloid, or single-element coil.

The materials used in basketry vary with the region, the availability of wild plants, and the craftsmen's preference. Palms are most common in tropical regions. Most of the baskets in Biblical times seem to have been made of cane.

The Bible mentions four kinds of baskets: *dud, kelub, tene,* and *sal.*

Although we do not know how they differed in their shape, size, or use, it is believed that *dud* was a carrying basket held in the hand (2 Ki. 10:7; Jer. 24:2). It may have been a large shallow basket similar to those used by the ancient Egyptians. Elsewhere *dud* means a pot in which meat was boiled. It is therefore believed to be a general expression signifying various vessels.

Kelub, mentioned in Amos 8:1, suggests a fruit basket, and in Jeremiah 5:27 it means a cage which was probably a roughly woven basket with a cover similar to that carried by a fowler for transporting his catch.

Tene was apparently a large deep basket in which grain and other similar products were placed (Dt. 28:5, 17) and in which the tithes were carried to the Temple (Dt. 26:2). Some scholars believe that it was jar-shaped.

Sal is believed to have been a small dish-shaped basket, possibly constructed of finer material.

In Biblical times, baskets served as containers of food (Gen. 40:16–18; Ex. 29:3, 23; Lev. 8:2, 26). Some baskets were used to bear the first fruits of the ground to the priest (Dt. 26:2, 4), as well as for secular purposes.

The Bible reports that in carrying out Pharaoh's command that every Hebrew male child be cast into the river (Ex. 1:22), Moses' family made a covered, waterproofed chest or basket of bulrushes or papyrus to protect the infant (2:3). Papyrus boats are also mentioned in Isaiah 18:2. In the Gospel story of the feeding of the crowds, twelve baskets are mentioned in which the leftovers of the five thousand were gathered (Matt. 14:20; Mk. 6:43; Lk. 9:17; Jn. 6:13).

Beekeeper

Although there is no reference to beekeeping in the Bible, scholars assert that they existed from about the fifth century B.C. to meet the increasing need for sweetening since sugar was unknown. The beekeeper cultivated bees for the production of honey and the pollination of crops. He gathered beehives using hand tools and inserted the honeycomb of the bees into the beehive or inducted wild swarming bees into the hive or prepared a honeycomb frame. He then placed some sort of screen plug into the hive entrance to confine the bees. He usually placed the hives near the source of pollen and nectar in orchards or clover fields. When he wished to inspect the hive and gather honeycomb, he burned either charcoal or cow dung to force the bees out. Then he scraped out parasites such as wax and moth larvae, and removed vermin such as birds and mice. He probably also destroyed diseased bee colonies and burned their hives or sterilized them.

Honey was abundant in Palestine, and there is repeated reference to it as a land "flowing with milk and honey" (Ex. 3:8, 17).

Honey was not only enjoyed for itself, but also as an accompaniment to other food (Pro. 24:13; Matt. 3:4; Mk. 1:6). Moreover, it was extensively used in making pastry (Ex. 16:31).

Philo and the Mishnah (second century A.D.) indicate that there were numerous beekeepers among Jews.

See *Farmer*.

Beggar

Though the Biblical Hebrew lacked a specific term for the professional beggar, begging was an ancient occupation. Professional beggars are implied in the statement that "the children of the wicked are cursed with beggary" (Ps. 109:10). As larger communities developed, the strong sense of kinship and neighborliness which had previously aided the needy diminished. This, coupled with widespread poverty, led to the rise of professional beggars.

The beggar is described as sitting along dusty roads on dung hills (1 Sam. 2:8) or awaiting the charitable at the gates of the Temple. Professional beggars were despised, apparently because many who made a career of alms-seeking were shiftless and not really victims of adversity. There were some who feigned diseases and handicaps in order to attract sympathy (Peah 8:9; Ket. 68a). Begging is clearly criticized in Ecclesiasticus 40:28–30. Nevertheless, to drive beggars away without giving them some alms was forbidden (B.B. 9a), and even non-Jews were to be given food and clothing (Tos. Git. 5.3.4; Yoreh Deah 251, 1 gloss). Women, however, did not beg from house to house, with the result that the Talmud regarded the support of a needy woman as more meritorious than the support of an improvident man (Hor. 3:7).

In the New Testament, Jesus is reported to have restored sight to a blind beggar at the Pool of Siloam (Jn. 9:8–11) and to the blind Bartimaeus begging along the Jericho road (Mk.

10:46–52). In the early Christian community, members were urged to assign a portion of their earnings to the needy (Acts 11:29, 30; Rom. 15:25–27).

Bodyguard

Bodyguards in Biblical times were mainly soldiers who guarded royalty and their families (Gen. 37:36, 39:1, 40:3), though occasionally civilians guarded persons of property. David was protected by a foreign guard (2 Sam. 23:22, 23). Rehoboam's guard supervised the royal shields in the Palace and the Temple area of Jerusalem (1 Ki. 14:27) where later a guard protected young King Jehoash when he was threatened by Athaliah (2 Ki. 11:19). A very lenient guard watched over Paul in Rome (Acts 28:16).

Probably bodyguards were selected on the basis of height, strength, agility, and military prowess.

See *Armor-Bearer, Runner, Soldier.*

Brewer

Although brewers are not mentioned in the Bible as an occupational group, there is archaeological evidence that there were brewers in Babylonia as far back as 6000 B.C. Barley, an important ingredient in beer, grew wild in Babylonia, which may be why it was the first known country to discover beer. Early fermented beverages may have derived from barley, grapes, or honey.

Beer was variously used as a libation, as a beverage, and as a medicine. The Hebrews probably learned the use of hops in producing beer after 587 B.C. when they were captured by the

Babylonians. The Bible does not reveal how beer was made, but the Jews undoubtedly drank it. Priests, however, were forbidden to drink beer or wine while officiating (Lev. 10:9).

The ancient brewer was also a baker. His raw material was grain and yeast. After it was soaked until it germinated, it was ground and molded into cakes which were partially baked. The cakes were then crumbled, placed in a jar of water, and left to ferment so that the result looked like soup.

Eventually, brewmasters probably became skilled in brewing, fermenting, lagering, and in the malting processes of beer production.

See *Baker, Vintner.*

Bricklayer and *Brickmaker*

In the Nile Valley, brickmaking and bricklaying date back to prehistoric times. In neolithic times (8000–4500 B.C.) brickmakers made bricks hand-shaped with thumb impressions in a herringbone pattern. A picture on the tomb of Thutmose III about 1460 B.C. depicts the then-current process of brickmaking and bricklaying. Some of the monuments of ancient Egypt made of sun-dried bricks still survive.

Bricks were the commonest building material in the ancient Biblical world and were made from a lump of mud or clay, usually rectangular, which was then dried and burnt. Burning the brick made it almost indestructible. Workers thoroughly soaked the clay, usually mixed it with straw, sand, or vegetable matter, and took it in baskets to the artisan who molded bricks by hand or kneaded them by intensive stamping of the feet or by using a wooden mold. The bricks were then laid out in long rows and left to dry. The size of the oblong-shaped bricks measured as much as twenty-one by ten by four inches. During the first two Christian centuries the standard size was nine inches square.

These early bricks often were inscribed with the name of the Pharaoh or the building in which they were to be used. In Babylon, bricks also bore the king's name and a dedicatory inscription in his honor.

Sun-dried bricks were typical in Mesopotamia and in Palestine. In Mesopotamia, they were often used in facings and pavements. City and house walls were of brick built on a stone foundation. Wooden beams were often injected into brickwork. In Egypt, this process had a dual advantage; it helped to eliminate or reduce warping, and since the mud structure dried out, the wooden beams made it firmer.

In Asia Minor and elsewhere, these wooden beams were often inserted in stone foundations and in mud-brick stone walls. This process of using brick upon wood over stone was used by Solomon in his construction of buildings in Jerusalem (1 Ki. 6:36, 7:12). Excavation of the Israelite Megiddo of Solomon's or of Ahab's period reveals that the technique was still practiced.

The ancient Hebrews in Egypt were described as bricklayers and brickmakers for Pharaoh during their sojourn there (Ex. 5: 6–19). This account accurately mirrors the process of brickmaking during the thirteenth and twelfth centuries B.C. These ancient bricklayers developed superior skill in their craft. The bricks were frequently laid out in intricate patterns. Isaiah (65:3) and the Torah (Ex. 20:25) chided Jews who preferred to use bricks instead of native stone for altars.

In performing his duties, the bricklayer laid his bricks to construct or repair walls, arches, and other structures. He probably measured distances from reference points and marked guidelines on a working surface to lay out his work. Then, using a trowel, he spread a soft layer of mortar as a base and binder for block. Next he applied mortar to the end of the block and placed it in the mortar bed. He tapped the block with the trowel to level, align, and embed it in mortar, providing for the desired thickness of the joint.

With his trowel he removed excess mortar from the face of the block. Using either the trowel or a pointed tool, he finished the mortar between the bricks. For spaces too small for a whole brick, he broke bricks to fit, using a hammer or the edge of the trowel.

Brick kilns have been found in Mesopotamia but not by the Nile or Jordan rivers. It is believed that the fiery furnace where "Daniel's three friends were thrown as punishment" (Dan. 3:6, 11, 16–23) may have been a brick kiln, one of those which furnished burnt bricks to Nebuchadnezzar's Babylon. On the other hand, in 2 Samuel 12:31, Jeremiah 43:9, and Nahum 3:14, *malben* is sometimes rendered as brick kiln, though, according to some scholars, inaccurately. The brick kilns of ancient Babylonia are believed to have looked like the huge pottery kiln excavated in Nippur.

From the Biblical account and contemporary papyri, it is clear that bricklayers were usually slaves who toiled under the supervision of severe taskmasters, who often flogged them to increase their production. There is a reference in the code of Hammurabi that indicates that bricklayers were paid five *she* a day or between ten and twenty cents. Their hours were, of course, long; their work arduous; and their general living conditions severe. But the work of the bricklayer was one of the most enduring of all vocations.

See *Architect, Mason, Stoneworker.*

Butcher

The closest specific reference to butcher in the Bible is "sar Ha-tabahim"—literally "captain of the butchers" but translated "butler" or "captain of the guards" (Gen. 40:3). We can reasonably conjecture, however, that in larger communities some persons slaughtered and quartered animals for the consumers' use. In 1 Corinthians 10:25 there is a reference to a shambles (meat market), and an excavation in Corinth during the first Christian century refers to "Lucius the butcher." Similarly, it is likely that persons skilled in this work served in the Temple of Jerusalem.

Pliny the Younger, 62–113 A.D. (Ep. 10, 96) refers to a guild of butchers in Rome who became concerned over the decline in the sale of sacrificial meat, which aroused official action against the church.

The tools of this occupation were knives, hooks, saws, and cleavers. Considerable manual dexterity and brawn were required. The occupation was probably learned by observation and some sort of apprenticeship.

The butcher was called "a partner of Amelek" in the Talmud (Kid. 82a), indicating that he was held in low esteem.

See *Bodyguard, Ritual Slaughterer.*

Calker and *Calking*

Calking is the process of driving various materials into the seams between the planks of ships in order to make the joints waterproof. The process of calking was known many centuries before Biblical times. In the Bible, workers of Tyre were famed as skilled calkers. They used pitch, tow, or bitumen (Ezek. 27: 9, 27). They may have combined this skill with other chores related to shipbuilding or repair.

See *Shipbuilder.*

Camel Driver

The domesticated camel was known in the Near East by 3000 B.C. and was used in a limited manner through the second millennium, although the ass was the main beast of burden. In the Bible, camels are first mentioned during the period of the Patriarchs (1900–1700 B.C.), much of whose wealth consisted of camels (Gen. 12:16, 24:10; Job 1:3, 17). They are mentioned twice as having used camels for transportation (Gen. 24:10, 31:17, 34). The camel seems to have been used by the Ishmaelites, Midianites, who decorated their camels with little golden crescents (Jg. 8:21), and the desert traders (Gen. 37:25), since it could travel for days without water. The camel was also prized as a beast of burden, as a provider of milk and clothing, and as useful in battle. Even its dung was used for fuel.

As commerce developed, there arose the occupation of the camel driver, who was responsible for his camel, passengers, and cargo. For speedy travel the camel driver used dromedaries (Isa. 60:6). He was paid for his services in money or in kind. He was subject to the vagaries of weather, blistering heat, and searing sandstorms as well as thieves who preyed on travelers. He was often away from his family.

David appears to have had a special official named Obil in charge of his camels (1 Chr. 27:30).

In Talmudic times, camel drivers were looked down upon—"One must not rear his son to be an ass driver or camel driver" (Kid. 4:13)—presumably because their morals were suspect.

See *Caravan Chief, Driver,* APPENDIX I.

Candymaker

In Biblical times, candies were made of dates, honey, nuts, and gum arabic and were exported to Tyre (Ezek. 27:17). Women were the principal candymakers and bakers of fancy cakes (1 Sam. 8:13). Sticky confections were sold at bazaars.

These early candymakers mixed together and cooked such ingredients as honey, corn syrup, butter, and gum base to produce sweetness of a definite flavor, texture, and color. They shaped the candy by spinning or by rolling it into strips ready for cutting. The royal family and the very rich were supplied with dainties prepared by experts (Gen. 49:20).

The ancients were clearly oblivious to weight-watching and dieting and commonly nibbled sweetmeats both during and between meals.

Captain

The term "captain," from the Hebrew *sar,* has such varied meanings as leader of thousands, hundreds, or fifties (1 Sam. 8:12), chief butler (Gen. 40:9), chief baker (Gen. 40:16), chief of the tribe (Ps. 68:27), and chief priest (Ez. 8:29).

In the New Testament, *chiliarchos,* usually translated "chief captain," means literally a commander of a thousand men, though it is commonly used as a term for any military officer (Mk. 6:21). In the Temple, police were employed who were governed by an official (Acts 28:16), translated "captain of the guard."

See *Baker, Bodyguard, Soldier.*

Caravan Chief

Caravans that carried substantial quantities of merchandise in ancient times were led by a caravan leader. From the early archives of the Assyrian traders at Kultepe we learn of a steady and extensive traffic between Kanish and Ashur. The trade was usually by donkey caravan that might consist of as many as six hundred donkeys and travel twelve to fifteen miles a day. Caravan leaders were given an allowance on setting out and kept diaries recording their expenses en route. At the end of their trip they gave a complete account of these expenses.

Merchants and travelers usually traveled in groups as protection against predatory animals and bandits. Local caravans headed by a chief delivered goods from one district to another mainly by ass and, less commonly, by camel. Unsettled political conditions sometimes disrupted traffic (Jg. 5:6). Most of the caravans mentioned in the Old Testament traded with Transjordan and Arabia.

Arab caravans carried mainly the profitable spices and incense which the rulers of Sheba may have monopolized (1 Ki. 10:2). Transjordanians sold or exchanged these products with Egyptians (Gen. 37:25). The caravan chief was probably selected because of his experience as a traveler, his integrity, and capacities in dealing with predatory humans and animals.

See *Camel Driver, Driver,* APPENDIX I.

Carpenter

Carpentry was practiced in Egypt many centuries before the most renowned carpenter in history, Jesus. According to the archaeologist Sir Flinders Petrie, ancient Egyptian carpenters built huge boats 150 feet long for transporting obelisks. They were also active in constructing temples, palaces, and tombs, as well as in building numerous irrigation pumps and repairing sluice gates in the network of the delta canals. Many Egyptian carpenters were also employed making wooden coffins and mummy cartonnages—the glued linen wrappings for the dead.

While the mechanically inclined members of the family undoubtedly built or repaired the agricultural utensils they needed for the family's requirements (such as carts, winnowing forks, plows, shafts for mattocks, boxes), for larger projects or more expert work, the professional carpenter was needed. In Biblical times, carpenters were usually Phoenicians, who seem to have done most of their shipbuilding at Tyre, where they built boats of cypress, masts of cedar, and oars of oak (Ezek. 27:5–6). The Phoenicians also built David's palace (2 Sam. 5:11) and Solomon's Temple as well as the later Temple (Ez. 3:7), and possibly did some of the repair work on the Temple (Ex. 25). Using imported hardwoods—ebony, sandalwood, and boxwood—they also built the upper floors of stone houses, the stairs and windows of synagogues, including the cherubs of the first Temple (1 Ki. 6:23).

For agricultural tools they used mainly mulberry wood, and for joining they used such domestic woods as cedar, cypress, oak, ash, and acacia (Isa. 44:14). Dowels and nails, dovetail and miter joints were used to join wood.

Many carpenter's tools dating from Bible times are now lodged at the University Museum at Philadelphia, Pennsylvania; they include compasses, nails, hammers (Jg. 5:26), pencils (Isa. 44:13), iron saws (some two-edged), planes, marking tools, an adz, a small chopper, files, chisels, and awls. Isaiah 44:13 also lists some additional carpenter's tools such as a plummet line and a square.

Some carpenters specialized in carving idols (Isa. 44:10–18) that were bought and worshiped. Others worked on bone and ivory (Ex. 31:5, 35:33).

Because of their nomadic origin, the Hebrews may have been slow in becoming skilled carpenters. Probably this is why David and Solomon had to import Tyrian carpenters to build the palace and the Temple. The Hebrew carpenters who repaired the Temple were later deported into captivity (Jer. 24:1) and Ezra again imported Phoenicians (Ez. 3:7).

There were guilds of carpenters (1 Chr. 4:14) who probably banded together to protect their common interests. The less gifted among them cut timber while the more skilled craftsmen engaged in carving and inlay work. (Paul Louis, *Ancient Rome at Work*, p. 47, refers to carpenters' guilds in Rome in the seventh century B.C.)

In Christian symbolism, the carpenter's square represents Jude and Thomas; the saw, St. James the Less. How esteemed the work of the carpenter was in the New Testament can be seen from the fact that Jesus is referred to as both the "carpenter" and the "carpenter's son" (Matt. 13:55). The Talmud, too, makes a number of references to carpenters: a carpenter's workshop (Tos. B.K. 6.25), carpenters' apprentices (Pes. 108a), and carpenters who carved artificial teeth (Yer. Shab. 6, 8c).

See *Architect, Artist, Furniture Designer, Ivory Carver, Mason, Shipbuilder, Wagonsmith, Wheelwright, Wood Carver,* APPENDIX IV.

Carpetmaker and *Rugmaker*

The verse, "I have decked my bed with coverings of tapestry. . . . with fine linen of Egypt" (Pro. 7:16), suggests the existence of carpet loomers who, we know from other sources, abounded in Biblical times. The carpet sewer, for example, sewed together sections of carpeting and finished edges by sewing or binding material by hand. He sewed decorative trimmings on rugs, borders, or runners and probably sewed together strips of padded material to fit beneath carpeting. There was also the rug braider who braided rugs by hand from strips of wool, cotton, and other materials. He selected strips to match, blend, or contrast colors and interwove three or more at a time to form a continuous braid. Then he laid the braid on a flat surface and coiled or bent it into shape, hand-stitching the ends together.

In the Bible, *midin* (Jg. 5:10) is sometimes translated "rich carpets"; Ganaz, translated "treasury," may include garments and carpets "of colored stuff" (Est. 3:9, 4:7). The word used in Judges 5:10 implies some object that people sit on. *Simicha,* which may also have been a rug, was the covering which Jael put over Sisera (Jg. 4:18) when, after fleeing from battle, he entered her tent. It may also have been a heavy cloak or a tent curtain.

See *Weaver.*

Cattleman and *Cattle Raising*

In Biblical times, human wealth revolved largely around cattle (Gen. 13:2). Abraham, Isaac, and Jacob and his twelve sons were shepherds (Gen. 46:34, 47:1, 3, 4, 6). From their cattle they derived their clothing, food, and tents. Cattle also served as sacrificial offerings. Consequently, herds and flocks were included in all blessings (Dt. 8:13, 28:4).

In the Bible, cattle is a broad term including goats, sheep, oxen, bullocks, heifers, camels, horses, and asses. The most numerous livestock were small cattle or sheep and goats known as *tson.* Horned cattle were raised successfully only where there was sufficient drinking water such as in the valley of the Jordan and in the Plain of Sharon, and especially in the western part of Bashan. Asses were abundant and highly useful (Gen. 12:16, 30:43; Jos. 7:24; 1 Sam. 8:16).

The Biblical cattle ranchers bred and raised cattle for food, for sale, and for sacrifices. They, their families, and servants supplied the cattle with hay and other forage when pasturage was low and provided salt licks as a supplement. They released bulls among the cows. There is no evidence that there was a knowledge of genetics in Biblical times. They utilized empirical and traditional methods.

The Bible forbade the hybridization of animals: "Thou shalt not let thy cattle gender with a diverse kind" (Lev. 19:19). Jacob's interesting tactic, increasing his flock at his father-in-law's expense by stripping the bark of branches of poplar, hazel, and chestnut trees and placing them in the watering troughs, apparently stimulated their reproductive desires and powers (Gen. 30:32–43).

See *Butcher, Cheese Maker, Dairyman, Farmer, Horse Breeder, Sheepshearer, Shepherd.*

Census Taker and *Census Taking*

Census taking occurred as early as the third millennium B.C. in Egypt when the Pharaohs took a biennial census which they later made an annual event. They surveyed the land, counted cattle and other property to assess taxes which were paid in gold, grains, hides, or in forced labor. Each province collected its own taxes. A Mesopotamian census list has been found spanning a period of five hundred years from the eighteenth century B.C. to about the time of Moses.

Records of the twelfth-century-B.C. Ramesside administration reveal the accounts of the government tax collectors and show that taxes were assessed per unit of land or per measure of grain. The story of Joseph reveals the tax imposed on agricultural yield (Gen. 47).

Besides its main purpose of providing revenue, the census was also necessary to provide a register of available manpower subject to forced labor or to military service. Conscription was by lot, as was the grant of land to those who had served in the army. Since the conscript faced death in combat, atonement and purificatory rites and other rituals were believed capable of averting the wrath of the gods.

The Bible records the counting of the secular tribes of Israel shortly after their arrival at Mt. Sinai (Num. 26; Ex. 30:11–16). Apparently, the Israelite tribes and their descendants both feared the taboo effect of head counting and resented being counted, because it led to taxes and conscription. They also considered it an infringement of their individual liberty.

The first royal census mentioned in the Bible was taken by David apparently to levy troops, to conscript forced labor, and to obtain revenue. David ordered this census over the protest of his general, Joab, who shared the popular fear of its possible evil consequences (2 Sam. 24:1–10). David's census lasted nine months and twenty days. Unfortunately, a plague broke out which confirmed the prevalent fear that head counting evokes baleful influences. Nevertheless, other censuses were taken during the days of Jotham, Jeroboam (1 Chr. 5:17), and Amaziah, 800–783 B.C. (2 Chr. 25:5). In the second chapter of Ezra and in the seventh chapter of Nehemiah we find census lists.

To avert the evil that was believed to lurk in head counting, the practice was instituted of collecting a half shekel from each person to be counted. When these were counted, the number of persons would then be known.

There are two censuses mentioned in the New Testament. One, conducted by the Roman Quirinus in the year 6–7 B.C., aroused the people to revolt (Acts 5:37). The second census, which was ordered by Augustus, is famous because it is believed to have brought Joseph and Mary to Bethlehem from Nazareth to be enrolled in the ancestral town of Joseph (Lk. 2:1–5).

See *Tax Collector*.

Charioteer

As far back as the third millennium there were charioteers in southern Mesopotamia who rode ass-drawn, heavy-wheeled vehicles in battle and on state occasions. During the second millennium, the Assyrians developed the chariot as one of their basic implements of war. It was a light, horse-drawn vehicle driven by a charioteer.

Ancient chariots had a crew of two to four charioteers. The Assyrians had three, the third holding a shield to protect the others, who either drove or held weapons. The Hebrews also had three, the third apparently serving as captain. There are a number of references to riders or charioteers and chariots in the Bible (Ezek. 27:20; 1 Ki. 22:34; 2 Ki. 9:21; 2 Chr. 18:33). Some charioteers such as Jehu were prone to speeding: "and his driving is like the driving of Jehu the son of Nimshi, for he driveth furiously" (2 Ki. 9:20). Solomon established chariot cities for his own army at Jerusalem and elsewhere. His army included fourteen hundred chariots (1 Ki. 9:15–19, 10:26).

To perform well in the arena, charioteers had to possess great strength and agility as well as calm nerves. They also went through a long and taxing training period (J. Carcopino, *Daily Life in Ancient Rome*, pp. 216–222). In Rome during the first century before Christ and after, the work of the charioteer was hazardous. He guided two horses by leaping from one to the other. He also waved weapons as he rode and engaged in mock warfare. While riding his galloping mount he alternately sat astride, knelt, lay down on the horse, snatched a piece of cloth from the track, and jumped over a chariot harnessed to four horses.

The traditional charioteer stood helmeted and erect in his chariot and carried a whip. He wore leggings around his calves and thighs. The color of his tunic indicated the side he was fighting for. His reins were tied around his body and he had a dagger at his side to cut himself loose should he become entangled. During a race, he had to be constantly on the alert. He had to look ahead to guide his mount and look behind to avoid being rammed or fouled by wily competitors. An error or accident could cost him his life.

Star charioteers became wealthy. One retired with a fortune of thirty-five million sesterces. A victorious charioteer was acclaimed by all, and his picture was hung almost everywhere in the city. He enjoyed certain immunities and was a popular idol.

See *Armorer, Driver, Harness Maker, Horse Breeder, Hunter, Soldier, Wagonsmith.*

Cheese Maker and *Cheese Making*

Cheese making probably started when man first took milk from wild or domestic animals. He soon discovered that unless he used the milk fairly soon, it became sour and formed an acid curd which by natural means released whey, leaving a semisolid curd. This was the first kind of cheese and this method of production is still used by primitive people.

In the Bible, there are references to curd and cheese; cheese of the kine was given to King David, revealing that milk from cows and possibly other animals was used for cheese before 1100 B.C. Twice in the Old Testament cheese was included in the list of provisions which David brought to his brothers (1 Sam. 17:18), and it was among the provisions which David received at Mahanaim (2 Sam. 17:29).

In Biblical times, cheese was manufactured by salting the strained curds, molding them into small disks about the size of a hand, and then drying them in the open air (Job 10:10). There were several varieties of cheese: *hemah* or cream (Pro. 30:33); *gebinah* or ordinary cheese (Job 10:10); and *hariz he-halab* (1 Sam. 17:18), probably akin to cottage cheese.

In post-Biblical days, cheese manufacturers belonged to a guild. Josephus (B.J. 5.4.1) refers to the valley of the cheese makers. The Talmud makes numerous references to the manufacture of a hard cheese (Shab. 96a).

When families later learned to improve their production of cheese, they kept their trade secrets, a situation still true of some cheese manufacturers.

See *Cattleman, Cook, Dairyman.*

Choirmaster

Choirmasters were probably Levites who conducted the Temple choir, which was composed of Levites. There were entire families of professional singers who officiated in the Temple. The choirmaster led their group in antiphonal singing (1 Chr. 15:16–24).

He probably auditioned and chose the members of the choir, directing them with an orchestral accompaniment. He may have composed and probably selected the music sung. He is believed to have been familiar with tonal and harmonic balances, dynamics, tempos, and shadings to achieve the desired results. His texts included the Pentateuch and the Psalms.

See *Chorister, Musician.*

Chorister and the *Choir*

Members of the Temple choir were trained to participate in the divine service. The first choir mentioned in the Bible was organized by the Levites for the Temple service and was accompanied by musicians. Two priests with silver trumpets blew the signal for the choir to begin (Tamid 7.3). The choir also sang at the offering of public sacrifices (2 Chr. 29:27) and at the wine libation (Maimonides, *Yad,* "Kele ha-Mikdash," 3).

The number of members in the choir ranged from a minimum of a dozen male singers (Ar. 2:6) to an unspecified maximum, and they ranged from thirty to fifty years of age when vocal powers often declined. Originally, members of the choir were required to have at least five years of training before they were accepted (Hul. 24). Young sons of the Levites were also allowed to sing with the choir "in order to add sweetness to the song." Apparently, the renditions of these youngsters were so stirring that it aroused the envy of the adult singers (Ar. 13b).

Levites were divided into twenty-four orders and each was assigned to serve a certain day (Ta'an. 27b). They served as doorkeepers, singers, or musicians. Each was given his post in the choir or orchestra and was prohibited from shifting. From the age of twenty-five to thirty, all members underwent training which included instruction in singing. The Talmud declares that this age restriction was practiced only at the Tabernacle, although at the Temple service, ability to sing and not age determined who was accepted as a Temple chorister (Hul. 24a).

When Solomon's Temple was dedicated, the sons of the

Levites accompanied the choir in singing God's praise (2 Chr. 5:13). The young Levites sang impressively with their soprano voices but were prohibited from using instruments and from entering the priests' hall in the Temple before the adult Levites began to sing. They had to stand on the ground below the adults (Ar. 13b). In addition to the young singers, the Temple choir had twelve adults.

The main service consisted of vocal rather than instrumental music (Suk. 50b). The Temple choir is believed to have been composed entirely of men despite 1 Chronicles 25:5, which refers to Heman's fourteen sons and three daughters, while Ezra mentions two hundred singing men and women among the returnees from Babylon to Jerusalem (Ez. 2:65). The women choristers sang dirges (2 Chr. 35:25).

Later, after the destruction of the Temple, an austere note entered when the rabbis issued a decree banning all instrumental or vocal music as a sign of national mourning (Git. 7a). Similarly, in orthodox synagogues women's voices were banned in choirs because "listening to a woman's voice leads to lusting after her" (Ber. 24a).

See *Choirmaster, Musician, Musical Instrument Maker.*

Circumcisor and *Circumcision*

Circumcision is a rite practiced by many people. In the Bible (Gen. 17) there is an account of its origin among Jews beginning with Abraham, who established it as a covenant between God and the Jews. It is also referred to as the Abrahamic covenant. Slaves acquired by Jews were required to undergo circumcision (Gen. 17:12), as were aliens who wished to participate in the Feast of Passover and those who wished to intermarry with Jews (Gen. 34:14).

Infant circumcision at the age of eight days became the practice among Jews (Gen. 17:12). Originally, circumcision appears to have been performed by the mother (Ex. 4:24–26), but eventually a religious functionary called a *mohel* performed the rite.

Though it was usually required that circumcision be performed on the eighth day of the infant's life, the rabbis permitted it to be postponed or even omitted if the infant was believed to be suffering from hemophilia. Circumcision is not a sacrament, and an uncircumcised Jewish child is considered a full Jew if its mother is a Jewess (Hul. 4b).

In performing this rite today, the *mohel* exercises care that sterile conditions prevail so as to protect the health of the child. To perform the operation, he may use a scalpel, a double-edge knife, or a clamp.

Among the reasons which have been advanced at various times for circumcision have been that it was a consecration of the generative powers, a puberty rite, or a means of facilitating cohabitation. Philo, Josephus, and Maimonides believed that it arose because of hygienic reasons.

At various times, Jews suffered martyrdom because of their adherence to the rite. Antiochus Epiphanes (175–163 B.C.) forbade it (1 Mac. 1, 48, 60; 2:46), and Jewish women risked their lives when they circumcised their sons despite the command. Emperor Hadrian (117–138 A.D.) also forbade circumcision on pain of death.

Clothier and *Clothing*

Early in the history of man, artistic persons emerged who were not content with clothing as mere protection against the elements. They used their imagination, artistic talents, and needle skills to create attractive and even lavish apparel.

Most of our knowledge of clothing worn in Biblical times comes from archaeological discoveries rather than from the Bible. Biblical references to clothing are usually general and imprecise. We know, however, that clothing in early times was made of the simplest fabric and design and was usually homemade.

Fabrics

Few textiles from Biblical times have been preserved in Palestine, but many have survived in the dry climate of Egypt. Among the Egyptian specimens are some which are six feet wide as well as narrow types made of linen and wool. They are found in both plain and patterned designs. Although the weaving was simple, the colors used in Biblical times were many.

Four fibers were most commonly used to produce cloth. Vegetable fibers were universally first spun to produce continuous yarns for weaving. Flax grew in limited quantities in Palestine and the quality produced in Galilee was considered comparable to that of Egypt. Assyria, too, had cotton fabrics from about 700 B.C. The cotton tree was introduced by King Sennacherib. Two centuries later there were cotton curtains, white and blue (Est. 1:6), at the king's palace in Susa, with linen and wool used as cords. While cotton grew in many countries, it flourished best or was spun in dampness or humidity in climates such as that of Egypt.

Egyptian linen was preferred because it was soft and pliant and made excellent, comfortable clothing. So precious were garments of fine linen that the Pharaoh presented them as gifts along with gold and jewels (Gen. 41:42). Durable sails were also made from it (Ezek. 27:7).

In earlier Biblical times, unbleached linen or cotton was used almost entirely, for although cotton could be dyed or printed with indigo fairly easily, linen was harder to dye. Some blue threads were found on the linen garments discovered in the cave with the Dead Sea Scrolls and at Dura-Europus on the Euphrates. The robe of the ephod, which covered the hips and thighs of the priest, was entirely made in blue (Ex. 28:31).

The two animal fibers commonly used for fabrics were silk and wool. In the Near East in Biblical times wool was most commonly used. Felt was made from the wool shed by sheep and goats. Spinning, which was already well established in early Biblical times, was first employed on wool about 1550 B.C. Exodus 35:25–26 mentions this in connection with the Tabernacle.

Animal fibers appear to have been dyed in Biblical times. In Palestine, dyers were located in towns such as Magdala on the Yarmuk River, at Tell Beit Mirsim, Gezer, and Luz. Any color mentioned in the Bible (except blue, which was used on cotton and linen), referred to a wool fabric. Virtually any color could be achieved with a blue and red dye plus the natural color of wool itself. Joseph's coat of many colors is believed to have been made of leather or wool felt with a woven binding to prevent it from tearing (Ex. 28:32).

Dress

One of the oldest sources of information on pre-Israelite apparel is supplied by Babylonian, Hittite, and Egyptian monuments, especially the famous Beni Hasan tomb painting that dates from about 2000 B.C. This painting reveals the colorful garments worn by both men and women; only two of these garments were white. These ancients wore their garments draped over one shoulder, leaving the other shoulder bare. The garment reached to slightly below the knee. Women's garments had a similar shape but were somewhat longer and more colorful than men's.

For men, the earliest known undergarment, the apron, was made of animal skins and was worn around the hips or loins. In time this developed into the undergarment called *ketonet,* a tunic worn next to the skin and removed at night (Gen. 9:21; 2 Sam. 6:20; Cant. 5:3). There were also *sedinim,* undergarments worn beneath the *ketonet,* which were made of fine linen (Jg. 14:12; Isa. 3:23). The undergarment was held together by a girdle made of linen (Jer. 13:1), or of leather (2 Ki. 1:8), or of gold (Dan. 10:5). When worn by officials, it was called *abnet* (Isa. 22:21). In later times (Ex. 20:26), priests wore a garment usually made of linen and similar to modern trousers, which was known as *miknasayim* (Ex. 28:42).

The cloak, called *meil* in Hebrew, was generally worn over the undergarment (1 Sam. 2:19, 15:27). Like similar garments of the high priests, it may have reached only to the knees. Many believe that it was a long-sleeved garment made of light fabric, possibly imported from Syria. Dignitaries usually wore the upper garment, *simlah,* over the *ketonet.* To wear only the *ketonet* was regarded as going naked.

Upper garments were made of material similar to the lower ones, either of wool or flax. Purple materials were imported from Phoenicia, byssus from Egypt, and artistic weaving and embroidery from Babylon (Jos. 7:21; Zeph. 1:8). Skilled tailors made white as well as colored garments for nobles that were similar to those found on Syrian figures on Egyptian monuments. Later, nobles wore over their garments a wide, many-folded mantle of state known as *adderet* or *ma'atafah* which was made of expensive material (Isa. 3:22) imported from Babylonia (Jos. 7:21).

The poor Israelite wore a rectangular piece of woolen cloth sewed together so that the front and the two openings on the sides for the arm were unstitched. At night, to keep warm he slept in the same garment (Ex. 22:27; Dt. 24:13). His upper garment, not usually worn at work, was made of poorer quality wool or flax. It had a wide fold at the breast which was often used as a pocket (Hag. 2:12).

The oldest sacred garment was the *ephod,* which was probably a simple loincloth (1 Sam. 22:18). While he ministered in the Temple, the ordinary priest wore a cloth covering his hips and thighs (Ex. 28:42), a long, embroidered linen tunic with sleeves, and an elegant belt of twined linen of blue, purple, and scarlet material (Ex. 28:8; 39:28). He wore costly, tailor-made robes on special occasions, after which they were immediately removed and set aside until needed again. These special robes were called *mahalazot* (Isa. 3:22) or *halifot* (Gen. 45:22), "changes," and were worn only during the Temple service. Priests, especially the high priest, wore a miter as a head covering with an inscribed gold plate at the front (Lev. 8:9).

For the kings of Israel and Judah and their families, expert tailors created richly colored robes and elegant gowns (2 Sam. 13:18). Some wore wigs, which were usually Persian (Isa. 3:24). Members of nobility had extensive and elegant wardrobes (2 Ki. 10:22) that were cared for by special keepers or valets

(2 Ki. 22:14). Clothes were also given as gifts (Gen. 45:22; Jg. 14:19; 2 Ki. 5:5).

Women's garments were basically the same as men's except that they were probably longer, made of finer materials, were more colorful, more elaborate, and required more skillful tailoring. Reference to luxurious and ornamented women's clothing is found in Isaiah 3:18, 23 and Ezekiel 16:10. Women also wore girdles (Isa. 3:24), but unlike those worn today, they were not undergarments. During the time of Ruth they wore a broad mantle in which they could carry such things as grain (Ru. 3:15). For women of nobility, tailors created a long train or veil (Isa. 47:2; Nah. 3:5). Women usually wore their best clothing on feast days (Ps. 45:8; Cant. 4:11).

Wool was probably worn daily by both men and women because it was long-wearing and warm. However, garments woven of both wool and linen were forbidden (Lev. 19:19; Dt. 22:11), a prohibition still observed by orthodox Jews today. Tailors also made silken garments, but because of their rarity and cost, only royalty and the wealthy could afford them (Ezek. 16:10). Such silken garments may have been woven and dyed.

Flax, from which linen is made, is mentioned in Joshua 2:6, suggesting that it was in common use, and this is confirmed by archaeological discoveries. Goods not manufactured into clothing at home were sent to such artisans as weavers (1 Sam. 17:7), dyers (Ezek. 23:15), and fullers, who bleached, washed, shrank, and pressed cloth.

Sandals were made of cowhide and other leather or of badger skins (Ezek. 16:10) and were worn by most people for protection against burning sands, rough terrain, or damp ground. In later times there were shoemakers who specialized in either men's or ladies' footwear.

In Talmudic times, the dress differed little from that mentioned in the Bible. From the rabbinical regulations governing the order in which one should remove his clothing before bathing, we learn about the typical clothing of the Jew of that period. In order of removal, they were: shoes, headwear, mantle, girdle, shirt, and a vest known by the Greek name *epikarsion.*

This last garment was worn by both men and women and was brought around one arm and knotted over the shoulder of the other (Nid. 48b; Derek Eretz. Rab. 10).

There are some interesting facts about colors popular in Talmudic times. White was worn at weddings and other festive occasions as well as on the New Year (Yer. R.H. 1.3). Mourners and excommunicated persons generally wore black (Yer. R.H. 1.3) as did those accused of adultery (Sot. 7a). Black shoes, however, were not worn because this was a typically non-Jewish practice (Ta'an. 22a), and Jewish women shunned red apparel because it was considered a licentious color (Ber. 20a). Jews were also urged not to wear the multicolored or purple garments of the heathen or their wide pantaloons (Sifre 81).

Because many of the articles of clothing mentioned in the Talmud have Greek names, it is believed that both in appearance and style Greek influence predominated at that time. Among these garments are the armless mantle of the laborer (Kel. 29:1), the *dalmatic* of the upper classes (Kel. 9:7), the handkerchief or *sudarium* (Sanh. 6:1), the felt hat or *pilenum* (Nid. 8:3), and the *stola* worn by both men and women (Yoma 7:1). There was also a kind of raincoat with attached hat known as *paemila,* which was used by dayworkers to protect their tunics from rain or snow (Yer. Hag. 1:8). Other clothes mentioned include *apilyon,* a felt cap or hat; *ma'aferei* or duster, or traveling coat with a hood; *minal,* which were either leather or felt shoes; and *sudar,* a scarf wound around the head and hanging down over the neck (Shab. 120a).

Tailor

As communities developed in size, number, and wealth, men and women craftsmen arose who designed and tailored the beautiful garments desired by royalty, priests, and the wealthy (Ex. 28:31–43). In 1 Chronicles 4:21 there is a reference to "the families of those who wrought fine linen." Scholars believe that a number of these finely made garments were exported, because they have been found in widely separated areas.

Tailors wove garments on the same type of looms as were

used for curtains. Since materials were expensive, garments were shaped in the same way that a sweater is knit. The tailor wove his tunic from cuff to cuff; the selvage, the sturdiest part of the fabric, came at the hems and at the neck opening where most stress occurred. He could easily make stripes in a wool robe by changing the color of the weft that ran up and down the tunic.

Expensive materials and methods were used for important priestly garments. The turban and breeches were made of plain linen, the coat of blue-and-white-checked linen, and the girdle also of plain linen. The breastplate and the ephod were of wool with gold and linen detail.

Embroidering

Embroiderers were busy pursuing their craft, especially among the Egyptians and Assyro-Babylonians who were highly skilled in ornamental needlework or cloth, but mostly in linen. They used many colors and designs, which may have been woven into the cloth or drawn in by needle or hook. The Bible refers to their work in a number of places (Ex. 26:36, 27:16, 28:39, 38:23; Jg. 5:30; Ezek. 16:10, 13, 27:7). It is believed that the mantle which tempted Achan (Jos. 7:21, 24) was of Babylonian manufacture and embroidered in gold (Ezek. 27:7). Josephus (Ant. 5.1.10) refers to the embroidered byssus from Egypt.

The Hebrews seem to have acquired embroidery skill early. Their embroiderers worked in wool, linen, or metal threads. Virtually all of their patrons were royalty, the priestly class, and other wealthy persons, though they also had some humbler clients (Ps. 45:13). The beautiful dyed garments of Sisera were embroidered on both sides (Jg. 5:30). The hangings of the Tabernacle were trimmed with fine needlework (Ex. 26:36, 27:16, 36:37, 38:18). The coats and girdles of the priests were beautifully decorated with fine needlework and woven work (Ex. 28:39, 39:29). Similarly, the ornamental pomegranates on the hem of the priest's ephod robe (Ex. 28:33) was of fine needlework. Some believe that Babylonian embroidered needlework that spread to other countries may have influenced the apparel of Israel's priests.

SUMMARY

Some sages declared that proper dress was more important than food. "The costly upon you, the inexpensive within you" (B.B. 52a). Another rabbi asserted, "Dress according to your means but eat below them" (Hul. 84b), while still another affirmed, "The glory of God is man, the glory of man is dress" (Derek Eretz Zuta 10). The scholar was expected to dress neatly, and he shamed his vocation if he went about with patched shoes or mended garments (Shab. 114a).

The Talmud declares that everyone should have two suits of clothes—one for weekdays and the other for the Sabbath (Yer. Peah 8.7). If a man cannot afford this, he should try to arrange his single suit differently on the Sabbath (Sanh. 113a). A bride was given a year to prepare her trousseau (Ket. 57a). A husband was required to give his wife at least one hat, a belt, three pairs of shoes (for the three festivals), and other clothing totaling fifty zuzim, or eight dollars (Ket. 64b).

In Talmudic times, wealthy Jews wore elegant clothes, including those decorated with gold embroidery (Yer. Yoma 7.3). Some also wore artificial hair (Er. 7b) processed by specialists. Others dyed their hair (B.B. 64b). Since considerable importance was attached to appearance during the time of Christ, tailors were undoubtedly kept busy. The commercial tailor is mentioned in Mishnaic literature (first and second centuries A.D.). He worked for private clients as well as for clothes dealers. Priestly garments were sewn by master tailors and there was a tailors' market in Jerusalem.

As indicated, many specialists were needed to meet the requirements of the Biblical consumer. We know little about the working conditions of these craftsmen. Although there were some small factories, most worked at home or in the homes of their masters. The income of the highly skilled craftsmen probably exceeded that of unskilled workers.

See *Dyer, Shoemaker, Silk Manufacturer, Spinner, Tanner, Wardrobe Keeper, Weaver.*

Cook and *Cuisine*

Cooking as an avocation is an ancient art that was usually performed by the women of the family (Gen. 18:6, 27:9; 1 Sam. 9:23; 2 Sam. 13:8), though men also performed this task (Jg. 6:19). Professional cooks were usually female slaves (Lk. 17:8). In wealthy homes and royal families, servants did the cooking, mainly in the preparation of the evening meal, which was the only real meal of the day. For the poor family this meal may have required an entire day's salary.

Cooking was done in the open, in the closed courtyards of houses in the cities, or in the living room. Cooks employed various methods to please the palates of their employers and guests. Meat was roasted in an oven, boiled in water, cooked in oil, or prepared on a griddle. Usually it was placed directly upon the coals or on a spit or grate. When meat was roasted, an entire animal was usually used and it was well cooked so that it could be easily pulled apart and eaten with the fingers. Most people preferred to boil their meat and fowl. Micah 3:2–3 refers to the stewing process. The sauce in which meat was cooked was called *marak* (Jg. 6:19). Broth was boiled and served in a separate dish. The Passover lamb was usually roasted and, eventually, roasting became the most popular method of cooking.

From the earliest times (Num. 11:5) fish, which was abundant and available in many varieties, was popular with Jews (Jer. 16:16; Ezek. 47:10; Eccl. 9:12). Fish lacking fins and scales, however, were forbidden (Lev. 11:9–12). Jesus and his followers ate boiled fish (Lk. 24:42; Jn. 21:9, 13). Fish was also roasted on a charcoal fire on a wooden or iron spit.

The earliest detailed menu on record is a description of a feast tendered by Ashurnasirpal II at the dedication of his new palace at Nimrud. The affair was attended by 69,574 persons and lasted for ten days. Details are found on a monument erected in 879 B.C. During the birthday banquet of Pharaoh at the time of Joseph (Gen. 40:20), food served included a variety of roast fowl, vegetables, roast beef, many pastries, and sweetmeats. In Palestine, however, the palace meals were far simpler until Solomon's time when lavish meals were again served.

In Biblical times the meals of the average person were very simple. Shortly after rising, he usually ate bread and olives. For lunch he ate either bread soaked in wine with a handful of parched corn or bread and grilled fish (Jn. 21:9, 13). His main meal was in the evening. Bread and milk were the main staples with fruits and vegetables added. Although many vegetables were eaten raw, lentils (Gen. 25:29; 2 Sam. 17:28) or greens (2 Ki. 4:38) were boiled in water or oil. The average person ate meat only on festal days or other special occasions.

In Talmudic times (*ca.* 1–500 A.D.) a typical meal began with an entree of some kind of pickled food to perk up the appetite (Ber. 6.7), followed by the main course, possibly fish, fruits, and vegetables, climaxed by dessert. During and after the meal, tidbits were eaten and a variety of wines and beer were imbibed. One rabbi declared that eating without drinking was suicidal (Shab. 41a). Among the drinks served was wine in ice (from Lebanon), wine flavored with myrrh (Meg. 15:23) or mixed with honey or pepper, vinegar, and black and red wines. It was believed that certain wines were good for the stomach while others were harmful (Yer. Shek. 48d).

The most popular forms of cooking utensils were a wide, shallow iron plate and a frying pan (Lev. 2:5–7; Ezek. 4:3). In early times these utensils lacked handles, but later two handles were added. Ordinary cooking dishes and pots were of unbaked, unglazed clay, although ritual vessels and a few special dishes were of copper. Deep-fat frying was done in a griddle. In the time of Isaiah and Jeremiah, the manufacturers of these pots made them in standard sizes and used trademarks to identify them. There were also copper kettles and pans, which were very costly. In connection with the Tabernacle (Ex. 25:29) and Solomon's Temple (1 Ki. 7:13–51), we find a list of various cooking utensils.

Archaeologists have found a large pot of bronze (1 Ki.

7:40; Ezek. 24:3) similar to the fleshpot (Ex. 16:3). The other utensils, such as the shallow pan, the kettle, and the caldron, are mentioned in 1 Samuel 2:14 and Jeremiah 1:13. After the Exile (587 B.C.) ordinary wealthy homes owned glazed vessels or metal dishes and, occasionally, even silver and golden vessels.

Knives to cut meat were first made of flint (Jos. 5:2) and later of bronze. Forks, other than a single, large, three-pronged one to lift pieces of meat out of the pot, were not used (1 Sam. 2:13).

In wealthy households, the cook doubtless planned menus, calculated the amount of food required for the meal, and requisitioned or bought it. He probably supervised other kitchen personnel engaged in preparing, cooking, or serving the meal. He cut, trimmed, and boned meats and poultry for cooking, and he carved the meat.

We have no record of recipes used in Biblical times. As to the training of cooks, though the Bible makes no reference to it, it probably consisted of some informal type of apprenticeship. Because of their access to food, cooks ate well, and if they pleased the palate of their employer, were probably well treated.

See *Baker, Fisherman, Potter.*

Counselor

Counselors were court officials who served as advisers to royalty (2 Chr. 25:16; Isa. 1:26, 3:3) and to members of the Sanhedrin. The advisers of Artaxerxes (Ez. 7:14) were his princely advisers (Est. 1:14). Some believe that these counselors exercised power second only to the monarch (Mic. 4:9; 2 Sam. 16:23; Mk. 4:9; Job 3:14). They were usually aristocrats who were men of the world and who possessed the sagacity, graces, and personality to win and retain the good will of their monarchs.

David's counselor was the illustrious Ahithophel (2 Sam. 16: 23). Rehoboam lost most of his kingdom and the fateful schism between Israel and Judah occurred because Rehoboam followed the advice of his young rather than his senior counselors (1 Ki. 12:6–14).

See *Ambassador, Dream Interpreter, Eunuch, Magician.*

Counterfeiter

There is incontestable evidence of the existence of counterfeiters in very early times. Many antique coins reveal the handiwork of ancient counterfeiters. The coins were forged and struck from inferior metals, then coated with silver. Many antique coins reveal a deep cut by a sharp instrument indicating that someone sought to determine whether the metal was genuine. Moreover, since the edges of coins did not become marked until the eighteenth century A.D., ancient forgers could snip off parts of golden weight with immunity. Consequently, to forestall such acts, it was necessary to weigh the coin again.

The Bible reveals awareness of these practices and denounces them. It demands, "Just balances, just weights (*epah, hin*) shall you have" (Lev. 19:36; Dt. 25:13; Am. 8:5). To assure honesty, tongues, bars, bracelets of gold and silver were apparently stamped with their weights by government officials.

See *Weights and Measures Inspector.*

Cupbearer

The butler involved in the story of Joseph (Gen. 40:1 ff.) was Pharaoh's cupbearer. A picture from about 2500 B.C. survives which shows King Ur-Nanshe of Lagash in Sumer drinking from a goblet and served by the cupbearer standing beside him.

Because of their close physical relationship with the monarchs, cupbearers often wielded great influence such as that exercised by Nehemiah, "cupbearer" to Artaxerxes I of Persia (*ca.* 465–423 B.C.), when he was appointed governor of Judea. During Solomon's reign, cupbearers were members of his retinue which, among other factors, impressed the Queen of Sheba during her visit (1 Ki. 10:5; 2 Chr. 9:4).

Pharaoh's butler in the Joseph story was imprisoned for displeasing his sovereign, but following Joseph's correct interpretation of his dream, he was restored to his former position (Gen. 40:1, 41:9).

The cupbearer's duties probably included supervision of the supply and quality of the beverages served (usually wine), serving the king, and testing the beverages before serving them to forestall attempts at poisoning the monarch.

Among the Assyrians, cupbearers were usually eunuchs, but not among the Persians. Consequently, though Nehemiah was a cupbearer, he is not believed to have been a eunuch. Herod the Great, however, had a cupbearer who was a eunuch (Jos. Ant. 16.8.1).

See *Eunuch, Steward, Waiter, Wine Steward.*

Custodian

In late Biblical times the custodian was usually a slave who attended a rich man's son, took him to school, and served as his tutor and companion until his charge was about sixteen years old. The Greeks employed such slaves (1 Cor. 4:15). Because of their close physical proximity, a warm relationship often developed between the boy and his custodian, who undoubtedly enjoyed a higher standard of living than many other working persons.

See *Teacher.*

Customs Clerk

Tolls on exported goods were collected in Biblical times at border towns (Ez. 4:20). The collectors probably assessed the value of the goods in order to determine the tolls to charge.

When Solomon controlled the frontier districts of Zobah, Damascus, Hauran, Ammon, Moab, and Edom, he dominated the entire caravan trade between Arabia and the north, from which his custom clerks collected tolls (1 Ki. 4:21). Matthew was a customs officer (Matt. 9:9) who later became a disciple. These officials probably maintained records of their receipts and disbursements.

See *Census Taker, Tax Collector.*

Dairyman

Milk was a favorite article of diet among the Hebrews. There is no specific mention of purveyors of milk in the Bible, but scholars believe that there were individuals who sold such dairy products as milk, butter (Pro. 30:33; Ps. 55:21), and cheese (1 Sam. 17:18; Job 10:10) to city residents. They were probably farmers who brought their products on donkey to the city. They may also have included middlemen who purchased dairy products from the farmer and sold them to the city residents.

See *Cattleman, Cheese Maker, Cook, Farmer.*

Dancer and *Dancing*

Nothing precise is known about the nature of Biblical dancing. It is believed that, as among all primitive peoples, there was a rhythmical and measured stepping to the accompaniment of music, singing, or beating of drums. In ancient and medieval times, Jewish dancing is believed to have consisted of gesticulations, violent leaps and bounds, and hopping in a circle rather than in graceful, soft, rhythmic movements.

Dancing among the Hebrews seems to have been mainly an expression of joy which perhaps may be corroborated by the use of the word *sahok*, usually translated as sporting, playing, or jesting (1 Sam. 18:7; 2 Sam. 6:5, 21; 1 Chr. 13:8, 15:29; Jer. 30:19, 31:4). Evidence of early Biblical dancing as characterized by violent leaping and movement may be found in the word *rakod,* meaning "to dance," but whose original meaning is "to leap like a lamb."

Another word referring to dancing in the Bible is *karkar* (2 Sam. 6:14, 16), which suggests a round dance and may refer to turning around upon the heels on one spot, typical of dervishes. Another dance was the choric dance, derived from *hol,* meaning to writhe or to turn (Lam. 5:15; Ps. 30:11–12; Cant. 7:1; 1 Sam. 18:6).

Other words conjectured to indicate the nature of Biblical dances are *pesah,* believed to refer to a limping dance (1 Ki. 18:26), and *hag,* meaning "holiday," possibly from the word *hug* meaning "circle" or "dancing in a circle."

In the Bible, dancing is often mentioned with religious functions. Scholars, too, affirm that the religious dance was the main feature of every festival. Originally, the dance may have been a procession around the altar or shrine, performed in a halting rhythm. It was also a prominent feature of religious feasts. At Shiloh, an annual feast occurred where the maidens danced (Jg. 21:19–21). Miriam and her maidens danced in thanksgiving for the successful crossing of the Red Sea (Ex. 15:20). Joyous folk-singing and folk-dancing occurred during the vintage festival when women were courted (Jg. 21:21). When the ark was returned to Jerusalem, "David danced before the Lord with all his might" (2 Sam. 6:14–16). There were religious dances relating to the story of Jephthah's daughter (Jg. 11:34). Women danced in honor of Saul and David when they returned victorious from battle (1 Sam. 18:6). Dancing and music were combined in praising the Lord (Ps. 149:3, 150:4). Some believe that the religious prostitutes, *kedashot,* who were attached to Canaanite sanctuaries, were also professional dancers. A number of seers resorted to dancing to arouse themselves to proper religious fervor (1 Sam. 10:10, 19:20–24), and their religious ecstacy proved infectious to their audience.

In the Talmud (Ta'an. 4.8), there is reference to a "marriage dance" which occurred in later Biblical times on the Day of Atonement and on the fifteenth of Ab. Nubile maidens wearing borrowed white gowns (so as not to embarrass the indigent) danced before eligible swains. The beautiful ones proclaimed their comeliness, while the plainer ones declaimed the transiency of physical beauty and the superior and more enduring virtue of character. Marriages often resulted from these dances (Ta'an. 30b). Some authorities believe that these dances were survivals of earlier marriage by capture.

Another public dance was the "torchlight procession," which occurred on the Festival of the Water Drawing during the Festival of Succoth (Suk. 5:1–4) when even the most prominent and dignified scholars participated. [Canticles 7:2 has been interpreted as either an ancient square dance or a sword dance.]

The Talmud also states that feasts often were climaxed with dancing, though we do not know whether these included professional dancers (Ned. 51a). It was considered a religious duty for guests to dance at a wedding in honor of the bride. Even dignified rabbis joined in the dancing. One waved a myrtle branch (Ket. 17a).

During Temple times, the Talmud relates that on the night of the first day of the Feast of Tabernacles, huge crowds carrying lamps of gold and vessels of water gathered in the women's court of the Temple. Every home in Jerusalem was brightly lit. Pious and distinguished men danced with torches in their hands and sang songs of joy and praise. The Levites made music with lyres, harps, cymbals, trumpets, and numerous other instruments (Suk. 51a; Maimonides, Yad Lulav 8.12.13).

A quaint passage in the Talmud reveals how much the ancient Jews loved to dance. It refers to Rabbi Eleazar's hope that "someday, the Holy One, Blessed be He, will give a dance for the righteous, and He will sit among them in the garden of Eden and each one will point the finger at Him, saying, as it is written [Isa. 25:9], 'Lo, this our God, we have waited for Him. . . . and we will be glad and rejoice in His salvation'" (Ta'an. at end).

In the Greco-Roman world, Herod employed professional dancers such as Salome (Mk. 6:22). Also in the New Testament, the prodigal son heard a company of dancers on his return (Lk. 15:25). Herodias' daughter's artistic dancing was designed to captivate her audience.

See *Actor, Musician.*

Doorkeeper

In the Bible, the terms "doorkeeper," "guard," and "porter" appear to be used interchangeably. Doorkeepers guarded the entrance to the Temple. They were Levites who were called "keepers of the threshold" (2 Ki. 22:4; 1 Chr. 9:19) or "keepers of the house" (Mk. 13:34), and they seem to have delighted in their assignments (Ps. 84:10).

There were also special doorkeepers of the Ark (1 Chr. 15:23), guards of private homes, and "keepers of the sheepfold" (Jn. 10:3). Sometimes doorkeepers were women (Acts 12:13; Mk. 14:66). There were many doorkeepers mentioned in Ezra (2:42) and Nehemiah (7:45).

See *Bodyguard, Police Official, Priest, Servant, Slave.*

Dream Interpreter and *Dreams*

Dreams are a universal phenomenon which from earliest times has been viewed by man as a supernatural communication. Man has always been baffled by his dreams; thus, eventually, there arose specialists who were believed to understand their meaning. Those who were credited with possessing this skill were usually rewarded with fees or gifts for their services and enjoyed the esteem of their fellow men.

In the ancient Near East, the Babylonians and Egyptians,

who were greatly preoccupied with dreams, used many such interpreters. Although this preoccupation was less true of the Hebrews, they, too, regarded certain dreams as a supernatural method of communication. While there was a close relationship in the Bible between dreams and prophecy (Jer. 23:25, 32; 1 Sam. 28:6), a revelation through dreams was held inferior to direct communication or confrontation with the Divinity like that attributed to Moses (Num. 12:6).

Most dreams in the Bible were intended for the benefit of the race rather than for that of the individual (Gen. 20:3, 28:12; Jg. 7:13; 1 Ki. 3:5). They are mainly of two kinds: those which parallel events of daily life (Gen. 40:8–17, 41:1–7; Eccl. 5:3), and those which communicate a message from God (Gen. 20:3–7; 1 Ki. 3:5–15; Acts 18:9).

The well-known dream interpreters in the Bible were Joseph (Gen. 40:12 ff., 18, 41:15 ff.) and Daniel (2:17 ff.).

The dream interpreter appears to have operated as follows: Clients came to him, usually troubled by their dreams, which they tried to reconstruct for his interpretation, as well as to give him other information about themselves. Basing his interpretation on their statements, along with his probably shrewd understanding of human nature, he may have employed some magical flourishes or incantations and come up with an acceptable interpretation.

In rabbinical literature, the earlier faith in the meaning of dreams continued. The Babylonian Talmud, which embraces the first five centuries A.D., was written in the land of the Chaldeans, noted for their magic. The tractate Berakot (55–58) is replete with dream interpretations, thereby indicating that the rabbis of the time believed that dreams were authentic communications. There was, however, a minority opinion in Jewish tradition that was skeptical toward dreams. Thus Ecclesiastes (5:3, 7, 8:1–8) regards dreams as vanity. Simeon ben Yohai about 150 A.D. averred that "as there is no grain without chaff, so there is no dream without vain things." His contemporary Rabbi Meir added, "Dreams do not help nor harm" (Hor. 13b). Another contemporary opinion was, "A sixtieth portion of every dream is true" (Ber. 57b). Philo, on the other hand, wrote five books on dreams, which he considered authentic communications.

Additional rabbinical views on dreams were:

> Every dream, except those occurring during fasting, means something.
>
> A dream uninterpreted is like a letter unread.
>
> An evil dream is better than a good one, for it leads to repentance. An evil dream is cancelled by the pain it causes, and the latter by joy. (Ber. 55a.)

Most of the ancient sages accepted dreams as valid communications. They distinguished, however, between good and evil dreams. "He who goes to bed in a cheerful mood will dream a good dream" (Shab. 30b). People prayed to be spared bad dreams (Ber. 60b), and one way believed to be effective in avoiding such dreams was by fasting (Shab. 11a). Another method employed to nullify evil dreams was to say in the presence of three persons, "I have had a good dream."

They reply, "Yes, it is good; let it be good; may God grant it to be good."

Similarly, reciting certain Biblical passages was believed to be effective in averting evil dreams. There is a prayer for good dreams in the Talmud (Ber. 55b) that is still recited and is found in the orthodox Jewish liturgy after the first and second priestly blessing.

Since the average person was usually regarded as incapable of interpreting his own dream (Yoma 28b), interpreters became necessary. They charged a regular fee in Talmudic times, usually one denarius or about sixteen cents in our currency. Rabbis were among these interpreters, and they were often consulted by pagan clients.

Because it was believed that the interpreter's explanation of the dream would be fulfilled, it was deemed prudent to present him with gifts to assure a favorable interpretation. One Chaldean interpreter who was consulted even by the sages was thus described: "Whoever gave him a fee received a favorable answer, while whoever gave no fee received an unfavorable one" (Ber. 56a).

Dream interpreters were in great demand. Jerusalem alone had twenty-four during the early centuries, and each was known to offer a different interpretation from those of his colleagues, but this did not lessen the popularity of the interpreters.

See *Counselor, Interpreter, Magician.*

Driver

In Biblical times, soldiers or slaves usually served as charioteers for royalty or for the wealthy classes. Ahab is mentioned as having spoken to the driver of his chariot after he was wounded in battle (1 Ki. 22:34). Jehu appears to have been a speeder because he is described as "driving furiously" (2 Ki. 9:20). Drivers drove various animals such as camels, asses, and, from about 1500 B.C., horses, and were probably responsible for the feeding and care of their animals. Royal drivers enjoyed the protection of guards to discourage raids by brigands. Some drivers who transported merchandise a considerable distance had to be away from home for substantial periods. It is likely that they were well remunerated for their efforts.

See *Camel Driver, Charioteer, Muleteer.*

Dyer and *Dyes*

Ras Shamra texts of about 1500 B.C. allude to the trade of dyeing, a vocation which later played an important role among the Hebrews. While the process is not mentioned in the Bible, there are references to dyed materials (Ex. 35:23, 25, 35; Jg. 5:30; Mk. 15:17; Acts 16:14).

The skins used for the Tabernacle were dyed scarlet by the juice of crushed cochineal insects found in oak trees. (Ex. 26:1, 31, 36:8). Solomon is mentioned as requesting work of Hiram of Tyre, a man "skilled in purple, crimson and blue fabrics" (2 Chr. 2:7). The Phoenicians appear to have had a monopoly on the making of purple from mollusks so that the ancient world depended on them for it. It was a black-purple or red-violet Tyrian or *imperial* dye prepared from mollusca purpura and murex found on the east Mediterranean coast and used for dyeing the very expensive garments worn by the nobility and the rich (Jg. 8:26; Pro. 31:22; Lk. 16:19; Rev. 18:12). This same costly purple was used in the Tabernacle fabric (Ex. 26), the Temple veil (2 Chr. 3:14), and the garments Jesus wore when he was tried (Jn. 19:2, 5). Lydia traded in cloth dyed in this fashion (Acts 16:14). In Palestine, yellow dyes were produced from ground pomegranate rind, while the Phoenicians used safflower and turmeric. Blue was made from indigo plants.

We have no information on how dyes were produced but we can make plausible inferences from surviving equipment and other data. At Tell Beit Mirsim on the edge of the Negeb about thirty homes approximately ten by twenty feet have been found which were used for dyeing. Each room had two round stone vats with small openings on top and retrieving drains around the rims. Masonry basins and benches were built either between or in front of the vats. Sometimes, an additional jar-vat was placed on the bench. Close by were other storage jars containing lime or potash for fixing the dyes. Thread, not the woven fabric, was dyed. It usually took two baths to perform the process; then the dye was thoroughly squeezed out and saved, while the thread was dried. In Palestine, the cold bath process was used, but the Egyptians may have used the hot bath process.

Similar Iron Age equipment and arrangements were found at Beth-shemesh and Tell en Nasbeh. In the latter, the benches seem to have been lacking. A Hellenistic dye plant was also found at Gezer showing continuance of the above type of installation. There was a furnace found in one excavated place indicating the use of hot dyes.

The Hebrews appear to have been proficient dyers, obtaining rich and enduring colors from murex shellfish which produce purple reds. Pomegranate bark produced black, while red was obtained from the roots of the madder plant. Wool was dyed in the coveted purple tones by soaking it overnight in grape juice sprinkled with powdered madder. The dyeing was completed with wood ashes and goats' dung. W. F. Albright (*The Archaeology of Palestine*) declares that dye vats were found in Debir where a center of the cloth industry was developed about 600 B.C. by the Hebrews after they arrived in southern Palestine. The Babylonians were known to dye their turbans (Ezek. 23:15), while the priests dyed their vestments.

Dyeing was conducted in factory centers where a guild of dyers seems to have operated (1 Chr. 4:21). These centers were near grazing land for herds and goats and near a plentiful water supply. A guild of purple dyers is mentioned on a tombstone inscription in Hierapolis. The ancient Thyatira, a Jewish center in Asia Minor, appears to have had a dye industry.

In Talmudic times, dyers were easily recognized by the red and blue threads which hung from one ear and the green and pale blue behind the other (Yer. Shab. 3b).

See *Clothier, Weaver.*

Embalmer and *Embalming*

In Biblical times, as today, among the Hebrews prompt burial of the dead was customary (Dt. 21:22, 23). The art of preserving the corpse from decay originated in Egypt. The embalmer removed the viscera for separate preservation and desiccated the body by packing it in salt and inserting spices in the orifices. He then packed the body with impregnated linen and wrapped the entire corpse in linen.

Though the Bible (Gen. 50:23–26) states that Jacob and Joseph were embalmed, the latter by his servants and physicians, this procedure was exceptional. Embalming was not ordinarily practiced among the Hebrews, as evidenced by the conditions of the bodies found in thousands of Canaanite tombs. They probably refrained from the practice because of their religious beliefs, their opposition to the Egyptian religion, and because of its prohibitive cost to the typically poor Israelite.

The embalming of Jacob and Joseph was meant to show their eminence and to preserve their bodies until interment in Canaan (Gen. 50:13; Ex. 13:19; Jos. 24:32), although in Joseph's case, his bones rather than his body are mentioned. The use of spices in the burial rites of Asa (2 Chr. 16:14) and Jesus (Jn. 19:39–40) was not to embalm but to purify them ceremonially. Embalming and mourning usually took seventy days, but Jacob's took forty (Gen. 50:1–3).

See *Apothecary*.

Eunuch

In ancient times, eunuchs were employed in the Far East and Middle East as harem officials and as confidential aides to rulers. In ancient China and Persia, they served as political advisers to rulers. Achaemenid Persians and Roman emperors Claudius, Nero, and Titus had many political eunuchs. Eunuchs also served as bodyguards, generals, and admirals.

Castration of human males was practiced in Assyria in the second millennium B.C. Persons were castrated either as punishment for crimes or as preparation for sale into slavery by their indigent parents. There were also voluntary eunuchs such as Origen and others who emasculated themselves or had the operation performed by others because they wished to free themselves from sexual desire (Matt. 19:12). By the third century A.D., there was a sect of eunuchs, the Valesi, who castrated themselves because they believed that they were thus serving the Lord.

The Hebrew word for eunuch, *saris,* usually means court officer, but it also means "castrate." Joseph's employer, Potiphar, though married, is nevertheless called a *saris* (Gen. 39:1). In Isaiah 56:3, the meaning of *saris* is clearly a eunuch. Eunuchs are mentioned as attendants to such kings as Ahab (1 Ki. 22:9) and Jehoram (2 Ki. 8:6). There were also eunuchs in the kingdom of Judah during Josiah's reign (2 Ki. 24:12; Jer. 29:2, 38:7). Generally, eunuchs were associated with polygamy and harems (2 Ki. 24:15; Jer. 41:16).

Some scholars believe that few Jews in Biblical times were eunuchs. Scriptures expressly forbid the practice (Dt. 23:1). Isaiah, however, requested that they be not excluded from the congregation (56:3). Josephus reveals that under Herod the Great one eunuch served as the royal cupbearer, another brought his supper, and the third put him to bed as well as managed the main affairs of the government (Ant. 16.8, 1). In the New

Testament, the word *eunouchas* is used and may not signify "castrate" (Acts 8:27). In Acts 12:20, the king's chamberlain (eunuch) supervised his bedchambers. In rabbinical literature, there is a distinction between congenitally born eunuchs and those emasculated by man. To emasculate a human being was considered a grave sin by the Talmud since the victim was deprived of the opportunity of "being fruitful and multiplying" (Shab. 111a). Consequently, a eunuch could not marry an Israelite woman.

See *Counselor, Cupbearer, Slave.*

Executioner

Executioners were employed by kings and were sometimes referred to as *razim*, runners (1 Sam. 22:17; 2 Ki. 10:25). They were recognized members of the royal retinue (1 Sam. 8:11; 2 Sam. 15:1), accompanying the king or his general into battle and bringing back an official report of its progress (2 Sam. 18:19).

Beheading by sword was a Roman rather than a typical Jewish form of execution. In the New Testament, there is a reference to an officer sent by Herod to behead John the Baptist (Mk. 6:27).

Although capital punishment was infrequently used, the Talmud indicates four methods used by the Jews: stoning, burning, decapitation, and strangulation (Sanh. 7).

Executioners probably combined executing with other duties.

See *Jailer, Police Official, Runner.*

Farmer and *Farming*

One of the earliest occupations of the Israelites was raising sheep and cattle. The most important flocks were sheep and goats with their essential milk and fleeces. The main domestic animals were camels, asses, dogs, sheep, goats, and often oxen. Horses, mules, and pigs, however, were not raised in Palestine. Poultry, which they later raised (about 500 B.C.), consisted chiefly of chickens, doves, geese, and pigeons. Beekeeping may not have started until about the middle of the fifth century B.C.

From the excavations of Jericho we learn that Palestine was one of the earliest agricultural centers of the world. As early as 7500 B.C. there was good farming and the land was irrigated. The hill country, too, was beginning to show signs of agriculture since there are relics from the Natufian period (*ca.* 10,000 B.C.).

The Israelites became farmers some time after they entered Palestine, where they learned the farming methods of the Canaanites. They lived in villages near their fields and eventually some of their villages grew into walled towns. During the day, the villages were quite empty since almost every able-bodied person was working in the fields. Even at night, many were busy protecting the crops. Owners and slaves, young men and women, children (Ru. 2; Isa. 61:5)—all, save the rich—worked hard from sunrise to sunset.

Farmer's Calendar

The regimen of the Palestinian farmer during the reigns of Saul and David is revealed by the famous Gezer calendar, a limestone plaque from 950 to 918 B.C. discovered by R. A. S. Macalister and translated by W. F. Albright. "His [a man's] two months are [spent in] olive harvest, his two months are grain planting, his two months is hoeing up of flax, his month of barley harvest, his month is harvest and feasting. His two months are vine tending; his month is summer fruit." (J. Pritchard, ed., *Ancient Near Eastern Texts*. Princeton, N.J.: Princeton University Press, 1951).

Few things grow easily in Palestine. Much of the land is stony and hilly and much of the farming is done on the hillsides. Even as early as the Middle Bronze Age (1950–1550 B.C.), farmers resorted to terracing to extend their arable land. However, some areas, such as the Jordan Valley, Bashan, and Esdraelon, were very fertile and produced two crops of grain in one year (Am. 7:1). A classic description of early Israelite farming is found in Isaiah 28:24–29.

Farmer's Tools

After the early rains in October, the farmer in Biblical times opened the farm season in November. He rose early to sow either by hand or from a box attached to a plow (Matt. 13:3–8; Lk. 8:5–15). In ancient Palestine, the farmer's plow was a forked bough with a piece of sharp metal attached. During the time of Saul, the Philistines monopolized iron, forcing Hebrew farmers to bring their metal shares on their homemade plows to the Philistines to be sharpened (1 Sam. 13:20). The farmer fertilized his soil, usually with the excrement left on the field (Lk. 13:8). He reaped with a short-handled sickle made of flint until about 1100 B.C. when iron implements became more common. Male and female reapers harvested small tufts of grain by grasping them with their left hands and cutting them with sickles held in their right hands (Dt. 16:9; Jl. 3:13). The Torah permitted plucking a small quantity of a neighbor's standing grain with the hands but not with a sickle (Dt. 23:25).

The farmer bound his sheaves into bundles which he carted to the threshing floor (Matt. 13:30). There he beat the ripe grains spread on the ground or on a stone wine-press floor (Jg. 6:11), using a staff or rod (Isa. 28:28). A flail, which some farmers still use, was a hand threshing instrument made of a wooden staff from which swung a short, thick stick.

Threshing floors were usually situated somewhere outside the village where the winds would help in the job of winnowing (Hos. 13:3). They were either of rock or of soil covered with clay. The sheaves were scattered about a foot deep on the floor and a ring of stones encircled them. In one method, animals were driven around until the grain was loosened and chopped into small pieces. Another, faster method employed a wooden sled with stones or iron fragments fastened into the underside that, when dragged, cut the grain. Using pitchforks, the farmer winnowed the grain by tossing it into the wind. The threshing period could extend to the end of August, or, with good harvests, until September.

After the winnowing, the grain was sifted with round screen trays (Lk. 22:31). Then it was stored (Matt. 3:12), and later transported to market by caravans (Isa. 30:6).

Seasons

There were two seasons in Palestine: the rainy season from October to April; and the dry season, which embraced the rest of the year, during which there might not be a drop of rain from the middle of May to the middle of October. If the rains came late, the farmer could be ruined. Consequently, he had to provide himself with storage places for water, which explains the many cisterns found in every major site in Palestine (2 Chr. 26:10; Neh. 9:25). Besides cisterns, early farmers in Palestine used springs and perennial streams such as Kishon, Jabbok, and Wadi Kufringa for artificial irrigation. Irrigation was widely practiced even in ancient times, especially for vineyards and vegetable gardens. The water was either carried or run into fields by water canals.

Crops

The chief crops in ancient Palestine were: grains (wheat, barley, spelt, cumin, millet, oats, rye, and rice), pulse, beans, peas, lentils, lettuce, endives, cucumbers, onions, leeks, garlic, looah, sesame (which also provided cooking fat), chervil, coriander, thyme, celery, cabbage, beets, turnips, mustard, radishes, rue, hyssop, lupine, fenugreek, purslane, mint, savory, dill. Other plants were flax, woad, cotton, madder, and gourds. Most extensively sown were wheat and barley.

The main fruits cultivated in ancient Palestine were grapes, melons, figs, dates, mulberries, pears, apples, sycamore figs, jujubes, peaches, carobs, olives (also a source of cooking fat), and pomegranates.

OLIVES

Of these fruits, the cultivation of the olive was one of the most important of the farmer's activities. In the Bible, the olive tree is called the king of the trees (Jg. 9:8) and symbolizes peace, beauty, and strength. The olive was used as a basic food and its oil both fried and seasoned foods. It fed oil wicks for illumination and served commercially as a medium of exchange. It was also a base for ointments and hair tonics and was used as an unguent in surgery. The roots of the olive tree made fine fuel and its branches were used to build booths during the Succoth festival.

FIGS

Figs, too, were common in high-lying sections of Palestine and grew in several varieties of colors. The fig tree thrived near dwellings and lived for centuries. Some produced several times a year. Green or winter figs (Cant. 2:13; Rev. 6:13) were on the branches during the winter and became ruddy during early spring, but they were small. Late figs, which came in August and September, were purplish, green, whitish, or nearly black. Both fresh and dried figs were pressed into cakes (1 Sam. 25:18) and were popular as food. They also made excellent poultices for boils (2 Ki. 20:7).

GRAPES

The high, stone-walled terraces of Samaria (Jer. 31:5) and the plains of Esdraelon had always been suitable for grapes. On the lower hills, such as Shephela, grapes and olives were both cultivated. The early Israelites stored their wine in clay jars or in skin bottles, mainly goatskin bags. The rich stored their wine in containers of pottery or skin. During the vintage period (September–December), the farmers sang vintage songs (Isa. 65:8), danced, courted, and often became drunk (Jg. 9:27).

Although grapes were variously used, their chief use was for wine. They were dried in the form of raisins or raisin cakes (1 Sam. 25:18) or made into jelly. The light sweet wines were used as a staple beverage. Wine was also exported from the Mediterranean islands.

The Farmer's Cuisine

The food of the Hebrews during the time of the patriarchs was similar to that of the desert nomads today. Common fare was parched corn, vegetables, beans, lentils, cucumbers, squash, all mixed with seasonings. For the poor, meat was a luxury and eaten only occasionally. Milk products, fruit, and bread were the basic foods.

Even the poor, however, enjoyed milk and butter. Where butter could be shipped in skin sacks, it was often used in payment of bills and taxes. There was a wide variety of cheeses, one of the best known and most popular being *labon*, a sort of yogurt. Many farmers also enjoyed an abundance of honey, some of which they exported to Tyre (Ezek. 27:17). Fish were also plentiful, as were nuts, which added variety to the menu.

Occupational Hazards

The labor and livelihood of the farmer were often threatened by such pests as ants, cankerworms, caterpillars, palmer worms (Jl. 2:25), field mice, tares, locusts (Ex. 10:14–15), wind, hail, mildew (Hag. 2:17). He was often bedeviled by the siroccos or hot winds from the eastern desert, which, blowing from the middle of September to the end of October, would cause growing things to wilt (Isa. 27:8, 40:6–8; Ezek. 17:10).

Farm Hands

Wealthy families hired farm hands who were of two types: those who received wages and maintenance and slave laborers who received only maintenance (room and board) but no wages. When they were freed, slaves were given gifts. Both types worked six days a week from sunrise to sunset and rested on the Sabbath. Hebrew day laborers were supposed to be paid at the end of each day (Lev. 19:13; Dt. 24:14). Many employers paid wages in kind, as did Laban to his son-in-law Jacob (Gen. 29:15, 30).

Wages

During Old Testament times in Palestine, "wages" usually consisted of food and clothing distributed by the family head to servants, their children, and their wives. The Hebrew prophets knew of inflationary times and spoke of wages as being put "into a bag with holes" (Hag. 1:6). The daily wage in New Testament times was according to Tobit 5:14 a drachma (less than twenty cents) for a day's work from sunrise to sunset.

The Hebrew farmer who lived in a village or a town aspired to own a vine and fig tree (1 Ki. 4:25). He also usually owned a few sheep yielding milk, cheese, and occasional meat meals. Other than during war or periods of crop failure, he probably ate and lived better than city dwellers. Though he had to toil unremittingly, was subject to the uncertainties of nature, and was often the victim of marauders, he nevertheless loved his plot of land and clung to it.

See *Beekeeper, Cattleman, Cheese Maker, Cook, Dairyman, Fisherman, Forester, Fruit Farmer, Gardener, Horse Breeder, Olive Oil Worker, Poultry Farmer, Sharecropper, Sheepshearer, Shepherd, Tree Surgeon, Vintner.*

Ferryman

One ferryman is mentioned in the Bible: "And the ferry boat passed to and fro to bring over the king's household and to do what he thought good" (2 Sam. 19:18). He probably received a small fee for his services and supplemented his income by engaging in other activities.

Fisherman and *Fishing*

Fishing as a vocation and a hobby was practiced early in Biblical lands. There is a tomb relief dating from about 2600 B.C. depicting three Egyptian fishermen pulling lines of net. Much later in history, about 704 B.C., we have a monument of Nineveh revealing an Assyrian fishing with a line. In the Bible, *dugah* signifies fishing (Am. 4:2) and *dayag* is a fisherman (Jer. 16:16; Ezek. 47:10).

The ancient Hebrews were fond of both fresh and salted fish (Num. 11:5), but they considered fishing hard work rather than a sport. They perceived that the physical exertions of fishing required a strong physique (Lk. 5:5). They and other peoples of antiquity fished in the Jordan, in the Dead Sea, and in the Mediterranean (Neh. 13:16). They also fished in the Nile (Isa. 19:8), in Lake Gennesaret, or the Sea of Galilee (Matt. 4:18), in the Tigris-Euphrates, in the Aegean Sea, in Lake Huleh, and in the Orontes.

Their fishing gear was the *mikmoret,* a dragnet which when loaded with fish sank to the bottom (Isa. 19:8; Hab. 1:15; Lk. 5:4), and the *herem,* a smaller net either drawn from the boat or drawn from the shore (Hab. 1:16–17). They also employed hook and line (Am. 4:2; Isa. 19:8; Hab. 1:15), and probably a harpoon or spear, (Job 41:1–2). After catching their haul, they either emptied it into their boat or dragged their nets to the shore (Matt. 13:48; Jn. 21:8). The fish were then sorted; those suitable for selling were placed in baskets and the others were discarded (Matt. 13:48).

Fish were either sold fresh to nearby communities or salted and marketed at such places as Jerusalem (Neh. 3:3, 13:16) and Acre (2 Chr. 33:14). Fishmongers hawked their merchandise to the town and city residents. Nehemiah 13:16 refers to the "men of Tyre who brought in fish and all manner of ware, and sold on the Sabbath unto the children of Judah and in Jerusalem." Nehemiah halted their activities by closing the city gates on the Sabbath.

Fishermen often worked in groups or guilds (Lk. 5:10). Sometimes they fished at night (Lk. 5:5). The New Testament refers to Jesus fishing (Lk. 5:1 ff.) and to his approval of it (Jn. 21:6). At least seven of the disciples were fishermen (Matt. 4:18, 21; Jn. 1:44). Some were partners and worked together (Lk. 5:7, 10). While fishing on the Sea of Galilee and probably elsewhere, they fished in small boats propelled by oars (Jn. 6:19) and apparently also by sails (Matt. 14:24).

The Bible does not specify fish by name but uses the terms *dag* and *nun* to signify all varieties of fish. Large fish are referred to collectively as *tannin,* though this also denotes mythological creatures. Leviticus 11:9 ff. divides fish into two groups: clean and unclean. Included among the former are those possessing fins and scales. Among the unclean are eels and shellfish. Jews are permitted to eat only the "clean" varieties.

From Biblical times (Num. 11:5) on, Jews have been very fond of fish, which usually graces their meals on Sabbaths and holy days. In the Talmud, large or small fish, salted or fresh, raw or cooked, were prized (Ned. 6:4). Chopped fish meat or tunny fish was sold and was very popular. The brine of salted fish and its fatty tail were used. A sort of smorgasbord of fish was also popular and oddly called *zahanah,* meaning foul odor. Apparently, it was believed to taste best when it was on the verge of decomposition (M.K. 11a).

Among the fish and sea foods mentioned in the Talmud, the most familiar are Spanish mackerel, the common tunny, triton, swordfish, herring, sprat, eel, muraena, sturgeon, and tonguefish.

Fish were used in Biblical and later times for purposes other than food. Fish oil served as fuel (Shab. 24b); fish skin and fish bones were used for writing materials (Shab. 108a) and for different implements (Kel. 10:1). Fish oil was sometimes mixed with olive oil (Bek. 29b).

Fishing is employed in the Bible as a symbol of God's judgment on nations and on individuals (Jer. 16:16; Ezek. 32:3). Jesus called to his disciples to become fishers of men (Matt. 4:19). The kingdom of heaven is compared to a dragnet (Matt. 13:47).

See *Cook.*

Forester

In Biblical times, a forester most likely was engaged mainly in custodial duties and in prevention of fires (Neh. 2:8). There were periods of local shortages of wood which led to temporary corrective though ineffective action. There are forests mentioned in the Bible which probably were protected by members of the king's entourage.

Mention is made of the "forest of Ephraim" where Absalom was slain (2 Sam. 18:6). It was in Gilead, forest of Hareth in the land of Judah that David sought refuge after returning from Moab (1 Sam. 22:5). From the forest "Ya'ar" on the road from Jericho to Bethel, the bears emerged who avenged Elisha (2 Ki. 2:24). In this forest, also, the Israelites, pursuing the Philistines, found honey (1 Sam. 14:25). In the forest "Horesh" Jotham built forts and towns (2 Chr. 27:4), while the forest

"Horeshah" was in the wilderness of "Ziph" where David sought refuge (1 Sam. 23:15–19). "Ya'ar ha negeb," "forest of the south" (Ezek. 20:46), may be a figure of rhetoric.

See *Farmer, Logger, Tree Surgeon.*

Fowler

Fowlers were professional birdcatchers in ancient times. Some snared birds in light traps made with noose cords which entangled the feet of the birds. There are a number of references to the fowler's snare (Hos. 9:8; Ps. 91:3, 124:7). Fowlers also captured birds, caged them, and placed them in a concealed spot outdoors so that their voices would attract other birds who would then be killed by the concealed bowman or by a throw stick (Ecclus. 11:30). Ancient fowlers also sewed the eyelids of captured birds and placed them in a camouflaged location where their cries would draw other birds who were then captured (Jer. 5:26).

Fowlers met a widespread demand for doves and other caged pets. Pigeons and doves were used for sacrifices while small birds tempted the palates of the gourmet.

See *Hunter.*

Fruit Farmer

Fruit farmers in the Holy Land and other countries cultivated mainly olives, figs, and grapes although they also cultivated almonds, apples, dates, melons, mulberries, pistachio nuts, pomegranates, and sycamore trees. The mandrake and the carob bean were eaten only occasionally.

Eating fruit from newly planted trees was forbidden until their fifth year (Lev. 19:23–25). Fruits such as grapes were dried (1 Sam. 25:18; Num. 6:3; Isa. 38:21). The fruit farmer sold his products to the town and city folk.

See *Farmer, Olive Oil Worker, Tree Surgeon.*

Fuller

The fuller was an old vocation, that of thickening and shrinking newly shorn wool and cleansing or finishing newly woven cloth after removing its natural oils. The Hebrew term "mikabes" (Mal. 3:2; 2 Ki. 18:17; Isa. 7:3, 36:2) refers to one employed in either of two occupations: cleaning of soiled garments of cloth or finishing of freshly woven cloth. It is believed that the cleansing of garments or cloth began in very early times. The work was both very time-consuming and vigorous.

To wash newly woven cloth thoroughly and to give its fabric proper texture and firmness, it was placed in hot water to which were added soapy detergents such as alkaline salts (Mal. 3:2). Then it was stamped on and worked over with a fulling billet (a metal instrument) while the cloth was scraped repeatedly and the wool evenly trimmed. Because of the foul odor that was emitted from fulling, the shops were situated outside the city limits near springs of water or large ponds. The fuller's field of Jerusalem is described as near the upper pool (Isa. 7:3, 36:2; 2 Ki. 18:17).

Since hand-woven garments were expensive and scarce in Bible times, the fuller's work was important. He appears to have also traded in textiles. There was an important fuller's guild in Rome during the seventh century B.C. and a tax was imposed on their work. The ruins of the guild's headquarters still survive and face the main forum.

See *Clothier, Weaver.*

Furniture Designer

In ancient times there were master carpenters who may be considered as the first furniture designers. These men lived in ancient Egypt where they designed beds (2 Ki. 4:10), stools, and throne chairs, the main types of ancient furniture. While few of these survive, we have many stone carvings and fresco paintings of furniture which give enduring evidence of early furniture.

The furniture designer's first beds were wooden and consisted of a simple frame supported by four legs. Great beds were found in the tombs of Tutankhamen. They were assembled with huge hooks and staples which could be dismantled and folded for storage or for moving. Beds were so uncommon that when the Pharaohs traveled, they took their own along. Instead of pillows, ivory head rests were used. This same pattern of furniture design was followed in Mesopotamia where wooden furniture was assembled by dovetailing or with dowels. Biblical references to beds are 1 Samuel 19:15, Deuteronomy 3:11, and Amos 6:4.

Mesopotamian furniture designers introduced three features that were later adopted by the Greeks and by the Romans: the decoration of the furniture legs with metal rings one above the other, like many bracelets on a woman's arm; heavy fringes on furniture covers; and typical furniture groupings consisting of a couch which was used for eating or conversation, a small table for refreshments, and the chairs. In Greece too, furniture was mainly couches, chairs, stools, tables, and chests.

These furniture designers used hammers, saws, and nails. They may also have made preliminary sketches of the designs they planned to execute.

In the Bible the word *kley* means "utensils" or "implements" and denotes all furnishings in the Tabernacle (Ex. 25:9, 31:7,

40:19; 1 Chr. 9:29). *Kley hemdah* (Nah. 2:9) means "precious things" but is also translated "pleasant furniture" by the King James Version.

See *Carpenter, Wood Carver.*

Gambler

There is no specific reference to gambling as an avocation or vocation in the Bible, although there is a wager recorded between Samson and the Philistines (Jg. 14:12–19) which relates to resolving a riddle. Many references are made to casting lots (Ps. 22:18), which was variously used to discern the Divine Will (Jn. 19:24), to detect culprits (Jos. 7:16–18; 1 Sam. 14:38–42), to divide an inheritance (Jos. 15:1; 16:1), and to settle disputes (Pro. 18:18). It is believed that Jews definitely learned to gamble only after their contact with Greek and Roman civilization about the fourth century B.C. Yet there are early historic references to what may have been gambling. At Mizpah, a little system of squares was found scratched into a smooth rock. Some scholars believe that pebbles were used for a game instead of draughts or chessmen. A gaming board and dice were found at Megiddo, and a beautifully inlaid board was found at Ur of the Chaldees dating from before 3000 B.C.

Some believe that betting may be referred to in the Biblical verses: "He that maketh haste to be rich shall not be unpunished" (Pro. 28:20), "He that hasteth after riches hath an evil eye and knoweth not that want shall overcome him" (Pro. 28:22), and "Wealth gotten by vanity shall be diminished, but he that gathereth by labor shall have increase" (Pro. 13:11).

Rabbinical law declares that if two people make a wager, though this is culpable, they must carry out its provisions based on the Biblical statement, "That which is gone out of thy lips thou shalt observe and do" (Dt. 23:23). The obligation, however, is moral, not legal.

There are two types of gambling mentioned in the Talmud: dice playing and pigeon racing. The former was shooting dice; the latter seems to have been betting on the flight of pigeons. Both were disapproved of by the rabbis "because they do not further the interest of society" (Sanh. 24b). Gambling for stakes was deemed akin to robbery. The gambler was considered unfit as a witness in a Jewish court of law (Sanh. 3:3; R.H. 1:8), although one opinion is that this restriction applies only to a professional gambler (Sanh. 24b).

The Talmud relates an interesting story wherein four hundred zuzim were lost by someone who bet that he could arouse Hillel's anger. He made three unsuccessful attempts until he ruefully admitted defeat (Sanh. 30b).

Maimonides in his commentary on the Mishnah asserted: "He who indulges in this game [gambling] spends his time on things which do not contribute to the well-being of his fellow man; and it is one of the principles of our religion that man ought to occupy himself in this world either with the study of the Torah in order to perfect his soul in the wisdom of the Torah, or in some useful work or handicraft or trade; but so that he find time sometime for the study of the Law."

Gardener and *Gardens*

Gardeners were commonly employed by royalty. Egyptian and Mesopotamian kings had beautiful gardens that no doubt were tended by knowledgeable slaves. Inside the lavish palace of the kings of Canaanite Ugarit was a garden court dating from about the fourteenth century B.C.

In the Bible, a garden is called *gan* or *gannah*. *Gan* appears originally to have referred to all kinds of gardens. In Biblical times, a garden evidently meant variously a vineyard, an orchard, a kitchen garden, or a royal garden. Among the gardens mentioned in the Bible, besides the Garden of Eden (Gen.

2:18), was the famous one Ahab appropriated from Naboth to make into his garden of herbs (1 Ki. 21:2). The Song of Solomon makes frequent reference to gardens (4:15–16, 6:2), as do Isaiah and others (Isa. 1:8, 30, 51:3, 58:11, 65:3, 66:17; Lk. 13:9; Jn. 18:1, 26; Jer. 29:5; Am. 4:9, 9:14). Among the most famous gardens was the Garden of Gethsemane (Jn. 18:1, 26). Occasionally, tombs were found in gardens (Jn. 19:41). Possibly because of their beauty and their luxuriant foliage, gardens were frequently used to worship idols (1 Ki. 15:13; Isa. 57:5).

There is no explicit reference to landscape architects in the Bible but a number of references suggest their presence. "Thou shalt be like a watered garden" (Isa. 58:11). "I made me gardens and orchards and planted" (Eccl. 2:5; Am. 9:14).

Gardeners were probably employed by royalty and the upper classes and undoubtedly worked hard at their duties. As mentioned in the story of Susannah, they divided gardens into beds which they laid out near water using cisterns and channels for irrigation. They must have struggled with the long and dry summer when the vegetation depended on the water supply (Num. 24:6). Cisterns and reservoirs collected the rain, and from these, by many conduits, the gardeners led the water in the evenings to refresh the gardens. No doubt, many a gardener despaired when, during periods of drought, he gloomily surveyed the withered leaves and wilted plants (Isa. 58:11). In John 20:15, there is a specific reference to a gardener: "she supposing he had been the gardener."

An overseer of the royal forests or *shomer-ha-pardes* is mentioned in Nehemiah 2:8. An orchard was called by the Persian word *pardes*, which later signified paradise. World-famous are the orange and lemon groves of Jaffa and Sidon, while the orchards around Damascus were also renowned. Toward evening, Biblical personages were drawn to the garden and the beautiful variety of fruits in season (Est. 7:7; Cant. 4:1 ff.).

The fondness of the Israelites for flowers may be seen from the fact that almost all of their artistic works have floral decorations such as the candelabra of the Tabernacle (Ex. 25:

33), the pillars of the Temple, and the molten sea with its brim decorated with flowers of lilies (1 Ki. 7:19–26). When the Israelites offered the first crop of fruits at the altar in Jerusalem on the Feast of Harvest (Ex. 23:16), they crowned it with the choicest flowers (Bik. 23).

We know that flowers were cultivated (Cant. 6:2) and probably, as in our time, crops of grain or vegetables were grown in the spaces between the trees. Gardens were planted on terraces on mountainsides (B.M. 10:4–6), and plants were occasionally raised in pots. Among the Palestinian plants of Greek origin were the box, iris, ivy, narcissus, mint, laurel, oleander, and rice.

Both in Biblical and Talmudic times, gardeners used dung, fine sand, the blood of animals, chaff, ashes, straw, leaves, scum of oil, and the remainder of the fruit of the field to fertilize their gardens and lands.

In post-Biblical times, there are many references to gardeners. Persian words such as *baga* and *bustana* appear in the Talmud revealing the practice of Persian horticulture. God is referred to by the Talmud as the first gardener, while Noah is credited as being the first human gardener. Other distinguished gardeners include Abraham and Solomon.

There are numerous references to gardens and parks in rabbinical literature. We learn that gardens were usually near the house (B.M. 105; Yer. B.B. 3.14b). The rabbis urged that gardens should be fenced in (B.B. 14a; Yer. B.B. 1.12d). There is a rose garden in Jerusalem, mentioned in the Mishnah, which is reputed to have flourished from the time of the prophets (Ma'as. 2:5). It was the only garden or park permitted in the Holy City (B.K. 82b). Other parks known during Mishnaic times (first two centuries after Christ) were those of Sebaste, Jericho, and Ashkelon (Ar. 3:2; 2:54). The Talmud declares that Solomon's Temple contained golden illustrations of various aromatic trees in full fruit, which exuded fragrant perfumes with the movement of the air (Yoma 39b). Philo states that many synagogues in Alexandria were surrounded by trees. We know that one sage, Rabina, employed a professional gardener.

Popular rabbinical proverbs regarding gardens were: "As the

gardener, so the garden." "Whoever rents one garden, may eat birds; whoever rents more than one garden at the same time, will be eaten by the birds" (Dukes, *Rabbinische Blumenlese*, Nos. 202, 456).

See *Architect, Tree Surgeon, Vintner.*

Glassmaker and *Glass*

Glassmaking is an art that may have first begun accidentally, as Pliny declares, by the fusion of sand and soda in an open fire. Certainly, glass can be made in this way. It is believed that the first conscious attempt to make glass came from the potter, artisan of the oldest of the arts dependent on fire. The development of colored glazes for coating pottery or stone beads appears to have anticipated the manufacture of articles made entirely of glass.

Sir Flinders Petrie (*Transactions of British Newcomen Society*, V, 72) states, "The earliest glaze known is that on stone beads of the Badarian age in Egypt about 12,000 B.C. This is green. . . ." The oldest pure glass is a molded amulet of deep lapis-lazuli color from about 7000 B.C.

The art of glass blowing is represented in tombs dating from the fifth dynasty in Egypt of the fourth millennium B.C. The manufacture of glass in Egypt became a continuous industry at the beginning of the eighteenth dynasty, and the remains of glassworks built about 1500 B.C. in Egypt survive. The glasswork of that period was excellent in both craftsmanship and durability, for the Egyptians possessed an astonishing knowledge of metallurgy and used tin oxide to make white opaque glass. Transparent glass, however, was uncommon. Pieces of glass found in tombs along with jewelry, although multicolored, are always opaque. From 1500 B.C. until the beginning of the Christian era, Egypt continued to be a glass manufacturing center with its main headquarters in Alexandria.

Before the advent of the blowpipe, glass vessels were made by winding rods of hot softened glass around a central core of sand built up on a metal rod. Alternately, the core would be dipped several times into a pot of molten glass, which would be gradually built to the desired thickness.

About 1200 B.C. the Egyptians mastered the art of pressing glass into open molds which led to the production of bowls, cups, dishes, all impossible to make by the sand-core method. Occasionally, hundreds of colored glass threads, each no more than a thousandth of an inch in diameter, would be applied to a vase, which would then be softened by reheating and pulled into bright, varied patterns. All this contributed to the high cost of the finished product. Next to Egypt, during Biblical times, Sidon was the main center of glass manufacturing in the Mediterranean world.

Glass was used almost entirely for personal adornment and, because of its costliness, was valued as if it were a precious gem. The only direct reference to glass in the Old Testament is in Job 28:17 where it is asserted that "the gold and the crystal cannot equal wisdom," implying that glass was very expensive. Glass seems to have been mentioned only poetically in the New Testament (Rev. 4:6, 15:2, 21:18–21). Paul declared, "For now we see through a glass darkly" (1 Cor. 13:12). Most scholars doubt the existence of a local glass industry in Biblical Palestine.

In Talmudic times, the Jews practiced glass blowing (Yer. Shab. 7.2), perhaps because many Jews lived near Belus with its sands. White glass was very costly (Hul. 84b; Ber. 31a) and its manufacture seems to have stopped after the destruction of the Second Temple in 70 A.D. (Sotah 48b; Suk. 4:6). Poorer persons used colored glasses (Tos. Peah 4).

Many objects were made either entirely or partly of glass: tables, spoons, bowls, bottles, drinking vessels (Kel. 30:1–4), beads, beds, lamps, cradles, seats, stools, paper knives and paperweights (Tos. Kel. 3:7). Jewish merchants sold these objects by weight (B.B. 89a; B.K. 31a).

See *Furniture Designer, Mirror Maker*.

Governor

This was an administrative officer appointed by kings to administer a definite territory or province. Joseph was a governor in Egypt (Gen. 42:6). Gedaliah was the Judean governor appointed by the Babylonian king (Jer. 40:5).

A governor might also be the absolute ruler of his area. The chief officers of the Temple were also known as governors. One Pashur put Jeremiah in stocks (Jer. 20:1, 2). There were "governors" of armies who served as the mayors of cities (1 Ki. 22:26; 2 Ki. 23:8). There were also "governors" of palaces.

In the New Testament, the word "governor" usually refers to Roman legates, procurators, and proconsuls (1 Pet. 2:14). Tenure was usually for one year, but many governors were reappointed. They administered the law and possessed powers of life and death (Matt. 10:18; Mk. 13:9; Lk. 21:12).

See *Judge, King, Proconsul, Procurator.*

Hairdresser and *Hair Styles*

Mankind's deeply rooted vanity and concern with personal appearance led to hairdressing as a career in the ancient Near East. Ancient Egypt boasted of expert hairdressers who dressed the natural hair and wigs of the royal families and the nobility, employing pins comparable to present-day hairpins. Mesopotamia, too, boasted of a variety of hair styles.

The Bible makes clear that women gave much time and attention to their hair, and they also employed skilled hairdressers (G. E. Wright, *Biblical Archaeology,* p. 191; 2 Ki. 9:30; Cant. 4:1, 6:5, 7:5). This must have been especially true of the royal family and the wealthier classes. The prophet Isaiah ridicules the many devices women used to curl and style their hair (3:24; 2 Ki. 9:30). Josephus refers to their custom of sprinkling gold dust on their hair to give it a golden appearance (Ant. 8.7.3).

In Biblical times most male and female Hebrews preferred their hair quite long. Absalom's long hair is mentioned rather approvingly (2 Sam. 14:25). Samson's strength was believed to reside in his uncut hair (Jg. 16:19). Barbers trimmed rather than cropped their clients' hair (2 Sam. 19:24). The trimming had to be done in specified ways: the forelock was not to be cut (Lev. 19:27) because this was typical of idolatrous cults (Dt. 14:1). Ezekiel also instructed the priests how to cut their hair (44:20).

The hair of the ancient Hebrews was usually black, a color considered symbolic of youth, while white hair symbolized old age (Eccl. 11:10). Herod allegedly dyed his hair black to look younger (Josephus, Ant. 16.8.1). Long black hair was considered a sign of virility.

Hairdressers and barbers cut their clients' hair at various intervals. Absalom, who gloried in his long hair, had it cut yearly. Most people, however, cut their hair more frequently.

Hair was not shaved off except on special occasions such as a period of mourning when part of the head, especially the front, was shaved. Israelites were also forbidden to follow the then-heathenish custom of shaving the head in a circle with only a strand remaining in the center (Lev. 19:27, 21:5). Although the Pentateuch prohibited shaving the head (Dt. 14:1; Lev. 21:5), the prophets suggest that it was a custom practiced by the people (Isa. 7:20; Jer. 7:29, 16:6; Ezek. 7:18; Am. 8:10; Mic. 1:16). Priests were forbidden to shave their heads, nor were they to follow the hair styles of the heathen. They were also to allow their hair to grow uncut, like the Nazarites, who vowed, for religious reasons, not to cut their hair.

While the Egyptians wore wigs, this custom did not develop among the Hebrews. The Assyrians wore their hair in several braids which extended to the nape of their necks. Samson's seven braids suggest that this may have been the style in Israel at that time (Jg. 16:13, 19).

Women's long tresses were praised as a sign of beauty (Cant. 4:1, 7:5). A woman cut her hair only when in deep mourning or degradation (Jer. 7:29; Dt. 21:12). In rabbinical literature, a woman's hair is considered so beautiful and so seductive that married women were urged to cover their hair as an act of modesty. When a pious mother, whose seven sons were successively high priests, was queried by what virtue she was so fortunate, she replied, "The beams of my house have never seen my hair" (Yoma 47a). Women in Talmudic times plaited their hair.

The rabbis termed a man who curled his hair as vain. They considered Joseph childish because at the age of seventeen he still curled his hair (Gen. R. 34), and they added that because Absalom was so vain about his hair, he was hung by it when he tried to escape from his father's soldiers following his insurrection.

Jews were prohibited from trimming their hair over their foreheads, but they were allowed to let it hang down over their temples in curls (Sifre, Ahare Mot, 13.9). One Jew, Abtalion ben Reuben, however, who associated with the court, was allowed to wear his hair in that disapproved style (B.K. 83a). Soldiers about to enter battle let their hair loose.

Interesting styles in haircutting prevailed in Talmudic times. The king had his hair cut daily, the high priest every week, and the ordinary priest every month. The high priest's hair was cut by having the top of one row of hair touching the root of the next (Sanh. 22b; Ned. 51a).

Pulling the hair of an opponent drew a fine of one hundred selaim.

Washing of the dead began with the hair since human hair was associated with the thoughts. During Talmudic times, prior to burial, a corpse was given a haircut (M.K. 1b).

By New Testament times, styles had changed and long hair was considered a "shame" (1 Cor. 11:14) in men, though women continued to wear their hair long, plaited, and virtually uncut. Jesus disapproved of the custom of swearing by one's hair (Matt. 5:36).

Training in hairdressing skills was probably acquired by observation and by some form of apprenticeship. Because this skill is a highly personal service, the occupation brought the practitioner into close proximity with the affluent, which automatically yielded certain material benefits as well as prestige.

See *Barber, Clothier, Perfumer, Spice Dealer.*

Harness Maker and *Repairman*

Among the scriptural references to harnesses and, by inference, to harness makers are: "Israel went up harnessed out of the land of Egypt" (Ex. 13:18). "Harness the horses and get up, ye horsemen" (Jer. 46:4). Additional references may be found in 1 Kings 20:11, 22:34; 2 Chronicles 9:24, 18:33.

The ancient harness maker used knives, awls, needles, and thread to cut the leather and shape, fit, and stitch the various parts of the harness together. He also repaired and replaced worn or damaged parts and made new harnesses. He cut leather strips from the hide and sewed them together by hand, and he frequently cleaned and dressed the harness. In New Testament times there was a street in Rome that harness makers occupied.

See *Saddle Maker, Tanner.*

Herald

An officer who publicly announced royal proclamations (Dan. 3:4; 1 Tim. 2:7; 2 Tim. 1:11; 2 Pet. 2:5) was a herald. He probably possessed a stentorian voice and read his proclamation from a scroll. As an officer of the government, he probably dressed in a dignified manner befitting his position.

The word "herald" is also used in "heralding good tidings" (Isa. 40:9, 41:27).

See *Letter Writer, Runner, Scribe, Town Crier.*

Historian

Archivists are known to have kept records of kings and kingdoms ever since the written word was commonly used. Archivists were employed by the Assyrians, Babylonians, Egyptians, Medes, and Persians. In Israel, from the time of David (2 Sam. 8:16, 20:24; 1 Chr. 18:15) there was a special royal officer or recorder, *sofer* or *maskir*, who recorded important events, advised the king, and preserved facts in the royal archives (Est. 6:1). Among other Hebrew kings who had court historians were Solomon, who along with David was served by Jehoshaphat (1 Ki. 4:3), and Hezekiah by Joab (Isa. 36:22; 2 Ki. 18:18). During the time of the Second Temple, there also must have been archives because Josephus cited a number of documents.

The books of Chronicles are historical books of the Bible, although the author is known only as the "Chronicler." W. F. Albright believes that Ezra was the chronicler of this period.

In Biblical times, Jews manifested a strong historical sense, as shown by the books from Genesis to Kings which recount the history of the Jews. It seems evident that there were historical records as *The Books of the Acts of Solomon* (1 Ki. 11:41) and *The Books of the Chronicles of the Kings of Judah* (2 Chr. 24:27).

According to C. H. Gordon in *The Ancient Near East*, "Other nations of the ancient Near East had annals but not real history in which personal character and motivation were delineated. The Hebrews achieved true historical composition by transferring human values from the epic to current events. The composition of real history is the greatest achievement of that period. It antedates Greek historiography by over five hundred years."

See *Librarian, Scribe.*

Horse Breeder

Some scholars believe that horses roamed wild in Natufian times (8000–10,000 years ago). The Mitanni (1500 B.C.) bred horses to enable them to subdue their neighbors, and wrote tractates on horses in Hittite cuneiform. Solomon imported and transshipped horses from Cilicia to Egypt. He probably also bred them despite the prohibition "he shall not multiply horses to himself" (Dt. 17:16). The price of a horse at that time was 150 shekels (1 Ki. 10:28–29).

Horse breeders fed, watered, and groomed their horses. Breeding may have been governed by the horse's ancestry, color, and other traits. In Roman times, during the first Christian centuries, horses were bred mainly for war, hunting, and sport, and rarely for use as draft animals.

See *Cattleman, Farmer.*

Housewife

The position of the woman in any society is an important index to the nature of that society. In ancient Israel, the husband enjoyed a proprietary right over his wife. He was the owner or master (ba'al) while she was the owned (beulah). In the Decalogue, she is included as part of his wealth along with his other property (Ex. 20:17). In this role she was unable to inherit property but she could own presents. She was also the mistress of the servants given to her at marriage, if her family were fairly affluent. Even these, however, became the property of her husband upon her death. Notwithstanding, the status of the Jewish wife was substantially higher than that prevailing among other nations in antiquity.

While the husband could exercise tyrannical power, the Bible offers evidence that a loving relationship often prevailed (Song of Solomon; 1 Sam. 18:20). Moreover, the wife was not defenseless or entirely at the mercy of her husband. Though he alone could exercise the right to divorce, she could desert him (Jg. 19:2) and turn to her blood relations. If he desired to leave her, he was required to give her a bill of divorce (Dt. 24:1), although "divorce was hateful to God" (Mal. 2:14–16; 1 Cor. 7:11). The husband also had other limitations on his power over her. He had to provide for her medical care even if she suffered from a prolonged illness (Ket. 51a), pay her ransom if she were captured, and on her death, she was to be provided with a proper funeral (Ket. 46b). The Talmud declares that he had to support her in better style than she had enjoyed before marriage (Ket. 48a, 61a). Even the poorest husband had to supply his wife with bread for at least two meals a day, with sufficient oil for eating and lighting, with wood for cooking, with fruit, vegetables, and wine where it was customary for women to drink wine.

On Sabbaths, he was required to supply her with three meals consisting of fish and meat. He was to give her a silver coin weekly for pocket money. If he were unable to provide her with the above, some authorities declare that he was compelled to give her a divorce (Hatan Sofer on Eben ha-Ezer 131, 132). Others, however, assert that he had to hire himself out to be a day laborer to support her. If he refused to support her, the court forced him to do so (Ket. 77a). If he mistreated her or lived in a disreputable neighborhood, she could leave his home and he was required to support her wherever she moved. He was required to supply her with clothing according to his station and to local custom.

He was to provide a home properly furnished consonant with his position and with local custom. Besides her clothing, suitable for the seasons of the year, and new shoes for each holy day, he was to provide her with bedding and kitchen utensils. Further, he was to provide her with ornaments and perfumes if those were customary. If he were unable to clothe her properly, he might be compelled to divorce her (Ket. 64b).

Frequency of cohabitation depended on his occupation (Ket. 61b). If he should persist in denying her rights of cohabitation, he might be compelled to divorce her.

If she predeceased him, he was to provide for her burial according to the custom of the land and his position. He was required to hire mourners if that was the custom, and to erect a tombstone, and to make other customary provisions. If he refused to do so, or if he were absent, the court might sell part of his property to meet the burial costs (Ket. 46a).

As for the duties of the housewife during Biblical times, besides her main duty of bearing and rearing children, she was busy from before dawn preparing food. This included the arduous grinding of the ears of corn into meal, a task which she usually did in a kneeling position. She gathered fuel; she fetched a supply of water which she carried from a spring or well. Because water was often scarce, she spent considerable time drawing milk from goats and sheep. Much of her time was spent cooking, baking, making and repairing clothing, ministering to the needs of her husband and children, and teaching her children. Proverbs 31:13–27 gives a vivid picture of the activities of the well-to-do lady.

The Talmud specifies the housewife's responsibilities. Besides baking, cooking, and washing, she was to nurse her children. If she had twins, her husband had to provide a nurse for one infant while she nursed the other (Ket. 59b). If she brought him a large dowry, she was exempt from housework save for such duties as comforting him and other signs of affection such as preparing his bed and serving at the table. Rabbi Eliezer declared that though she brought one hundred slaves, her husband might insist on her working in wool (namely, spinning) lest idleness should lead her into intrigues—"idleness leads to immorality." Rabbi Simeon ben Gamaliel counseled that the husband should not allow his wife to be idle as it would dispose her toward melancholia. However, a married woman was never required to work in the field. The Talmud suggests that housewives might maintain their cheerfulness by playing chess.

Since playing chess or raising animals was not deemed an occupation (Ket. 52b, 61b), more purposeful activities appear to have been suggested for her.

In Talmudic times housewives were often authorized by their husbands to operate shops. Widows were appointed guardians of their infant children. Consequently, some women were familiar with business (Ket. 9:4–5). The housewife was not expected to go out too frequently (Gen. R. 45:2) and was expected to act modestly even when alone with her husband (Shab. 140b). The highest praise of a wife was that she fulfilled the wishes of her husband (Ned. 66b).

The Talmud contains many favorable passages regarding women. "If your wife is small, bend down and whisper in her ear," or consult with her in worldly matters (B.M. 59b). "A husband should love his wife as himself and honor her more than himself" (Sanh. 76b; Yeb. 62b). "He should not torment her for God counts her tears." "One who honors his wife will be rewarded with wealth" (B.M. 59b). "He who sees his wife die before him has, as it were, seen the destruction of the Temple: his world is darkened, his step is slow, his mind is heavy. The wife dies in the husband's death; he in hers" (Sanh. 22a).

The role of the housewife in the New Testament does not differ radically from that in the Old Testament. Jesus occasionally made allusions to her domestic duties. "A woman loses a coin and searches for it" (Lk. 15:8). "Two women will be grinding grain at a mill" (Lk. 17:35). Women served as deaconesses in the early Church (Rom. 16:1). The subordination of women is stressed along with the virtue of modesty and piety. They were expected to manifest mainly domestic virtues as evidence of their piety and faith.

In short, as in all times, the role of the housewife was varied. Her duties were arduous, but her life was sweetened by the regard and love of her mate and her children.

See APPENDIX III.

Hunter and *Hunting*

While many persons hunted for pleasure and protection in antiquity, there were individuals who engaged in hunting as a vocation or as a means of supplementing their food supply. The Egyptian and Assyrian kings and nobles were very fond of hunting, and their monuments portray them in many hunting scenes. While the Mesopotamians hunted wild beasts such as lions, the Egyptians accompanied by dogs and cats caught game and predatory birds.

There are a considerable number of references to hunting in

the Old Testament. Nimrod was "a mighty hunter before the Lord" (Gen. 10:9); Esau was a cunning hunter (Gen. 25:27); and Ishmael, too, was known as a hunter (Gen. 21:20). Israelites who settled in Canaan continued to hunt wild game. Some dangerous animals such as the bear and the lion whose habitats were in Palestine were slain by Samson and David.

Techniques employed to bag animals and fowl were varied. They included the use of pitfalls and nets to entrap the lion (Ezek. 19:4–8), bows and arrows (Gen. 27:3), the sling (1 Sam. 17:40), the snare (Ps. 91:3), spears, swords, and clubs against wild animals (1 Sam. 17:40; Ps. 23:4). The battue method of hunting, in use from ancient times until the present, was probably used. The villagers formed a cordon, beat on the ground, yelled loudly, and pounded drums or sticks, thereby driving the frightened quarry into a blind canyon or into a group of nets or into a pit where it was dispatched. Possible references to this method may be found in Job 18:11; Psalms 18:5; Isaiah 24:17–18; Jeremiah 48:43–4. In ancient Near Eastern art, there are scenes depicting hunting with a lasso and spear. There are far more references in the Old Testament to the fowler and his nets and snares than to the hunter, because Palestine is located in the main flight routes of the migratory birds. Josephus refers to hunting dogs (*Ant.* 4.8.9), to Herod as a mighty hunter (*Ant.* 157, 16.10.3), and to horses that were used regularly for the chase in post-Biblical times.

Jews generally were either indifferent or opposed to hunting. They later developed a revulsion toward the killing of animals for sport. Among the animals they hunted for food were the gazelle, hart, roebuck, and wild goat (Dt. 12:15, 22, 14:5). The partridge was probably the bird mainly hunted in Biblical times (1 Sam. 26:20), and a tame partridge in a cave was used as a decoy (Sir. 11:30). Neither beast nor bird was allowed to be eaten unless the blood had been "poured out" (Lev. 17:13; Dt. 12:16). Jewish dietary laws later required that animals be mercifully slaughtered by a shohet before being eaten.

As city life and trade developed, the economic importance of hunting declined. However, Leviticus 17:13 deals with a law regarding hunting and one of the Proverbs also deals with it (12:27).

Hunting is mentioned infrequently in post-Biblical times. There are scant references to hunting in the Talmud (Ab. Zar. 18b; Hul. 60b; B.B. 75a). The general attitude expressed was that hunting was a cruel and un-Jewish activity. One medieval rabbi declared, "He who hunts game with dogs as gentiles do, will not enjoy the life to come."

See *Fowler.*

Innkeeper

The Bible contains references to lodging places where caravans or parties of travelers rested for the night (Gen. 42:27, 43:21; Ex. 4:24). In early Biblical times, inns must have been very simple and designed to provide elementary shelter rather than luxurious accommodations. They are believed to have been unfurnished and may have had niches in the walls where travelers spent the night. The Hebrew word for inn is *malon* (Jos. 4:3; Lk. 10:34). It signified a camping place for an individual (Jer. 9:2), for a family (Ex. 4:24), for a caravan, and even for a nation (Jos. 4:3, 8). There was a special word for host or innkeeper, *faudake.*

By New Testament times, the number of travelers had so greatly increased that the need for inns became critical (Lk. 10:34–35). Moreover, their appointments and comforts had improved. However, Joseph and Mary are described as having been unable to find room at the inn in Bethlehem (Lk. 2:7). Tradition has it that there was an inn near Bethlehem, Gerut, built by Chimham (2 Sam. 19:37–40). The good Samaritan is mentioned as having left his patient at an inn (Lk. 10:34).

In the Talmud, a company of Levites is recorded as having left one of their comrades at an inn when he became ill on the way to Zoar (Yeb. 16:7). Rabbi Ishmael bar Jose stated that his father customarily prayed at an inn (Yer. Ber. 4:7). When inns became sufficiently spacious, cattle as well as their owners were accommodated (Ab. Zar. 2:1).

Josephus (Ant. 15.5.1; B.J. 1.21.7) speaks of "public inns." The Mishnah (Yeb. 16:7) declares that the word of an innkeeper was doubted, and the Mishnah (Ab. Zar. 2:4) places innkeepers on the lowest scale of degradation. Female innkeepers may have been as loose as Rahab (Jos. 2:1). The ancient innkeeper appears generally to have limited his services to a bare minimum of shelter and food.

See *Tavern Keeper.*

Interpreter

Although international commerce and diplomatic relationships that date far back in history required interpreters, there are only a few passages in Scriptures which refer to them. Joseph, feigning ignorance of the language of his brothers, used an interpreter to communicate with them (Gen. 42:23). Other passages mentioning interpreters are 2 Chronicles 32:31; Isaiah 43:27.

Because their work brought them into close contact with important persons, interpreters probably enjoyed considerable prestige and preferments. We have no evidence of a formal training program for them, but they were probably well-traveled persons with a facility in languages.

In the New Testament the word "interpreter" refers to explaining the speech of those possessing the gift of tongues (1 Cor. 14:28), expounders of Scriptures (Lk. 24:27), or translators of foreign languages (Acts 19:6). Interpreters also solved riddles, interpreted dreams (Gen. 40, 41:13; Job 33:23), and served as intermediaries between God and man.

See *Dream Interpreter, Priest.*

Ivory Carver and *Carvings*

Ivory workers, such as carvers, were practicing their craft as far back as 3400 B.C. Ivory and bone were worked in Palestine to make furniture, figurines, and other costly objects. Ivory was carved mainly in panels, in the round or in open work, namely, in relief. Most ivory used in Palestine came from Syrian elephants which inhabited the upper Euphrates until exterminated in the late first millennium B.C.

The abundant ivory carvings that have been found are beautifully executed. They are excellent both in technique and ingenuity of pattern. Among the ivories of the Canaanites has been found an ointment vase in female form with a hand-shaped stopper (thirteenth century B.C.). In Tell Beit Mirsim, an unguent spoon was found fashioned like a swimming woman catching a duck. Incised panels from Megiddo depict animated scenes.

Ivories discovered at Samaria, dating from the time of Ahab, reveal the commingling of Assyrian, Egyptian, and Syro-Hittite influence dominated by the Phoenician. Because they are similar in workmanship to the ivories found at Arslan Tash (Syria) and Nimrud (Iraq), it is conjectured that they may have been the product of a guild of craftsmen. Some are inlaid with colored stone, glass, gold, and lapis lazuli. Typical designs are the cherub and the lotus patterns. There are also panels with a woman's head, with crouching and suckling animals, and with Egyptian figures and motifs, particularly the kneeling infant, Horus.

An eighth-century-B.C. Israelite carving is a cosmetic palette and jar found in Hazor which has a simple, hatched pattern. Among other excavated items carved in ivory are articles of furniture made for royal and other wealthy homes, caskets decorated with ivory carvings, amulets, combs, boxes, game boards, mirrors, and spoon handles. In 1 Kings 10:22 there is reference to Solomon's fleet of ships which once every three years brought gold, silver, and ivory. In Ezekiel 27:15 there is reference to Dedan or Rhodes in connection with horns of ivory (tusks).

Display and ownership of ivory were an obvious sign of wealth and luxury (Am. 3:15, 6:4). The ivory carver was engaged in carving the inlaid decoration on thrones (1 Ki. 10:18; 2 Chr. 9:17), on houses (1 Ki. 22:39; Ps. 45:8; Am. 3:15), on beds (Am. 6:4), and possibly on decks of ships (Ezek. 27:6).

The carver's tools included files (Jer. 10:4), bow drills and wooden mallets (Jg. 5:26), scraping instruments, and various chisels and awls.

See *Artist, Seal Maker.*

Ivory Merchant

Most ivory used in Syria and Palestine came from Syrian elephants, which roamed the upper Euphrates until they were slaughtered to extinction in the late first millennium B.C. Ocean-going vessels manned by Phoenicians who decorated their vessels with ivory plaques (Ezek. 27:6) transported tusks from India to Babylonia (2 Chr. 9:17, 21).

Merchants did well with ivory. It was a form of wealth (1 Ki. 10:18, 22; Rev. 18:12) that was used for thrones overlaid with gold, for couches (Am. 6:4), for furnishings, and for paneling rooms or palaces (1 Ki. 22:39) as well as being widely used in manufacturing small objects. Thus, for example, in the Israelite period of Palestine, ivories from Samaria and Hazor were used to make beautiful spoons, flasks, unguent vases, and ladies' combs.

See *Merchant,* APPENDIX I.

Jailer

Prisons in antiquity lacked the complicated features of modern penitentiaries. They were generally small and primitive. Egyptian prisons were forced-labor compounds where persons awaiting trial were kept. In Judah, the guardrooms of the police guards served as a temporary prison for Jeremiah (32:2, 8, 12).

When there were prisoners, a guard was necessary, and when there were considerable numbers of prisoners, there was someone who served in the capacity of warden. He either combined the duties of a guard and warden or performed only in a supervisory role.

Prisoners were confined in a *bor,* which was apparently a dungeon (Ex. 12:29; Jer. 37:16, 38:6; Lam. 3:53). Joseph and Pharaoh's steward were imprisoned in a Beth-sohar (house of confinement) believed to be a fortress for prisoners (Gen. 39:20–23). After his capture by the Philistines, Samson was imprisoned (Jg. 16:21, 25). There are four places of detention mentioned in connection with Jeremiah (37:15–16), and all imply stern solitary imprisonment. Other prophets imprisoned were the seer Hanani (2 Chr. 16:10) and the prophet Micaiah (1 Ki. 22:27; 2 Chr. 18:26). Kings, too, such as Hoshea of Israel (2 Ki. 17:4), Jehoiachin (Jer. 24:1), and Zedekiah (Jer. 52:11) were imprisoned.

During New Testament times, Jewish prisons probably were similar to the Greek and Roman models. According to Josephus, John the Baptist's prison (Matt. 14:3, 10) was the castle of Machaerus. Peter and John were apparently imprisoned in a public ward (Acts 4:3, 5:18). Paul was also imprisoned (2 Cor. 6:5; Acts 16:24, 28:30).

See *Police Official.*

Jeweler and *Jewelry*

The tendency of even the most primitive natives to adorn themselves with some form of simple decorative material has been widely observed. In Palestine, the use of jewelry is believed to have been common as far back as the Natufian period about 10,000 years ago. These early inhabitants wore necklaces and head ornaments of shell, bone, and fish vertebrae. Jewels have been valued from the earliest times for a variety of reasons. Man has long had an interest in personal adornment which jewels satisfy. He has also been prone to believe jewelry exercised magic powers. Moreover, jewels were an effective hedge against sudden economic or social changes.

Hebrews, too, eventually learned the art of jewelry making. They shaped wires of gold and silver into beautiful lacy forms often studded with jewels. One can find the modern counterpart of these craftsmen squatting with their fining pots for purifying the metal (Pro. 17:3) in old Jerusalem or in the jewelry stalls of Damascus.

In the Bible, jewels were used variously for the high priest's insignia (Ex. 28:15–21, 39:8–14), for personal adornment (Ex. 11:2; Isa. 3:20, 21, 61:10), for royal crowns (2 Sam. 12:30), for the royal sanctuary (2 Chr. 3:6), for the royal treasury (1 Ki. 10:11; 1 Chr. 29:2), and for gifts (Gen. 44:2; 1 Ki. 10:2), although it is difficult to identify exactly the jewels mentioned.

The early Hebrews possessed only limited quantities of precious stones or decorative minerals. Among the collections found in Megiddo, Gezer, and Ezion-geber from the fifteenth to fourteenth centuries B.C. have been necklaces of agate, alabaster, carnelian, and beads with a few precious stones. Aside from an early amount of manufactured jewelry from Egypt (Ex. 11:2, 12:35), and other booty (Num. 31:50; Jg. 8:26), jewels entered Palestine through regional distribution, especially through the traders of Phoenicia (Ezek. 28:13). There is some reason to believe that foreign merchants had factories in the Samaria of Omri's period. The art of cutting and polishing stones probably developed into a local craft after the uncut stones were imported.

In ancient times makers of jewelry were generally endowed with artistic ability and possessed of good manual dexterity. They either made or repaired jewelry. They formed models of articles from wax or metal, and used carving tools. After they placed the wax model in the casting ring, they poured plaster into the ring to form the mold. They then inserted the plaster mold into a furnace or fire to melt the wax. This was followed by casting the metal model from the plaster mold, for which they used hand tools to cut, saw, file, and polish. Pieces of jewelry were soldered together and the soldered ends smoothed. The beauty of natural colors was enhanced by engraving. These ancient Hebrew jewelers made bracelets, coronets, ear and nose rings, armlets and anklets, gold nets for the hair, elegant cosmetic cases, and pendant and gem seals.

In Biblical times, only the well-to-do could afford jewelry. Most Hebrews were too poor to own any (1 Ki. 10:2; Ezek. 27:22).

Upon the Exodus from Egypt, the Hebrews asked their neighbors for jewels of silver and jewels of gold (Ex. 11:2).

David acquired treasures such as the jeweled crown of King Ammon (2 Sam. 12:30). Later, other crowns were accumulated. In Solomon's reign, the royal collection contained precious metal and gems, many of which had been presented to the kings and governors of Arabia. The queen of Sheba brought Solomon gold and precious stones (1 Ki. 10:2–10), and his Temple altar was illuminated with golden candlesticks standing near one hundred golden basins (2 Chr. 4:7). The second Isaiah denounced those who hired goldsmiths to make idols (46:6).

There were undoubtedly merchants who sold various forms

of jewelry to the rich and to royal families. They bought and sold jewelry for the luxury trade.

Because the possession of jewels was often unsafe and subject to thievery in Biblical times, those who owned jewelry either wore it, hid it on their person, or buried it in the ground (Jos. 7:2; Pro. 2:4). A cache of jewelry was found under the floor of a palace room in Megiddo.

Ancient jewelry may be found in various museums in the world, such as the Oriental Institute of Chicago, Egyptian National Museum, the National Museum of Lebanon, Palestine Archaeological Museum, and the University Museum in Philadelphia, Pennsylvania.

See *Artist, Metalworker, Refiner, Seal Maker.*

Judge

Even in the most primitive societies, there are certain persons who enjoy the esteem of their peers and who function as judges. Usually, they are the elders or successful warriors. In Exodus 18, there are indications that ancient judges were originally priests who pronounced oracles. They were the heads of the families (Gen. 38:24) and the elders of the city (Dt. 21:19). The chief judge of a kingdom was the king (2 Sam. 15:2–4). Military leaders such as Othniel, Ehud, Gideon, and Jephthah (Jg. 3:7–10, 12:7) were leaders as well as judges. Also serving as judges were Eli the priest (1 Sam. 4:13), Samuel (1 Sam. 7:15), Deborah (Jg. 4:4), and Samson.

Exodus describes how Moses followed his father-in-law's (Jethro's) advice and appointed judges for every "small matter" while Moses rendered decisions on "great matters." The system which Moses introduced of judges handling various gradations of problems seems to have ceased with his death.

During the time of the Judges (1225–1020 B.C.), the military leaders apparently assumed the role of judges. A well-known nonmilitary leader was Samuel who was a circuit judge with headquarters in Ramah (1 Sam. 7:15, 12:3). When the monarchy was established, the king and his officers became the highest legal authorities, and the king became the final court of appeals (2 Sam. 12:5, 16; 1 Ki. 3:28).

David is recorded as having appointed six thousand Levites as judges and officers (1 Chr. 23:4, 26:29). Jehoshaphat, king of Judah (871 B.C.), appointed judges for all the fortified cities. In Jerusalem, he appointed the high priest to judge all religious matters. For the king's secular affairs, he appointed someone known as "the ruler over the house of Judah" (1 Chr. 19:5–11).

Ezra (fifth century B.C.) was ordered by the king of Persia to appoint magistrates and judges (Ez. 7:25, 10:12). In the Talmud, the rabbis speak of the judges who were members of the Great Sanhedrin (seventy-one members) and the Lesser Sanhedrin (twenty-three members) and the court of three during the second commonwealth.

To become a member of these courts, one had to be appointed by the chief of the Sanhedrin or by three of its members (San. 13b). Only such a judge could decide a criminal case. Generally, all Israelites were deemed qualified to serve as judges in civil matters, but only priests, Levites, and Israelites of spotless character and ancestry could judge a criminal case (Sanh. 4:2). The Palestinian Talmud barred women from serving as judges (Yoma 43b).

The qualifications of a judge were knowledge of the Law and integrity. The Talmud specifies that he be "wise, humble, fearful of sinning, of good reputation and popular" (Tos. Sanh. 7:1). To become a member of the Sanhedrin, it was necessary to possess wisdom, a knowledge of foreign languages and of sciences, to be of good height, and possess an appearance which commanded respect (Sanh. 17a). An old man, a eunuch, or a childless man was not appointed. Also disqualified were professional gamblers, such as dice players and pigeon racers, those who lent money on interest or who profiteered (Sanh. 3:3). Others also excluded were shepherds, tax farmers, tax collectors (Sanh. 25b), robbers, extortioners, and all suspected of dishonesty (Tos. Sanh. 5:5). Banned, too, were those disqualified from testifying (Nid. 49a) and those related to any of the litigants (Sanh. 3:4). There was no fixed age limit for a judge (Shab. 56b).

Judges were viewed as performing sacred duties; deliberating over a decision was described as "inquiring of God" (Ex. 18:15). Moses is frequently described as bringing a case to God before rendering a decision (Ex. 18:19). In Talmudic times, men were said to have refused appointments unless other members of the court were worthy and respectable men (Sheb. 30b). The rabbis urged that all cases be heard before a regular court of at least three judges and preferably a larger court (Sanh. 8a).

Once the members of the Sanhedrin rendered a decision in harmony with the Law, the same court could not again arbitrate, even if both parties desired it (Sanh. 6b). There was no interpreter between the judge and parties concerned except when the judge understood a language but could not speak it fluently (M.K. 6b). The judge tried to arbitrate but could not compel a decision save when orphans were involved or when the case could not be legally established.

Only ordained judges could decide penal cases. When prompt and decisive action was necessary, the local courts frequently extended their authority and imposed corporal punishment, confiscated property, and even asked non-Jewish government officials to enforce compliance to their jurisdiction (Sanh. 46a). Later, rabbis leaned toward the principle that the law of the land should be observed so long as it did not clash with Jewish law.

Forty days before the destruction of the Temple, the Sanhedrin moved from the Temple precincts to a place called "trade hall." From this time on, Jewish courts have had no jurisdiction involving capital punishment (Ab. Zar. 8b). The Romans, following the unsuccessful Bar Cochba revolt, forbade Jews to sit as judges in cases involving fines or corporal punishment (Sanh. 14a).

A judge's duties were often trying: "He who shuns the judicial office rids himself of hatred, robbery and vain swearing" (Ab. 4:9). He was often rewarded for his effort by ingratitude. "Seven classes of persons will have no portion in the world to come: a scribe, a teacher of children, the best of physicians, the judge of a city, an enchanter, a synagogue beadle and a butcher" (Aboth de Rabbi Nathan 36); "the just judge, however, causes the Divine Presence to alight upon Israel" (Sanh. 7a).

It was preferred that a case should be decided by at least three judges, rather than one (Ab. 4:10), though one judge could render a decision if the litigants agreed and there was no other competent judge (Sanh. 5a). A case involving a trifling amount merited the same deliberation as one dealing with a great sum (Sanh. 8a). Both parties should be treated alike and with the same respect (Sanh. 30a). Witnesses were to be examined thoroughly by the judge who was cautioned to avoid suggesting an answer which might be false (Ab. 1:19).

The professional ethics demanded of judges was high (Dt. 16:19; Ex. 23:8). The Bible forbids bribery though it does not indicate a penalty for it. It is, however, included among the crimes for which the curse was pronounced on Mt. Ebal (Dt. 27:25). Later laws declare that bribery was punishable by thirty-nine stripes in accordance with the general view that when the punishment for a crime is not specifically mentioned in the Bible, corporal punishment is to be administered.

Many Biblical passages indicate that at various times, especially during the kingship, bribes often perverted justice. Bribes were even taken to shed blood (Ezek. 22:12; Am. 5:12; Mic. 7:3). Isaiah eloquently denounced bribery (Isa. 1:23, 5:23, 33:15). Takers of bribes were also denounced by the Psalmist (Ps. 15:5) and in Proverbs (17:23). The sons of Samuel were the only example of persons named for accepting bribes. Later, the rabbis held both the giver and taker of bribes as guilty (Sanh. 23:2).

In the Mishnah, there is a rule that the decision of a judge who accepts pay for rendering a decision is to be voided (Mish. Bekorot 46). This is interpreted as applying when he accepts payment after he has rendered his decision, or if he has accepted it from only one of the litigants. Elsewhere in the Talmud (Ket. 105a), Karna, a criminal judge of Babylonia, accepted a fee to reimburse him for his loss of time from each of the litigants before he tried a case. The Talmud debates this issue and concurs with him that judges should be reimbursed for the earnings which they lost while not pursuing their usual nonjuristic occupation. Another judge would not sit on a case unless the litigants provided a substitute to perform his normal work while he served as a judge. This is the only form of compensation which judges were allowed to accept. In short, judges were honorary, voluntary positions rather than paid posts. Under later law, judges were paid for their services.

See *King, Lawyer, Police Official, Priest, Rabbi, Scribe.*

King

Kings were rulers who governed their subjects; they usually enjoyed the privilege of transmitting their authority to their offspring. The Hebrew word for king, "Melek" (Gen. 39:20), also designates the Deity (1 Sam. 12:12). Other names for Hebrew kings were *princes* and the *Lord's anointed.*

In the ancient Near East, there were generally three kinds of kings: the petty rulers of the Palestine cities, who were often of foreign origin and ruled over the city-state with the help of the military aristocracy; the Mesopotamian and Egyptian kings of the Biblical period, whose rule was considered divinely ordained; and the completely national kings of the Transjordanian peoples who were related to the Hebrews.

The first attempt to introduce a king into Israel was an offer of the throne to Gideon (Jg. 8:22), but he rejected it (8:23). A number of factors nevertheless led to the need for a central authority. The decline of the clan, the widespread acceptance of settled civilization, and the crucial need for greater political unity all contributed to the demand for a king. Probably the climaxing factor was the critical political situation under the Philistine yoke (1 Sam. 3, 7). The communities that had escaped Philistine oppression suffered from invading Transjordanian Ammonites (1 Sam. 11:1–7) and Amalekites (1 Sam. 14:48).

During the early period of the Jewish monarchy, there was no definite transmission of royal power. Thus, after Saul's death, Judah accepted David's rule (2 Sam. 2:4) while the north and Transjordanian tribes accepted that of Saul's son Mephibosheth (2 Sam. 9:10). The right of primogeniture did not always operate. One example was Abimelech's claim to Gideon's throne (Jg. 9:2). The maternal side of the king's lineage apparently played a role in the succession of the Davidic throne.

The main duties of the king varied. He was a military leader who was expected to lead the army in battle (1 Sam. 8:20). Saul did so against the Amalekites (1 Sam. 15:5), Ahab against the Syrians (1 Ki. 22:30), and Jehoram against the Moabites (2 Ki. 3:6–12).

The king was also the supreme judge who supported the rights of the widow and the poor and adjudicated occasional disputes (2 Sam. 12:1–6; 1 Ki. 3:16–28). Normally, however, justice was dispensed without provision for further appeal (Dt. 19:12, 21:21). The king also had authority over priests and could punish them (1 Sam. 22:11–18; 1 Ki. 2:26–27). Sometimes, as with Asa, he reformed the cult (1 Ki. 15:12–15). Some kings, such as Saul, performed priestly functions (1 Sam. 13:10).

The Jewish king was not an absolute monarch. The elders entered into a contract with the new king (2 Sam. 5:3; 2 Ki. 11:17), and his rights and duties were defined and deposited in the central sanctuary (1 Sam. 10:25), probably during the anointment ceremony. Proof of the limited power of the Jewish king was that David could win Bath-sheba from Uriah only by stratagem (2 Sam. 11). Similarly, Ahab could seize Naboth's field and execute him only after a legal trial although the charges were false (1 Ki. 21:8–14). Nathan the prophet denounced David (2 Sam. 12:1–18), and Elijah rebuked Ahab for their violation of the Law (1 Ki. 21:17–24). Some monarchs, however, such as Solomon and Manasseh, flouted the Law.

The revenue of the king came from gifts (1 Sam. 16:20), from booty gained from wars (2 Sam. 8:1–14), from general taxes, which Solomon seems to have been the first to introduce (1 Ki. 4:7–19, 27–28), and from the income of their own estates. Solomon earned considerable income from his mining activities, his merchant marine, and his traffic in horses. Imposts were also levied on merchants who passed through the Holy Land.

The coronation of a Jewish king was probably impressive. Solomon was brought on a mule accompanied by foreign mercenaries. A sacrifice was probably offered (1 Ki. 1:9) at the holy place and Solomon was then anointed by the priest Zadok (1 Ki. 1:38–39) and by the prophet Nathan, after which a trumpet was blown and the people shouted, "Long live King Solomon." A festive procession accompanied by the new king from the Temple to the throne followed. He then took his place and received the homage of the officials and the royal princes (1 Ki. 1:40, 53). A covenant was made between the Lord, the king, and the people. He was given a new throne name. Thus, Eliakim became Jehoiakim (2 Ki. 23:34) and Mattaniah became Zedekiah (2 Ki. 24:17).

Although in the Near East, kings were believed to be divine, in Israel they became holy by elevation to office (2 Sam. 1:14, 16). Consequently, even though David had the opportunity to slay his adversary Saul, he refrained (1 Sam. 26:9) because he considered the king as representing a divine power. The king symbolized the Lord's blessing, prosperity, harmony, and peace. He was sometimes called "the light of Israel" (2 Sam. 21:17).

See *Governor, Judge, Proconsul, Procurator, Queen.*

Labor Recruiter

There is ample reason to believe that during Solomon's reign, his vast building projects required the services of many skilled artisans who were not available in Israel. Consequently, the services of a labor recruiter who knew where and how to gather the needed manpower was necessary (1 Ki. 5:6, 9, 15, 16). He undoubtedly informed his prospects of salaries and working conditions.

See APPENDIX III, APPENDIX IV.

Laundress

There is no mention of the occupation of laundress in Scriptures. Undoubtedly, however, the royal families and the rich enjoyed the services of slaves who did their laundry. Washerwomen used a cleanser or detergent, *borit* (Mal. 3:2; Jer. 2:22), which probably means "lye" but which is often translated as "soap."

Washing was usually done in a running body of water. Washerwomen probably combined their laundry work with other domestic duties.

Lawyer

There is a record of a trial in Sumer in 1850 B.C. in which there were members of the Citizens Assembly at Nippur who prosecuted a person accused of murder while two of the Assembly spoke as his defense attorneys. Many centuries later in Greece the lawyer was not a specially trained person practicing before a judge who gave his verdict on the basis of law. He was rather the litigant's friend who spoke for him before the litigant's peers who in turn rendered their decision on the basis of the case as they saw it.

Among the Jews, a lawyer in Biblical times was one learned in the Law of Moses. The Greek term occurs in Luke, in Titus, and in Matthew. It signifies those absorbed in legalistic discussions and in Mark 12:28 seems synonymous with "scribes."

Lawyers are viewed negatively in the New Testament. They are among those who are cited as against Jesus' "healing activities on the Sabbath" (Lk. 14:3) and who rejected John the Baptist (Lk. 7:20). They are also described as neglecting justice and placing intolerable burdens on their fellow men (Lk. 11:45–46). They reject sound knowledge and hinder those who search for it (Lk. 11:52). Most of these charges are attributed to Jesus. However, according to scholars, these views do not accurately portray the lawyer-scholars of the period. These rabbinical lawyers, according to G. F. Moore, R. T. Herford, L. Finkelstein, and others, were dedicated scholars whose main function was to study, explain, and apply the Law to contemporary conditions. Many qualified as judges. They were members of the Sanhedrin as well as the main speakers at religious assemblies (Mk. 1:22). They received no payment for their services, but earned their livelihood from other occupations.

See *Judge, Rabbi, Scribe.*

Letter Writer

King David and his successors employed special secretaries whose duties consisted of writing letters and circulars. Such functionaries still exist in countries where there is a high rate of illiteracy. Throughout antiquity, there were professional letter writers who, for a small fee, would compose letters to meet their clients' needs.

The first recorded letter mentioned in the Bible was written by David to Joab and delivered by Uriah (2 Sam. 11:14). During Talmudic times, there was an upsurge of commerce which was accompanied by a sharp rise in correspondence requiring the services of letter writers. This increase in the use of letter writers was not due to illiteracy among Jews, but rather to the need of a corps of business correspondents. A Talmudic statement (Sanh. 17a) urges scholars not to reside in towns lacking professional letter writers.

The Talmud records the original text of two letters, one written by the community of Jerusalem to that of Alexandria and referring to the visit there of Judah ben Tabbai, the other sent by Gamaliel I to the Jews of Upper and Lower Galilee and referring to the insertion of an additional month in the year (Yer. Hag. 2; Sanh. 11b).

Most of the New Testament consists of twenty-one letters or Epistles. There are also letters of introduction mentioned in 2 Corinthians 3:1, Acts 18:27, and 1 Corinthians 16:3. Correspondence among prominent persons was usually sent sealed. When Sanballat sent an open letter to Nehemiah, the act was considered flagrantly contemptuous (Neh. 6:5).

See *Postal Employee, Scribe.*

Librarian

Librarians are known to have functioned very early in history. In 2700 B.C. King Dedkere Isesi had an archival library and a librarian, Senezemib. Thutmose III (*ca.* fifteenth century B.C.) also had a palace library. A thousand years before Abraham most of the cities of the Near East had collections of books. About 2000 B.C. there were already millions of tablets of written documents dealing with religious and medical subjects and annals. Abstracts of archives were engraved on Egyptian walls where they are still visible. At the time of the Exodus (*ca.* 1300 B.C.) there were probably libraries staffed by librarians in all palaces, temples, and record offices. The book of Deuteronomy turned up in the Temple library (2 Ki. 22:8; 2 Chr. 34:14). Remains of two archival libraries have been found in Lachish near Megiddo dating from about the fourteenth century B.C.

The palace collections of Israel contained, besides archives, religious and literary works. References to "the books" in Daniel 9:2 may indicate a synagogue library; 2 Maccabees 2:13 mentions that Nehemiah founded a library; and Ezra 6:1 refers to the "house of books," a common Egyptian term for library.

The work of the librarian is evident from a Sumerian "book list," or the first library catalogue, which dates from about 3500 B.C. In Alexandria during the fourth century B.C., Ptolemy Philadelphus had an enormous library which housed thousands of the books then available and to which scholars flocked. The library had regular librarians and its catalogues were among the first efforts in bibliography.

See *Historian, Scribe.*

Locksmith

The first lock was probably a rock placed by a cave man in prehistoric times across the mouth of the cave and rolled back each morning. The oldest lock extant is an Egyptian pin tumbler lock found in the ruins of Nineveh. Modern cylindrical door locks still operate on this same tumbler principle. Keys and locks were usually made from wood, but the Romans made multicolored locks out of brass and ivory. Isaiah is believed to have referred to a lock when he declared, "And the key of the House of David will I lay upon his shoulder" (22:22).

We do not know whether the locksmith engaged in this skill exclusively or in other related activities. It is likely that the services of the locksmith were in greater demand in larger communities than in farm areas where neighbors have trusted each other from time immemorial.

Logger

There were loggers in Biblical times who chopped trees to specified lengths, lashed the trunks together, and, when necessary, floated them down waterways. Thus Hiram sent David cedars and firs from the forests of Lebanon (2 Sam. 5:11) for the Jerusalem palace of Solomon and for the Temple (1 Ki. 9:11; 2 Chr. 2).

Woods of various trees had many purposes. Besides the construction of royal palaces, wood was used for food vessels (Lev. 11:32), carts (1 Sam. 6:14), idols (Dt. 29:17), boats (Gen. 6:14), and burnt offerings (Lev. 1:7), as well as in furniture, musical instruments, and farm implements.

See *Forester*.

Magician and *Magic*

Magic was practiced throughout the ancient world under two categories: black or evil magic, and white or benevolent magic. Black magic aimed at malevolent results and involved curses, incantations, and consorting with evil spirits for such purposes as harming an adversary. White magic attempted to ward off harmful effects of black magic and to enlist the aid of hidden powers in favor of a suppliant.

The Egyptian priests who practiced sorcery formed a special class. As royal magicians, they were at the beck and call of the royal family. These priestly scholars were attached to the temples and were required to be of unblemished appearance. Undergoing long periods of preparation followed by initiation into the rites, they studied the art of the *House of Life,* which contained the textbooks of the system. At the completion of their training, they could recite the proper spell for every occasion, and they knew all the ceremonies and traditions related to sorcery. They became the *hartumim,* magicians of the Bible (Gen. 41:8).

The Egyptian magicians predicted the future by using cups (Gen. 44:5, 15), a trick that they may have learned from the Babylonians. The rite involved adding a drop of oil to a cup of water and then forecasting the future from the shape formed by the drops or from the way the light fell on the drops. Another method was to add a drop of water to a cup of oil.

In Mesopotamia, too, sorcery was a highly skilled vocation demanding long study and considerable knowledge. Magic rituals were performed as early as the third millennium B.C. when the movements of the body were coordinated with the magic incantations. A popular method of forecasting the future was to inspect the livers of sacrificial animals, closely observing all omens and subsequent events. This was done by keeping a record of the configurations of the livers. To do this, clay models of livers were made and observations and the points to be watched were inscribed on them. Such models dating back to the second millennium B.C. were found at Mari (Syria).

The Bible cites Egypt and Babylonia as the sources of occult practices (Ex. 7; Isa. 47:9–15), and both countries undoubtedly influenced Israel in this direction. The demons of Jewish folklore were not independent of God, nor were they His equal, but they were bound to acknowledge His superiority and to obey Him when requested (Num. 20–24; Mk. 3:22–23). Various types of occult practitioners are mentioned in Deuteronomy 18:10–11 and their rites are forbidden as idolatrous (2 Ki. 21:6; 2 Chr. 33:6). In the New Testament, demonology was practiced by such Jews as Simon Magus (Acts 8:9) and Elymas (Acts 13:8).

Magic and its practitioners were considered potent (Mic. 5:1; Jer. 27:9; Ex. 7:9–25). The most common medium of witchcraft was human speech, which was universally believed to possess limitless power. "Open not thy mouth for evil" (Ber. 19a). When a magician spoke at the right time and place and under proper conditions, he was believed to be invincible. Commonly employed for magical purposes was the esoteric name of God. For centuries the Hebrew letters YHWH and permutations of other names of angels and demons were considered effective talismans. Besides the magic word and formula, there were magical objects used to avert the evil eye. Women, children, and even animals were guarded by amulets and talismans, which consisted of either natural objects (such as parts of an animal or plant) or paper with magical writing. Copies of the Bible were believed to possess protective power and were taken along on journeys. The phylacteries which are worn and the mezuzoth which are affixed to the doorposts by Biblical command (Dt. 11:20) were probably regarded as protective devices.

In the Pseudepigrapha, the Book of Enoch (9:7) states that the angels taught the daughters of men incantations and exorcisms, and the cutting of roots, and also revealed to them the healing plants. The Book of Tobit describes the prevalent belief that the heart, liver, and gall were effective vehicles of magic. Tobias regained his sight when his eyes were anointed with the gall of a fish (8:2, 11:11–13). In Jubilees 10 we read of Noah's apparently magical book of healing.

The most common form of magic was the love charm, especially the one used for an illicit affair. Women seemed to predominate in practicing this form of magic. Consequently, magic and adultery are often linked (2 Ki. 9:22; Nah. 3:4; Mal. 3:5). The Bible forbids the wearing of charms (Isa. 3:18–23), often found in the form of earrings used by snake charmers and occult whisperers.

Divination is one of the main branches of the occult. Although the Bible condemned divination, it persisted, and as late as the second century B.C. Ben Sira condemned it (Ecclus. 3:2). Samuel, Saul, Jonathan, David, Elijah, Elisha, and others used divination in various forms without incurring censure. Nor did it seem possible to curb man's irresistible desire to pierce the mystery of the future.

Another form of divination was stargazing, which was condemned by the Bible (Isa. 44:25; Dan. 2:27, 4:7; Job 38:33). Reading the heavens, these practitioners would advise on the lucky and unlucky days. Probably most of the ancient East had professional astrologers to whom people turned. The astrologers drew horoscopes and their patrons followed their suggestions.

Another form of the occult is rhabdomancy or the throwing of sticks or arrows up in the air. Omens were inferred from their position when they fell (Ezek. 21:21; Hos. 4:13). Casting of lots was also used to determine future events or to discern the will of God (Jos. 18:10). The choice of the goat to be sacrificed on the Day of Atonement (Lev. 16), the detection of a guilty person (Jos. 7:14–15), the search by Haman for a propitious day to destroy the Jews (Est. 3:7) are further examples. Some examples in the New Testament are the allocation of Christ's clothes (Matt. 27:35) and the choice of Mathias (Acts 1:15–26).

Trials by ordeal were also used to establish guilt or innocence of a wife accused of engaging in extramarital relations (Num.

5:11–28). Necromancy was the practice of consulting with the dead (Dt. 18:11; 1 Sam. 28:8; 2 Ki. 21:6), but was condemned by the Law (Lev. 19:31; Isa. 8:19, 20).

Myomancy, another method of divination, employed rats or mice (Isa. 66:17). The cries or other behavior of the rodents were believed to forecast evil. The mice and golden emerods mentioned in 1 Samuel 6:4 were charms symbolizing some magical qualities.

Some examples of what may be described as sympathetic magic are the use of mandrakes to cause conception (Gen. 30:14–18), and Jacob's use of peeled rods (Gen. 30:37–41), which in verse 40 suggests that selective breeding occurred. In 1 Samuel 7:6, Samuel pours water on the earth in what appears to have been sympathetic magic to induce a storm. In Judges 16 we read of the unusual potency residing in Samson's hair. In Job 3:8, Job asked that the day of his birth be cursed by those who are ready to rouse up Leviathan. This is believed to allude to the magicians who were thought to arouse a dragon to swallow the sun during an eclipse.

The Urim and Thummim, whose exact nature is unknown, may have been some pouchlike object fastened to the ephod (the official garment worn by priests) and kept in the high priest's breastplate (Ex. 28:15–25). It was employed to penetrate the future, to declare the innocent and the guilty, to divide the land, and to decide issues of war and peace. While performing with the Urim and Thummim, the priest wore his robes and the breastplate of judgment.

Another practitioner of the occult was the *menahesh* or enchanter employed by Laban (Gen. 30:27), by Balaam (Num. 23), and by the Aramaean servants of Benhadad when they awaited a good omen (1 Ki. 20:33). The *menahash* was also a prognosticator (Lev. 19:26; Dt. 18:10; 2 Ki. 21:6).

The *meonen* practiced augury, conjured, or produced hallucinations. Another interpretation is that he was someone who studied the formation of the clouds and their dispersal. The *meonen* was believed to be a master of thunder and rain as manifested by Samuel and Elijah or a sort of weather prophet (Jg. 9:37; 2 Ki. 21:26; Mic. 5:12). Some, however, believe that he was a soothsayer who hummed mysteriously while performing.

The *kosem* was a professionally trained diviner who would throw himself into a trance before predicting future events. Balaam is the first-mentioned example of this type in the Bible (Num. 24:4). The *hober*—the word signifies binding, probably with amulets and charms—was a charmer who gathered animals for good or evil purposes.

Dream interpreters were widely consulted by non-Israelites. The interpretations of various dreams were listed in handbooks for the use of magicians; one dates back to the nineteenth century B.C. As for the Jews, the Bible makes clear that they understood the meaning of their dreams. Joseph and Daniel are the well-known dream interpreters of the Bible (Gen. 40:12, 41:15). Daniel, who is pictured as the divinely inspired interpreter of dreams (1:20, 2:2), replaced Babylonian wise men, Chaldeans, soothsayers, and magicians.

The *kasdim* or Chaldeans were a special class of occultists mentioned in the book of Daniel who are coupled with magicians. Necromancers appeared to be numerous in Biblical times and they were denounced for invoking "ghosts and familiar spirits" (Dt. 18:11). Saul and other kings attempted to rid the country of their influence; yet, ironically, Saul consulted the witch of Endor (1 Sam. 28:7–25). Despite official opposition, there seems to have been an almost irresistible desire to consult ancestors and the recent dead through the services of mediums known as "familiar spirits."

The Babylonian Talmud offers interesting examples of the wide diffusion of magic. While it prohibits its practice, a knowledge of magic was deemed important for members of the Sanhedrin and the judiciary. The most learned scholars were deeply versed in the occult, and the influence of magic was so great that even scholars succumbed to it. Though they did not practice it for personal gain or for unlawful purposes, they occasionally sought to foil black magic with white magic.

See *Counselor, Dream Interpreter, Interpreter, Snake Charmer, Weather Forecaster.*

Marble Setter

Marble setters who paved the marble floors of public buildings were known as *marmorii*. They cut, tooled, and set marble to produce ornamental surfaces on floors. They trimmed, faced, and cut marble to proper size and spread mortar on the bottom of the block and on the sides of adjacent blocks. They then set the block in position and tamped it into place, pouring grout in the joints between the blocks, after which they filled the joints between the slabs with plaster and pointed the joints with a trowel or wooden paddle.

Marble, which was found in many colors in the Middle East, was popular in temples (1 Chr. 29:2), palaces (Est. 1:6), and other structures. Marble setters inlaid pillars, flooring, and wall inlay. Marble is cited in the list of "precious" or luxury commodities (Rev. 18:12).

See *Architect, Mason, Stoneworker.*

Mason

There are a number of references in the Bible to a variety of construction men who built temples, palaces, and a variety of public buildings in Biblical times. "What are the names of the men that built this building?" (Ez. 5:4). "He shall build the Temple of the Lord" (Zec. 6:12; 2 Chr. 34:11; 1 Ki. 7:1; Dan. 9:25). According to 1 Kings 7:1, Solomon's palace took thirteen years to construct.

Mainly slaves or captives of war (1 Ki. 9:15; 2 Chr. 2:18), the construction workers performed a variety of tasks—removing and cleaning forms, dismantling old forms by the use of a hammer, using a shovel to level the earth to fine grade specifications.

Before building the forms, they probably sorted and stacked lumber according to size. Many workers erected shoring and braces. They dug ditches and excavated for foundations using picks and shovels. They then loaded and unloaded and moved building material (2 Chr. 34:11).

Functioning as a distinct occupational group were the masons who worked for royalty and created public buildings. Because stone was expensive to transport and difficult to work with, it was generally not used in the construction of private homes. Masons were employed to work with the harder stones for the Temple and other large buildings since the native limestone was too soft. These harder stones were usually quarried in the Lebanon area from which they were imported (1 Ki. 6:7).

Employing many of the same tools as the carpenter, the mason sawed the limestone (1 Ki. 7:9) and trimmed it with a pickax. When he quarried large blocks of stone, he would hammer in wooden wedges and soak them until the stone cracked under the force of their expansion. This method was widely used in the ancient Near East. Large metal forge hammers crushed stone by repeated pounding.

The mason also built mausoleums in natural caves in the hills (Isa. 22:16) such as those found at Beth-shemesh (eighth century B.C.) and Beit She'arim (first century B.C.). Masons cut cisterns at Gibeon, Jericho, Lachish, Megiddo—which required the removal of about a half-million cubic yards of limestone by hand.

From the tenth century B.C., picked and marginally drafted masonry was used. These ancient stones reveal a narrow border or stonecutters' guide along or across the face of the stone. During the Hellenistic period, Herodian buildings at Jerusalem, Machpelah, and other places show how enormous blocks of stone were aligned without mortar so that even now one cannot insert a knife blade between the joints. Similar excellent masonry is visible at Megiddo, dating back to the ninth century B.C. Masons often left their unique stamp on their work. One example is that of the steps of the Capernaum synagogue. Masons' inscriptions are also visible at Shebna's tomb, the Siloan tunnel, and the Samarian fragment.

Contractors were usually master masons who worked along with their employees. Sometimes, their work force might number sixty people. These contractors were held responsible for the quality of the work performed under their supervision and were liable for punishment for careless work (A. Zimmern, *The Greek Commonwealth,* pp. 262–263). As contractors, they probably possessed a knowledge of estimating and their duties included conferring with their clients and supervising their staff and the progress of construction.

See *Architect, Bricklayer, Marble Setter, Stoneworker.*

Master

Many of the well-to-do in Biblical times had no specific occupation. They maintained themselves through their inherited wealth or the wealth they accumulated as landowners, cattle dealers, or as occasional traders. Most of their wealth consisted of land, cattle, and slaves.

Many landowners of moderate means worked along with their employees or slaves, managing their properties, marketing their surplus of food either through sale or barter. They also supervised their households and probably participated in local affairs.

The master was, of course, the head of the house (Ex. 22:8), the owner and master of the slaves and servants (Ex. 21:4–8; Dt. 23:15; Jg. 19:11; 1 Sam. 30:13).

Merchant and *Peddler*

Retailing, the distribution and sale of goods, is probably the oldest and most widespread phase of trade. Tools, ornaments, and weapons dating from the earliest times have been found far from the origin of their manufacture, having evidently been carried by traders. There was a well-defined retail trade in Babylonia in 2000 B.C. and earlier, for towns even then had shopkeepers, peddlers, and traders, some of whom traveled extensively. Linked with retailers was the export, import, and wholesale trade.

The early Hebrews had little to trade except surplus animals and produce. As the farming villages developed, the farmers brought grains, wines, oil, pottery, textiles, tools, dyes, leather, or metal products to market, either to sell or to exchange them with other farmers. Some scholars contend that the wealth of the patriarchs in cattle and servants may have been acquired by trade. Abraham, for example, is now believed to have led caravans of from two hundred to six hundred donkeys in Palestine and Syria.

With the development of roads and the increased population, markets and merchants also increased. Commercial stands sprang up near shrines, and religious centers like Jerusalem (Neh. 13:20), Damascus, and Samaria also became trading centers. The traveling merchant either carried his merchandise directly to his customers or to markets (Neh. 13:16), using camels, mules, asses, oxen, or slaves to do so (Gen. 24:10).

During Solomon's reign, the merchants multiplied, as did their business activities. During Ahab's reign the right to have *huzot*—streets or a special market place in the market of Damascus—was obtained from Benhadad (1 Ki. 20:34).

Evidences of retail trade in the Bible are references to Bakers' Street (Jer. 37:21), the Fish Gate (Neh. 3:3), Fullers' Field (2 Ki. 18:17; Isa. 7:3), and the Valley of Craftsmen (1 Chr. 4:14). Josephus mentions bazaars of wool and clothing merchants (B.J. 5.8.1). Lydia was a renowned trader of purple dye from the city of Thyatira (Acts 16:14).

During Maccabean times, it became an established custom for the villagers to bring their products into town once a month. Still later, they extended it to twice a week, on Mondays and Thursdays. At Gaza, Acre, and Botna, there were large fairs where slaves and horses were sold (Yer. Ab. Zar. 1.4). In Talmudic times, goods were sold by contract (Shab. 120b) and paid by bills which were sold for cash before maturing (B.M. 4:9). Merchants communicated by parcel post and regular mail (Shab. 10:4, 19a; R.H. 9b). Local authorities tried to fix prices to protect the consumer (B.M. 5:7). Merchants' profits were usually between 20 and 30 per cent though sometimes they ran as high as 100 per cent (W. W. Tarn, *Hellenistic Civilization*, p. 250).

Hawkers and peddlers were familiar figures in Biblical times (Gen. 37:28; Pro. 31:24; Neh. 3:32, 13:20; Matt. 13:45). The *soher*, literally wanderer, was usually a Canaanite (Gen. 23:16) who dealt with products such as fine apparel or spices, old silver, iron, salt, or wool (Pro. 31:24; Isa. 3:18–24, 23:8; Job 41:6), which were not generally available in most communities. Nehemiah refers to the fish and manner of ware which *rohelim*, peddlers, brought to town (13:20). In Song of Solomon 3:6 there is a reference suggesting that spices were a main item traded. This is also confirmed by the Talmud (B.B. 22a).

When the Jews were dispersed after their loss of independence in 587 B.C., they began to turn toward commercial pursuits. The Talmud cites a number of references to this and declares that resident merchants of a town must not interfere with the trade of the peddlers since Ezra ordained that peddlers be allowed to sell their goods in the cities so that cosmetics might be available to Jewish women (B.B. 22a).

Both in the Bible and in other literature, traders and shopkeepers were usually considered dishonest and immoral (Dt. 25:13; Pro. 11:1, 20:23). Hosea refers to the peddler as one whose hands are "the balances of deceit" (12:7), referring to their often crooked weights and measures. In Ecclesiasticus 26:29 we find a similar thought: "A merchant will hardly keep himself from doing wrong and a huckster shall not be freed from sin." The Talmud alludes to their dubious honesty, their proneness to tale-bearing and garrulity (Yer. Peah 16a), and their tendency to engage in intrigues (Yeb. 62b).

See *Ivory Merchant, Spice Dealer, Warehouseman, Water Seller,* APPENDIX I.

Metalworker and *Metals*

About 1200 B.C., the Palestinians were familiar with the processes of mining, smelting, refining, and working gold, silver, and copper. As objects found in excavations reveal, these pre-Israelite Palestinians showed good technical ability. The smiths manufactured many metal vessels and implements both for war and for peace, including knives, scissors, daggers, swords, lances, spearheads, plow blades, tips for oxgoads, sickles, forks, axletrees, axes, smaller pins, rings, seals, fibulae, images, figurines, hair curlers, and small instruments.

After the development of Solomon's copper and iron mines and smelting plants in the Wadi Arabah and Ezion-geber, mass-production methods were introduced in working with metals. Undoubtedly, many workers were employed in Biblical times extracting and working with metals.

Ore shaped into blocks, ingots, rings, or disks was usually shipped to the smith's workshop. Here it was refined in a furnace to which the draft was forced through clay pipes from the bellows (generally a sewn goatskin or sheepskin). The molten metal was poured from ladles or buckets into stone or clay molds, or beaten on an anvil (Isa. 41:7) with a forge hammer.

Varieties of Metal

There is no general name for metals in the Bible, but the following are mentioned: antimony (Jer. 4:30), copper (Ex. 27:1–8), electrum (Ezek. 1:4), gold (Isa. 40:19), iron (Gen. 4:22), lead (Num. 31:22), silver (Gen. 13:2; Ex. 26:19), and tin (Num. 31:22). The Hebrews knew about gold, which was found at Ophir, Havilah, and Uphaz, and they used their own ships to transport it (1 Ki. 9:28, 22:49). In the markets of Tyre, they purchased silver, iron, tin, and lead (Ezek. 27:12). Copper utensils came from Javan (Ezek. 27:13).

Biblical Tools

Tools used to manufacture metals were the *pa'am,* hammer or ax (Isa. 41:7), *makkabah* (Isa. 44:12), *pattish* (Isa. 41:7), *melkahayim,* tongs (Isa. 6:6), *garzen,* hatchet (Dt. 19:5), *mappuah,* bellows (Jer. 6:29), *marzef,* fining pot for silver, and *kur,* a melting furnace for gold (Pro. 17:3). Ezekiel describes the technical process of metal casting in 22:18–22.

In Talmudic times, the anvil (*saddan*), the spade (Ps. 74:5–6), the shovel, and the grinder were used (Kel. 17:7).

Bronze Worker

Bronze is believed to have first appeared in Palestine at the beginning of the Middle Bronze Age (1950 B.C.). A few bronze studs were found at Jericho that are even earlier and may have been brought by the Amorites from Syria. Many tombs at Jericho had bronze rings set with scarabs made locally.

In Lachish, a bronze toggle pin, a figurine, and a pin from about the sixteenth century B.C. have been discovered. More bronze articles have been discovered at Megiddo. After David conquered Hadadezer of Damascus, he is reported to have removed "very much bronze (brass)" from two of the Syrian cities (2 Sam. 8:8). Similarly, when the Chaldeans captured Jerusalem in 587 B.C., they carried off all the copper and bronze they could capture (2 Ki. 25:13–17; Jer. 52:17–23).

Solomon used copper extensively to beautify and furnish the Temple (1 Ki. 7:13; 2 Chr. 3:15, 4:9) and imported a bronze expert from Tyre to supervise the project. The casting of the bronze was done in the Jordan Valley.

Coppersmith

The Hebrew word *nehoshet* means not only copper but copper alloy. Probably in the earliest times, swords and axes were cast in copper alloy (1 Ki. 7:45). Metalworkers or smiths were probably the first full-time industrial specialists (Gen. 4:

22), and the tribe of Kenites were probably smiths. In a wall painting of Beni Hasan about 1890 B.C., a traveling band of tinkers is depicted.

The archaeologist Nelson Glueck discovered a number of large copper mines and smelting centers belonging to Solomon and dating from the tenth century B.C. They were found in the Wadi Arabah, Israel, and included slag heaps, ruins of workmen's quarters and towns, flues for draft, and furnaces for producing metals.

Solomon employed copper workers, thus making Ezion-geber (1 Ki. 9:26) a Pittsburgh of that period. One of Solomon's greatest copper centers was Khirbet Nahas, the city of copper in the valley of smiths, about sixteen and a half miles south of the Dead Sea.

Goldsmith

Goldsmiths are often mentioned in the Bible. They made wire by cutting sheet gold into narrow threads (Ex. 39:3). They made jewelry or idols, either of solid gold or beaten gold (Isa. 40:19, 41:7, 46:6; Jer. 10:4, 51:17). In constructing the Tabernacles, they used both cast and beaten gold. They also hammered out the lamp stand and lamp trimmers (Ex. 25:31 ff.). There were two linked cherubs (Ex. 25:18) on each side of the slab of pure gold resting on the ark in the Tabernacles. The Talmud mentions seven varieties of gold, but it is difficult to identify them.

Ironworker

In the Bible, ironworking is associated with Tubal-cain (Gen. 4:22). The use of iron in Palestine seems to have grown slowly because it was difficult to produce. The first iron smelted was not sufficiently hard. Iron had to be heated, but copper and bronze could be worked cold.

Hebrew tradition maintains that the Canaanites had iron at the time of Joshua's invasion before the arrival of the Philistines about 1190 B.C. Since Og of Bashan is mentioned as having an iron bed (Dt. 3:11), it suggests that an iron mine may have existed in Transjordan as early as Moses' time. The passage in Deuteronomy 8:9 stating that the Promised Land was one whose stones are iron and out of whose hills copper can be dug implies that iron and copper mining may have been known in Moses' time.

References in Jos. 6:24, 22:8 and Numbers 31:22 allude to iron or iron products. Although it is uncertain whether the Philistines introduced iron to Palestine, they soon obtained a substantial supply of it as the story of Goliath suggests (1 Sam. 17). His spear tips alone are reputed to have weighed over sixteen pounds.

To keep the Hebrews under their control, the Philistines denied them the use of Hebrew smiths; thus, the Philistines prevented them from equipping themselves with up-to-date weapons. Consequently, when the Hebrews needed to sharpen or repair their tools, they were forced to turn to Philistine smiths, who charged them very high fees (1 Sam. 13:19–22).

Iron tools were also used during David's time in Transjordan (2 Sam. 12:31). During Solomon's time, iron ore and copper were mined and smelted along the Wadi Arabah area.

Lead Worker

Lead is included in the Biblical list of metals (Num. 31:22; Ezek. 22:18, 20). Lead sulfide ore was found in Asia Minor; Mesopotamian merchants traded in lead. Lead workers made many objects such as heavy covers (Zec. 5:7, 8), weights for fish nets, sinkers (Ex. 15:10) for sounding lines and plummets. Job 19:24 refers to lead poured into forms, cut in stone, or to a lead tablet inscribed with an iron pan. Workers in lead may have also worked with other metals.

Silversmith

The first allusions to silver in the Bible are in Genesis 13:2. Abraham was very rich in silver and paid four hundred shekels of weighed silver to Ephron for the Cave of Machpelah (Gen.

23:16). Midianite merchants bought Joseph from his brothers for twenty pieces of silver (Gen. 37:28). Two talents weight of silver were offered to Gehazi, servant of Elisha, by the healed Syrian, Naaman (2 Ki. 5:23). There are also references to the processes of mining and refining of silver (Job 28:1; Mal. 3:3).

Silver was used in a number of ways: it was mainly prized as a standard for business dealings (Gen. 23:15–16) and for wealth (Gen. 13:2, 24:35; Ex. 25:3; Num. 22:18). It was highly valued as jewelry and charm amulets (Jg. 8:26). Besides its conversion into bars or coins as money, silver also was turned into sacred musical instruments such as trumpets (Num. 10:2), portable ornaments in buildings, and images (Ex. 20:23; Jg. 17:1–5; Acts 19:24). One of the most valuable pieces of silver artwork is the Persian bowl in the New York Metropolitan Museum of Art, which bears the cuneiform inscription that it was made for Artaxerxes I (464–424 B.C.). Silver also went into sockets, pillar trim, fillets, and hooks of the Tabernacle (Ex. 26:19), into the candlesticks and tables of the Temple, and into the royal crown, which was made of silver and gold (Zec. 6:11). In Acts 19:25, there is a reference to a guild of silversmiths.

The silversmith assembled and repaired silverware. He used an intensive fire to heat the silver until it became sufficiently softened for reworking. He wired parts such as legs and handles to the body to prepare it for soldering. Then, after he had soldered the parts, he filled in holes and cracks with silver solder.

The silversmith hammered out deformities, leveled, and traced punches. He used pliers to shape the object into the form he desired. To ornament his handiwork, he used a saw and hammer to pierce and cut. He usually performed his work while squatting on the ground.

Folklore

Metals played a curious role in superstition and sorcery. It was believed that a person bitten by a mad dog would be cured if he drank from a copper tube for twelve months. In a severe case, he was to use a golden tube (Yoma 84a). Amulets were usually written on metal tablets. Coins or gold ornaments were placed in the clothing or in the shoes of a bridegroom because it was believed to foil the power of witches. Water that came into contact with iron was believed to prevent poisoning. Yemenite Jews have long worn iron bands on their arms and feet in the belief that this gives them additional strength.

See *Assayer, Jeweler, Miner, Mining Engineer.*

Midwife

The midwife assisted mothers at childbirth. During the delivery, Hebrew, Egyptian, and Mesopotamian women crouched upon a birth stool or a pair of bricks or stones called *abnayim* (Ex. 1:15). The midwife seized the infant, severed its umbilical cord, washed the child with water using salt as an antiseptic, wrapped it (Ezek. 16:4), and announced its arrival to the father (Jer. 20:15).

Some scholars believe that midwives were not commonly used, pointing to the fact that in Egypt where the Israelites were most fertile only two midwives, Shifrah and Puah, are mentioned (Ex. 1:15–16). Undoubtedly, when midwives were unavailable, relatives or friends aided in delivery.

The Talmud states that the midwife tied the umbilical cord, cleaned the child, and whispered comforting words to the mother. She was permitted to violate the Sabbath when performing her duties since all religious laws may be suspended when a life is at stake (Shab. 1c, Yer. Shab. 18.3). In Talmudic times, midwives also aided in delivering domestic animals (Hul. 43a).

We do not know how midwives acquired their skill, but probably it was through observation, practical training, and experience.

See *Nurse, Physician.*

Miller

Most Biblical families ground their own corn. Normally, women ground corn (Ex. 11:5; Matt. 24:41), but prisoners were sometimes assigned to this chore (Isa. 47:2; Lam. 5:13). Larger types of rotary querns drawn by animals were also used (Matt. 24:41). Because the Israelite depended on his hand mill for daily bread, he was forbidden to give it in pledge (Dt. 24:6), especially since the daily baking of bread required many grindings (Ex. 11:5; Gen. 18:6).

The oldest common method of grinding corn was to spread it on a flat stone and rub it with a round stone. During the Iron Age (1200–970 B.C.) the rotary quern had become common. It consisted of two circular stone slabs, each about eighteen inches across; the top one was pierced through to revolve on a pivot attached to the lower stone. The handle was a wooden stick protruding from a hole near the outer edge of the upper stone. The grain came through the pivot hole in the upper stone which then, as it turned, crushed the corn so that the flour spilled from between the two stones onto the ground. During the grinding process, if animals were not used, two women sat on the ground by the mill opposite each other and turned the upper millstone by alternately manipulating a wooden handle placed near the outer rim. Then each used her right hand to pour grain from a nearby basket. The meal poured onto a cloth placed under the millstone (Matt. 24:41).

As towns developed and the population increased, millers became occupational specialists and ground grain for many families. In New Testament times, public millers had large wholesale mills and granaries like those which have been unearthed at Pompeii as well as at Ostia, port city of Rome.

Miner, Mining, and *Ores*

Men engaged in mining before the dawn of history. Flint, copper, and tin were used during the Stone and Bronze Ages. Probably, the first step in the history of mining was the alluvial mining of gold in the gravels deposited by rivers or by post-glacial floods. Outcrop mining—the surface mining of ores found in the top strata of the earth or in the veins of rocks—was the earliest source of copper, lead, silver, and iron. Even before the Iron Age (twelfth to tenth century B.C.) underground mining with shafts and galleries was practiced in many regions and used in the Stone Age.

The Fertile Crescent, which includes Mesopotamia, the Nile Delta, Palestine, and Syria, contains chains of well-mineralized rocks supplying ores of copper, gold, silver, tin, lead, and iron. On the south can be found granite, diorite, and porphyry. Some of the rocks contain gold, silver, iron, turquoise, and semi-precious stones along with various building stones.

NONMETALLIC MATERIALS

Egypt had granite, diorite, and other igneous rocks along with sandstones and limestones. In Palestine, east of the upper Jordan, were basalt, limestone, and sandstone. Huge standing stones were quarried and erected in neolithic times. Limestone was easily worked and used for the excavations of cisterns, tombs, and the making of waterpots (Jer. 2:13; Jn. 2:6).

Flint tools have been found in Palestine dating back more than six thousand years ago. Stone Age men made flint arrow-heads, scrapers, chisels, and knives. Flint was excellent material for providing a sharp cutting edge. Zipporah, wife of Moses, circumcised her son with a flint knife (Ex. 4:25).

Marble was a crystalline limestone, usually white or cream-colored, found in Assyria, southern Greece, and Crete. "Marble stones in abundance" are mentioned in 1 Chronicles 29:22.

METALS

Originally, pure gold, copper, bronze, and iron were used in their natural form without alloys. Silver was often alloyed with gold. Copper ores were extracted from surface outcrops. More than one thousand years before Abraham in Ur, the working of copper was advanced through mining.

Mining for turquoise and copper began in Egypt before 3000 B.C. at Maghara and Serabit el Khadim in west Sinai. Shafts more than one hundred feet deep have been found in Egyptian mines. Tunnels ventilated by shafts were driven into hillsides, and pillars supported the roof. First, stone tools were used, but later bronze and stone tools were used jointly. Wedges and fire were employed to split the rock, and the miners separated the ore by crushing, washing, and hand-picking. Baskets were used to transport the ore and drainage tunnels were built to drain off surplus water. Smelting was generally done at the location in clay crucibles with charcoal and primitive bellows. Many old sites still reveal such slag heaps and crucibles.

Gold was generally alloyed with various amounts of silver. It was abundant in the alluvium of the eastern desert of Egypt, and was also found in the western coast of Arabia, the Aegean Islands, western Asia Minor, and the mountains of Armenia and Persia.

The most important furnishings in the Mosaic Tabernacle (Ex. 25) and in Solomon's Temple (1 Ki. 6) were made of gold. Natural silver ore may have occurred but silver was usually extracted from the sulphide ore of lead (galena). Its main sources were Asia Minor, Armenia, and Persia, the islands of the Aegean, and Laurion in southern Greece. Silver was abundant in Biblical times (Jer. 6:29–30).

Nehoshet is variously translated "copper," "bronze," or "brass." Thus brass in the Bible may be any one of the three, though true brass, which is an alloy of copper and zinc, came into use later about 1000 B.C.

Copper ores were found in Armenia, Syria, Persia, Midian, east Egypt, and Sinai. The surface copper ores are bright green and blue carbonates which were used in Egypt and elsewhere as eye paint. This metal was used in the Tabernacle and Temple and also for such household articles as basins, mirrors, ewers, idols, musical instruments, and armor.

Iron was known in its native form in ancient times (Gen. 4:22). The Hittites are believed to have been the first to smelt iron. When their kingdom terminated, their knowledge spread elsewhere. The Philistines brought the art to Palestine and became famous as a nation of smiths to the disadvantage of the Israelites (Jg. 1:19; 1 Sam. 13:19–22).

Iron was found in abundance in the Wadi Arabah between the Dead Sea and the Gulf of Aqaba; iron ores abounded near Mount Carmel, Mount Hermon, southwest Midian, Cyprus, Syria, the Pontus coast of Asia Minor, and in the Aegean Islands. Both copper and iron were mined by Solomon. An excellent description of Solomon's copper mines is found in Nelson Glueck's *The Other Side of the Jordan* and R. J. Forbes's *Metallurgy in Antiquity*.

Tin is mentioned in the Bible only in lists of metals, but the dark heavy oxide ore cassiterite was extracted chiefly from streams and not mined until about Roman times.

Lead is also mentioned in a few lists of metals in the Bible. It was sometimes used as tablets for inscriptions (Job. 19:24).

There are a number of passages in Scriptures pointing to mining as an occupation, and these have been corroborated by archaeological findings. The promised land is described as one "whose stones are iron and out of whose hills thou mayest dig copper" (Dt. 8:9). In Genesis 4:22, the genetic lists declare that Tubal-cain was the founder of metal crafts, which presupposes that mining existed to provide the metal. The most vivid Biblical description of mining is found in Job 28:1–11. Job exhibits familiarity with the hazards of mining and with mining procedures in remote locations: "They open shafts in a valley away from where men live. . . . They search out . . . the ore in the gloom (28:3–4). In Job 28:1, the word *motsa,* mine, suggests a place where silver may be found.

The Sinai mines, which were worked at various periods from predynastic times to the twentieth dynasty, were among the principal sources from which Egypt obtained her copper supply. During the Iron I–II Age (1200–600 B.C.) the copper deposits of the Wadi Arabah were intensively mined, as shown by the remains of mining and smelting camps filled with shards of that period.

The Kenites are said to have been the first to exploit the mines during that period, since their center was at Sela near the copper mines (Num. 24:21). The Hebrews probably learned mining and smelting from them. Until the time of David, the Philistines monopolized iron (1 Sam. 13:19–22). Some believe that Israel may have engaged in mining in the peninsula of Sinai, while journeying to Canaan. Following the establishment of the Hebrew monarchy, the Hebrew kings vied with the Edomite rulers over control of the valuable mineral resources of the Arabah. This, along with rivalry over access to the Gulf of Aqaba, probably was largely responsible for the wars between Judah and Edom from David to Jehoshaphat, and from Amaziah to Ahaz.

In the northern part of the Arabah, the main mining center was Khirbet Nahas (copper ruin), about sixteen and one-half miles south of the Dead Sea, near the vast ore deposits of the Wadis Gheweibeh and Jariyeh. Some identify it with Ir-nahash, "snake-city" (1 Chr. 4:12). In south Arabah, the most important mining center was in Men'iyyeh on the west side of the Arabah about twenty-two miles from the head of the Gulf where, according to Glueck, there are vast deposits of copper ore. The presence of iron slag in the Arabah is considered as proof that iron and copper were mined there during the Iron Age.

At the two main camps were large walled enclosures, probably inhabited by gangs of slave laborers. Miners were usually slaves, convicts, or prisoners of war. It is likely that, as with most miners, their work was arduous, their days long and backbreaking, and that they lived under primitive conditions. They used picks and wooden shovels, wedges and stone hammers to break the ore, as well as draft animals and humans to load and to transport their product.

One Agatharchides gives a harrowing account of the working conditions in the Nubian gold mines, which the Ptolemies worked with slaves, convicts, and prisoners of war: "The younger men crawling with lamps on their foreheads, tunneled the quartz by hand, following the veins of gold. The hewn quartz was dragged out by the children, and the older men broke it small with hammers; the fragments were then, preparatory to washing, ground to dust in spar mills, turned not by oxen but by women, three to a spar and naked. They were guarded by armed Nubians; all were fettered and flogged, and were worked without rest or care for their bodies"; and all, says Agatharchides drily, welcomed death when it came (W. W. Tarn, *Hellenistic Civilization*, p. 254).

The occupation of mining was greatly advanced with the development of metal tools, the alternate use of fire and cold water which shattered the rock, as well as by smelting and drainage by adits.

See *Metalworker, Mining Engineer.*

Mining Engineer

While mining engineers in our modern sense were, of course, nonexistent in Biblical times, there were experts on extracting minerals from the earth. They planned and supervised the construction of mine shafts and tunnels, developed means of extracting the minerals, and planned methods of transporting the minerals to the surface. They directed the operation of the mines and probably supervised safety measures. Solomon probably employed such persons for his copper mines in Ezion-geber. They are believed to have been Phoenicians. Job 28:1–2 suggests the existence of mining engineers.

See *Metalworker, Miner.*

Mirror Maker and *Mirrors*

Many mirrors have been found by archaeologists. They were usually made of polished metal as implied in Exodus 38:8, since glass mirrors were not available until late Roman times. Many artisans were employed making them, though we do not know whether they made mirrors exclusively.

These ancient metal mirrors have been found along with jewelry and articles of women's apparel. The mirrors are round, sometimes of one piece, sometimes lacking a handle, but more commonly having one of wood or ivory. Most of the mirrors found in Palestine and Syria date from the postexilic period to the Roman times. Their handles were decorated with engraved dots, circles, and volutes; they belong to the fashioned art of the Mediterranean seaboard, combining Aegean, Anatolian, Egyptian, and Mesopotamian influences. The unpolished side of the mirror was usually bare.

The laver of the Tabernacle (a copper vessel which the priests used for ablutions) was made by smelting the bronze mirrors of the women who ministered at the door of the tent of meeting. Job 37:18 likens the sky to a "molten mirror," obviously of metal. Consequently, the translation of "mirror" as *looking-glass* is considered fallacious. Similarly, the translation of *glasses* in Isaiah 3:23 is considered incorrect, and although it is conceded that the objects might have been mirrors, they were not made of glass.

Mirrors were highly prized in antiquity, and royalty often exchanged them as gifts.

See *Glassmaker, Metalworker.*

Money-Changer

"Shulhani," or one who sits at a table, was a money-changer. During the existence of the Temple, when pilgrims from distant points came to Jerusalem, the money-changer changed the currency of one country or province to that of another and changed small coins to larger currency, for which services a small fee was paid.

The half-shekel which Scriptures required annually of every adult male Jew was to be paid in Tyrian silver coins. The Mishnah (Shek. 1.3) declares that the tables of the money-changers were set up in the provinces on the fifteenth day of Adar, one month before Passover, to accelerate regional collections. Ten days later, when the pilgrims from foreign countries arrived in increasing numbers, the money-changers moved their tables to the Temple precincts.

In the New Testament, Jesus is described as "cleansing" the Temple by driving out those who traded in animals or birds for sacrifice (Matt. 21:12 ff.; Mk. 11:15 ff.; Lk. 19:45; Jn. 2:15 ff.). He overthrew the tables of the money-changers and, according to Mark, forbade anyone to carry a vessel through the Temple area, an act which has puzzled many scholars. The incident is usually explained as a protest against the commercialization of religion. Some scholars, however, maintain that Jesus was not opposed to the maintenance of the Temple and the sacrificial system, but they believe that the violent act may have been a protest against the excessive charge (equivalent to about thirty-one cents) imposed by the money-changers for their services. We know that profiteering in the sale of sacrificial doves evoked the disapproval of Simeon ben Gamaliel, a leader of the Pharisees, who reduced the number of mandatory sacrifices, thus forcing the price down (Ker. 1.7).

Whether the allegation of overcharging was true or not, ill feeling against the money-changers may have existed. Moreover, in the last days of the Temple, to win or retain their office, the Temple authorities often bribed Roman officials. These actions incurred the displeasure of the people.

See *Banker, Money Lender, Pawnbroker,* APPENDIX II.

Money Lender and *Loans*

From the beginning of the second millennium B.C., the practice of charging interest for loans had become common. Interest rates varied from a low of 12 per cent in Greece to 30 per cent in Egypt. In Babylonia, however, rates of 20 per cent were typical. For an advance of grain, interest of 25 per cent to 33 per cent was common, while short-term loans of fifteen days cost as high as 300 per cent.

The Bible forbade Jews to take interest for loans to their coreligionists (Ex. 22:25; Dt. 23:19; Lev. 25:35–38). This prohibition included interest on loans of silver, chattel, or produce. But this ban did not seem to halt the practice. Abuses in charging interest were denounced by the prophets (Ezek. 18:8, 13, 17, 22:12; Neh. 5:6–13). Proverbs, too, affirms that riches acquired through usury are unstable and will not benefit their owner (28:8).

The background of this prohibition against interest relates to the fact that until late in their history, the Hebrews were mainly engaged in agricultural and pastoral occupations. The loans referred to were not to aid business ventures, but rather to relieve poor, distressed persons who, without this aid, might be forced to sell themselves into slavery (Lev. 25:47 ff.). Thus, the loan was philanthropic rather than economic. As urban life developed and the economy became more complex, capital was needed for business expansion, and loans bearing interest became inevitable.

When a loan was made, the borrower surrendered a piece of his movable property to the creditor as surety. Indispensable objects of daily living were not to be taken as such pledges. (Dt. 24:6). Thus, a garment offered as a pledge had to be returned before nightfall (Ex. 22:26–27; Dt. 24:12–13) since the poor man usually covered himself at night with this garment.

The debtor pledged his son, daughter, or slave at the disposal of the creditor in case of failure to repay the loan. During Nehemiah's time, some Jews who had mortgaged their lands and vineyards were forced to surrender their children as sureties (Neh. 5:2–3). A rich or good friend could also serve as surety. There are many references in Proverbs urging caution in serving as surety especially for strangers (Pro. 6:1, 11:15, 17:18, 20:16).

The New Testament mentions the jailing of an insolvent debtor (Matt. 18:23–30; Lk. 12:58–59). In Rome, a creditor could seize an insolvent debtor, put him to work, or place him in chains. Jesus twice referred approvingly to the investment of money with bankers (Matt. 25:27; Lk. 19:23).

See *Banker, Pawnbroker,* APPENDIX II.

Mourner and *Mourning*

An occupation, now defunct, that existed in Biblical times was professional mourning (2 Chr. 35:25; Eccles. 12:5; Ezek. 27:32; Am. 5:16). The professional mourner was hired for a fee to eulogize and to bemoan the death of the departed. Probably because of their wider emotional range and more intensive modes of expression, most of these professional mourners were women. They were variously called *sharot,* singing women; *mekonot,* mourning women; or *hachamot,* cunning women (Jer. 9:17).

The professional mourner practiced certain techniques. In Palestine during the second and first millenniums, mourning included rending one's garments, wearing sackcloth, tearing out tufts of hair until the head was bald, cutting the beard, lacerating the body, scattering dust on the head, weeping and wailing, and beating the breast. Jews were forbidden to round the corners of their heads, mar the corners of their beards, make incisions in their flesh, or tattoo themselves when they mourned the dead, nor were they to rend their garments and make a baldness between their eyes (Lev. 19:27–8, 21:10–11; Dt. 14:1). Mourners also engaged in occult practices that were apparently transmitted from generation to generation (Jer. 9:20). Further, they composed poems lauding the deceased and describing the transiency of life. The length of the poems depended on the importance of the deceased and possibly on the amount of the anticipated fee. The poems were recited or chanted with piercing cries calculated to stir the audience.

Fragments of funeral elegies found in the Bible include the elegies of David for Saul and Jonathan (2 Sam. 1:17–27) and for Abner (2 Sam. 3:33–34). There are also lamentations for communities such as those of Jeremiah as well as his satirical laments for Babylon, Tyre, and Egypt (Isa. 14:4–21; Ezek. 27:2 ff., 32:2–10).

The mourner's lament generally had three main parts: (1) The eulogy was usually florid (Ezek. 19:1–14) and extolled the bravery of the deceased in war (2 Sam. 1:25, 27; Ezek. 32:27), and his unsurpassed and distinctive personal qualities (2 Sam. 1:19; Isa. 14:10–11; Ezek. 27:32). (2) The second aspect was usually introduced by the words *Ach* or *Achaw*, "how" or "what." In case of violent death, the lament was poignant and frequently demanded retribution or a curse upon the enemy (2 Sam. 1:21). The happiness which the enemy may have derived from the death (2 Sam. 1:21) was denounced (2 Sam. 1:20; Lam. 1:3, 7, 21). The present sad state of the mourners was compared with former conditions (Isa. 14:11; Ezek. 19:9, 31:11). The repellent qualities of the lower regions were compared with life on earth. (3) The third phase was consolatory and offered to the good memory left by the departed, the posterity who would immortalize his name, and the conviction that the proper performance of the funeral rites would ease the sorrow of the mourners. An impressive example is the lament for Judas Maccabeus (1 Mac. 9:21).

The Hebrew elegy is a composition employing a verse whose

second part is always shorter than the first (Ps. 136; Isa. 1:9; Jon. 2:3). Some believe that there may have been laments in the form of a dialogue. The refrain may have been chanted by the choir: "How are the mighty fallen" (2 Sam. 1:19, 25, 27); "Go down and be laid with the uncircumcised" (Ezek. 33: 19 ff.); "Alas, alas, thou great city" (Rev. 18:10).

During the lament, the flute was usually played, probably because of its capacity for high tones (Jer. 48:36). The Mishnah declares that even the poorest funeral must have at least two flutes and a wailing woman (Ket. 4.4), which also seems to have been the practice in New Testament times (Matt. 9:23). Interestingly, God's name was not mentioned during the lamentation (2 Sam. 1:17 ff., 3:33 ff.).

Muleteer

The muleteer drove his mule, which was usually heavily laden. He probably groomed, fed, watered, and cleaned its stable as well as loaded and unloaded the animal. He was probably fed or paid a fee for his services (J. Carcopino, *Daily Life in Ancient Rome,* p. 182).

Among the references to traveling by mule are 2 Samuel 13:29; 1 Kings 1:33; 1 Chronicles 12:40; Esther 8:10; Isaiah 66:20.

See *Camel Driver, Charioteer, Driver,* APPENDIX I.

Musical Instrument Maker and *Musical Instruments*

The varied musical instruments mentioned in the Bible were made by artisans, but we know little about their construction. Some instruments, however, that shed some light on the subject have been found among the Egyptians. Depending on the kind of instrument, a variety of tools were used. Makers of wooden instruments used saws, planes, and hammers, while makers of brass, bronze, or copper instruments used heat to hammer or mold the instrument into the desired shape. Many instrument makers also played the instruments they made and were itinerant minstrels. They were also skilled in making other objects of wood or metal, and they may also have been diviners (2 Ki. 3:15). They were undoubtedly paid fees for their services.

Musical instruments were constructed of wood or metal—bronze, copper, silver, or gold—or bones and shell. The harp was often made of precious wood and metal. We know what some of them looked like, but we do not know how they sounded. A few ancient instruments have survived, but they are too fragile to be played. By far the oldest Jewish musical instrument is the *shofar* or ram's horn (Jos. 6:4, 6, 8, 13), which is still used in synagogues prior to and during the High Holy days. The Bible accounts for its origin in Genesis 22:13. Four Sumerian lyres, possibly harps, discovered in Ur by the archaeologist Sir Leonard Woolley, are to be found in the University Museum at Philadelphia, Pennsylvania, the British Museum, and the Baghdad Museum. The Sumerians also possessed long vertical reed flutes, double pipes or oboes, and short silver flutes. Drums, as well as metal rattles and animal horns, were used to accompany singers.

Among the instruments used at Temple services were the reed pipe (1 Sam. 10:5; 1 Ki. 1:40) probably used by David, and the double pipe, *ugab,* or oboe (*chalil*). Musicians also used trumpets at Sinai (Ex. 19:16) made of beaten or turned silver. Trumpets were also used to summon the congregation to meetings, to signal on various occasions such as danger, war, peace (2 Sam. 2:28), festivals (Ps. 81:3), and holy days (Num. 10:1–11).

Some other instruments used in Biblical times were:

Kinnor: Small, portable, stringed instrument made of wood trimmed with metal and fitted with twisted grass and sheep gut strings.

Nebel: Bottle-shaped stringed instrument (1 Sam. 10:5).

Organ: Panpipes; reed stems attached together and blown obliquely (Gen. 4:21; Job 21:12, 30:31; Ps. 150:4).

Castanets: Rattle-like oval hoops with a handle; fastened across the hoop were metal rods threaded with loose strings that jingled (2 Sam. 6:5).

Sackbut: Small, high-pitched harp, or a large, multi-stringed, and deep-toned harp (Dan. 3:5, 7, 10, 15).

Trimbrels or *Tambourines:* Small hand drum inscribed on Egyptian and Assyrian monuments; its parchment was believed to have been rigidly fixed. Mentioned in Exodus 15:20.

Dulcimer: Thought to have been a bagpipe. The real dulcimer used in King James Version, consisted of strings stretched over a rectangular box which served as a sounding board. The strings were struck with hammers. This instrument is considered the forerunner of the piano. Daniel 3:5, 10, 15.

Harp: Wooden framework, either oval, square, or triangular, with eight or nine stretched animal strings. Held against the body, it was plucked with either the fingers or a plectrum (Gen. 4:21; 1 Sam. 16:23). *Psaltery* was similarly plucked.

Lute: A later model of the harp, containing three wooden sides and ten strings (1 Sam. 10:5; 2 Sam. 6:5; 1 Chr. 15:16, 20).

See *Choirmaster, Chorister, Musician.*

Musician and *Music*

Very early in history, man expressed himself musically by singing or by playing some musical instrument. There were talented persons who sang and played various instruments without pursuing music as a career, but there is evidence of professional singers and instrumentalists in the Bible (2 Sam. 19:35; Eccl. 2:8).

It is generally believed that professional musicians among the Hebrews arose during the time of David (1000 B.C.), although even earlier in Egypt and Assyria the professional musician was well known. Before the establishment of the monarchy under Saul, women were the major musicians. The famous women musicians of the Bible were Miriam, Deborah, Jephthah's daughter, and the women who hailed young David when he returned victoriously from battle (1 Sam. 18:6–7). With the advent of professional musicians in the Temple and the royal courts, the number of professional women singers seems to have diminished.

Although the Bible mentions Jubal as the "father of all such that handle the harp and the pipe" (Gen. 4:21), it is believed that early Hebrew traveling players and minstrels were musicians as well as diviners who, besides playing, repaired metal products (2 Ki. 3:15). There are two other references to minstrels in the Bible: "the singers in front, the minstrels last" (Ps. 68:25), and "the sound of harpers and minstrels, of flute players and trumpeters shall be heard in thee no more" (Rev. 18:22). Probably, in return for their services, they were given food, lodging, and money. Minstrels sang to their own accompaniment or to that of others.

Later, the prestige of the trained singers and instrumentalists rose, and they became high-ranking functionaries next only to the king and princes. Sometimes they were so revered that they were spared the death penalty suffered by others who had committed similar crimes. They were exempt from ordinary work and from paying tribute (Ez. 7:24) and were supported by the state through the allotment of "holy things" (Neh. 12:47).

There were musical guilds among the Hebrews. When the Temple musicians organized a guild, membership eventually became hereditary and passed from father to son. According to 1 Chronicles 25, the heads of these guilds, Asaph, Jeduthun, and Heman, led twenty-four groups embracing 288 Levite musicians. The names of the Biblical musical hereditary guilds are believed to be found in the Psalms "for the sons of Korah."

In ancient times, the Hebrews were admired for their musical talent. There is a carved relief of the eighth century B.C. depicting Hebrew musicians playing at the Assyrian court of Sennacherib. In Psalm 137:3 their conqueror is recorded as asking, "Sing us of the songs of Zion." In Hellenistic times the Roman geographer Strabo declared that the singing girls of Palestine were the most musical in the world.

What is not known about the vocation of musicians is the nature of the formal training and the working conditions. Though many may have been self-taught, it is likely that there was some form of instruction.

In Biblical times music was an important element in religious worship. There were families of professional singers who officiated in the Temple. The congregation's participation seems to have been limited to such responses as "Amen" or "Hallelujah" or "His mercy endureth forever." Antiphonal singing, or the singing of choruses in response to each other, characterized the Temple liturgical service (1 Chr. 15:16–24). In later times, Agrippa II allowed musicians to wear white priestly garments. While singing, they were stationed east of the altar in the Temple (2 Chr. 5:12).

When the walls of Jerusalem were dedicated, Nehemiah arranged the Levitical singers into two large choruses which marched around the city walls in different directions, then stood opposite each other at the Temple and sang alternating hymns of praise to God.

In Amos 5:23, 6:5, and Isaiah 5:12 we read that the feasts following the sacrifices were accompanied by music. Music was also important in other aspects of life. Various popular folk festivals were accompanied by music and dancing in which females joined. Music was played at harvest festivals (Jg. 9:27, 21:21), at the marriage or accession of kings (1 Ki. 1:40; Ps. 45:9), and at family festivals (Gen. 31:27; Jer. 25:10). At funerals, professional mourners and flautists (Matt. 9:23) performed. Other occasions for music were the completion of house roofings and sheep-shearing festivals. The shepherd in the field whiled away his time playing his reed pipe (1 Sam. 16:18;

Lam. 5:14). David was probably the first music therapist when he played his harp to dispel Saul's melancholy (1 Sam. 16:16 ff.).

Curt Sachs, the musicologist, asserts that Jewish vocal music found in Jewish communities of Iran, Iraq, and Yemen is three thousand years old. Chapter III of *Habakkuk*, "For the Chief Musician," refers to a song to be accompanied on stringed instruments. When the Jews returned from Babylonian captivity, the Temple liturgy developed. Priestly musicians played trumpets, Levites played the cymbals (Ez. 3:10), while the religious leaders "sang one to another" (Ez. 3:11).

Joshua ben Hananiah, who had been a member of the Levitical choir in the Temple (Ar. 11b), described how the choristers went in a group to the synagogue from the orchestra by the altar (Suk. 53a) and participated in both services. The choral singing was cantillation, a recitation which depended on the rhythm and sequence of the words of the text rather than on the notes of the tune. The syntactical structure of the sentence, rather than the metrical form of the musical phrase, influenced the music. The style of singing is believed to have been shrill, nasal, alternately full of beauty and sudden accentuated notes.

It is believed that the reason we do not have the details of the Temple musical practice may be due to the Levites' refusal to reveal their trade secrets. We do not know whether the Hebrews had a musical notation, but great care was taken to protect the secrets of musical technique and the meaning of technical terms. This knowledge was transmitted orally and is now irretrievably lost.

The Psalter was the Temple hymnbook, which was chanted by the Temple choir and accompanied by the Temple orchestra. Harmony in our sense of the word did not exist; the main purpose was to make "a joyful noise unto God" (Ps. 66:1). The psalms were sung antiphonally by two choirs or by a choir, soloist, and congregation.

After the destruction of the Temple in 70 A.D., the music which accompanied the Temple service was forbidden.

There are a number of references to music in the New Testament: Luke 7:32; Matthew 9:23; Mark 14:26; 1 Corinthians 14:7. In describing the fall of Babylon (symbolizing Rome), Christ is quoted as having declared that in the great city there would be no more harpers or minstrels, trumpeters or flute players (Rev. 18:22).

See *Choirmaster, Chorister, Musical Instrument Maker.*

Nurse

Generally, members of the immediate family and friends served as nurses in Biblical times. It is likely that women's natural inclinations led them to wash, feed, and minister to the sick. Women served as midwives.

There does not seem to have been any formal training of nurses.

See *Midwife, Physician.*

Nursemaid

Nursemaids were known in Biblical times and performed any of the following activities: they prepared and served meals for their charges, including the feeding of infants; they probably bathed and dressed young children, played with them or observed their play, and accompanied them on walks and outings; they probably also kept the children's quarters tidy. Moses' mother served as his nursemaid while she was working for his adoptive mother (Ex. 2:7). Deborah served as the nursemaid to Rebekah (Gen. 35:8) and remained on with the family. Nursemaids who seemed also to have been governesses were Naomi (Ru. 4:16) and the governess of Mephibosheth (2 Sam. 4:4).

See *Custodian, Midwife.*

Olive Oil Worker and *Olive Oil*

Many persons in antiquity were engaged in raising olives and in producing and selling olive oil. Oil was used extensively and was one of Palestine's main agricultural products. Although sesame oil was also used extensively in Mesopotamia, the approximately two hundred Biblical references to oil allude to olive oil. To obtain olives for oil production, before the olives were ripe they were either shaken from a tree or beaten down by striking the branches with a light pole.

The prime olives were crushed with the bare feet (Mic. 6:15) or were pounded with a large stone. The pulp was then poured into a basket where it was gently shaken to and fro. The baskets served as strainers and the oil was collected in jars or other containers. Then the liquid was poured into another vessel. After the oil had floated and was purified, the top layer was skimmed off and became known as "beaten" or pure oil. This pure oil was used for the lamp that continually burned in the sanctuary (Ex. 29:40; Num. 28:5). Such oil was also a portion of Solomon's annual payment to Hiram (1 Ki. 5:11).

The second step consisted in heating the olive pulp and again putting it into the vat. Pressure was applied by a large beam, one end of which was placed into a niche in the wall and the other end weighted with stones. The oil produced was allowed to stand until the sediment had subsided. Sometimes salt was used to purify it and the product was called *shemen.*

Olive oil production for ordinary domestic use was similar to the production of wine. The simplest kind of oil press was a shallow trough hewn into native rock from which there was a conducting channel carrying the oil to a lower trough or oil vat.

The Mishnah reveals that the olives from Tekoah were best, followed by those from Regeb. Olives were harvested in September and October, and a good tree could yield from ten to fifteen gallons of oil a year.

Olive oil served many purposes. It was used for food, for anointing kings (1 Sam. 10:1, 16:1), for priests (Lev. 8:30), for prophets (Isa. 61:1), and for polishing warriors' shields (Isa. 21:5; 2 Sam. 1:21). It was also customary for ordinary people to anoint themselves with oil daily after bathing (Ru. 3:3). Guests arriving at a banquet were also anointed (Ps. 23:5; Am. 6:6; Lk. 7:46).

Olive oil was considered a gift of God (Jer. 31:12; Jl. 2:19). The Bible declares that oil, grain, and wine will be denied when Israel disobeys God's wishes (Dt. 28:5; Jl. 1:10; Hag. 1:11).

Oil was shipped considerable distances and was included among the cargo of Babylon. During Biblical times there was a guild of olive seethers (producers of oil by the heating method) in Palestine (Mish. Kel. 5:5, 8:8).

See *Farmer, Fruit Farmer.*

Overseer

There were several types of overseers in early Biblical times. One type of overseer was the superintendent of a labor gang in Egypt who carried a long rod for punishing laggards, and was a severe taskmaster (Ex. 1:11). When the Israelites under David and Solomon employed forced labor (2 Sam. 20:24), they used overseers. Overseers were also employed in building and repairing the Temple (2 Chr. 2:18; 34:13, 17). Joseph is also called a supervisor in the sense of prime minister (Gen. 39: 4–5), and he urged Pharaoh to appoint other supervisors (Gen. 41:34).

The leader of the singers returning from exile was called an "overseer" (Neh. 12:42). Similarly, overseers accompanied Nehemiah (11:9). In the New Testament, the elders of Ephesus are termed "overseers of the church" (Acts 20:28).

Overseers were clearly unpopular. Discipline was harsh and personnel relations in the modern sense was unknown. Proverbs 6:6–7 informs us pointedly that ants work willingly without an overseer.

See *Taskmaster.*

Painter, House

Painting of buildings or articles is scarcely mentioned in the Bible. Nevertheless, painting was extensively practiced. In Palestine as far back as the neolithic period, designs and scenes were painted on house walls in Teleilat el Ghassul. About 1200 B.C. at Megiddo the mud-plaster walls of a palace court were painted in a variety of colors and patterns. The tombs and temples of Egypt were painted in various colors: reds, yellows, greens, and blues. Capitals of columns and the columns themselves were painted by the Greeks. Traces of color have been found in Sidon tombs.

See *Artist.*

Pawnbroker

Pawnbrokers were known in China about three thousand years ago, and were functioning in Greece and Rome before Christ. They estimated the pawn or pledge value of articles such as jewelry and other valuables and lent money to customers. They scrutinized articles brought to them to determine their condition and value and verified the value of gold or silver articles by weighing them or by employing acid tests to validate carat content and purity. When pledges were redeemed the pawnbroker computed the interest (*Encyclopaedia Britannica,* xvii, 405).

There is no specific mention of a pawnbroker in the Bible. However, security was given in the form of a pledge of some personal effect for small temporary loans (Dt. 24:10; Job 24:3), the mortgage of real estate (Neh. 5) on the surety of a guarantor (Prov. 6:1–5). In view of the previous references, some form of pawnbroker may have existed in ancient Israel.

See *Money Lender.*

Paymaster

The paymasters were "the workmen that had the oversight of the house of the Lord," viz. the foremen. "Howbeit there was no reckoning made with them of the money that was delivered into their hand; for they dealt faithfully" (2 Ki. 22:5–7). Joab is mentioned as a paymaster (2 Chr. 34:8–12). We have no further elaboration of their activities in the Bible, but we can reasonably conjecture that they were expected to keep a record of their receipts and disbursements.

While most large building projects were built with slaves or forced labor, some skilled free persons were employed for administrative and supervisory tasks, thus requiring the services of a paymaster. Moreover, pay was also disbursed even to slaves in kind such as food or clothing. During the reigns of Kings Jehoash and Josiah (639–609 B.C.) of Judah, construction workers were paid wages that they received through their own representatives.

See *Accountant, Treasurer.*

Perfumer and *Perfumes*

The art of making perfume was known in the Near East about four thousand years ago. During the eighteenth century B.C., the great palace at Mari had its own perfumery which supplied huge quantities of ointments and perfumes to the royal family, officials, and soldiers. The perfumes were used for personal hygiene, festivals, and royal banquets. Palace perfumeries appear to have been common in antiquity. In 1 Samuel 8:13, the typical king is cited as requiring the services of perfumers, cooks, and bakers. We also find a reference to the use of perfumes by the repatriated troops of King Ahab (*ca.* 730 B.C.) in 2 Chronicles 28:15.

Because of the widespread use of perfumes, there were probably a considerable number of persons employed both in its manufacture and in its use. This is demonstrated by the existence of a guild of perfumers (Neh. 3:8).

The ingredients that the perfumer used came from various countries: the Red Sea provided onycha; Arabia, bdellium, frankincense, and myrrh; Persia, galbanum; India, aloes and nard; Ceylon, cinnamon; Somaliland, frankincense; Palestine, stacte and saffron. From 1 Kings 10:10, we learn of the large supply of spices which the Queen of Sheba gave Solomon.

The methods employed by the perfumer were related to cooking and depended on the raw materials and their ultimate use. The ancients did not employ our modern method of distilling an essence. Generally, fresh flowers were squeezed by compressing them into a bag, by soaking them in fat and constantly changing them, or by dipping the flowers into hot fats or oils at 65 degrees Centigrade (the most common method).

The perfumer artfully blended different scents. From Exodus 30:23 we learn that the sacred anointing oil consisted of myrrh, cinnamon, aromatic cane, and cassia. Originally, the holy incense of the Bible consisted of four blended scents: stacte, onycha, galbanum, and frankincense. Later, in the Herodian temple, seven other perfumes were used: myrrh, cassia, nard, saffron, castus, cinnamon, and aromatic cane. The sacred perfume was used to anoint the Tabernacle, its furnishings, and the Aaronic priests (Ex. 30:22–33). It was forbidden to use the formulas of the holy oil and incense for secular purposes. Exodus 30:33 and 1 Chronicles 9:30 refer to priests commissioned by David and Saul to make perfumes for the Tabernacle.

While perfumes were used extensively as a cosmetic (Ru. 3:3; Est. 2:12), they were used also in funeral ceremonies such as the embalming of Jacob (Gen. 50:2–3) and of Joseph (Gen. 50:26), on the bier of King Asa (2 Chr. 16:14), and in the wrapping of Jesus' body (Jn. 19:39–42).

Kings and the wealthy perfumed their garments and furniture (Cant. 4:11; Ps. 45:8). Harlots also sprinkled their beds and themselves with various perfumes (Pro. 7:17). Since considerable skill was needed to produce perfumes, the perfumer probably ranked higher than most other skilled workers and enjoyed a higher standard of living.

See *Apothecary*, *Spice Dealer*.

Philosopher

Among the Greeks and Romans, philosophers were men who charged fees for their lectures and discussions, though occasionally they remitted fees to those unable to pay. Their subject matter was broad, embracing almost all knowledge then available. Their main purpose was to discover the ultimate meaning of the universe, and the reasons for and meaning of all phenomena.

The Church Fathers opposed the philosophers of their time because the philosophers generally regarded the chief purpose of life as pleasure and denied the providence of God. The apostle Paul bids the Colossians to beware lest they be spoiled by philosophers (Col. 2:8). Luke also reports that the Epicurean and Stoic philosophers made a jest of Paul's discourses and denied God's providence (Acts 17:18).

The ancient philosophers differed sharply in their philosophy and behavior. Some led highly moral and ethical lives while many indulged in gluttony, immorality, and self-aggrandizement. Their work brought them into close contact with youth as well as with adults, both of whom were often influenced by their claim that their teachings offered a satisfying and rational code of life.

The public's attitude toward the philosopher ranged from high esteem to intense distrust and ridicule. The wealthy paid philosophers to live with them as companions, educators, and as spiritual advisers. Nero, Trajan, and Aurelius had philosophers residing at their court. On the other hand, they were also the butt of popular jokes, of criticism from such intellectuals as Quintilian and Lucian, as well as of some monarchs.

See *Rabbi, Teacher.*

Physician and *Medicine*

Among the ancients, Egyptian medicine is the best known, though it was mainly magical in nature. Their early physicians were often temple priests organized under a chief who dealt principally with hygiene and diet. They prescribed emetics on three days in every thirty—the so-called "Egyptian days," which were later regarded as unlucky. They used ointments, potions, and poultices. Among the drugs they used were cedar oil, alum, brains, honey, salt, sycamore bark, sulphate of copper, liver, the heart and blood of different animals, oil of camomile, and stag's horn.

Doctors were so highly esteemed in Egypt that sometimes they were deified. One such was Imhotep, who was physician to King Zoser about 3000 B.C. Temples were erected to him and to other physicians. These early doctors may have possessed some surgical skill but their knowledge of anatomy seems to have been scant. Egyptian doctors served as embalmers (Gen. 50:12) and as apothecaries, preparing tonics, hair pomades, and other cosmetics.

About 2000 B.C. considerable medical progress was made in Mesopotamia. The surgical procedures mentioned in the code of Hammurabi suggest a high level of medical organization and a rudimentary knowledge of anatomy. Hundreds of mineral and animal drugs were used. The most common were asafetida, castor oil, cedar, fig, mandrake, henbane, mustard, myrrh, mint, poppy, and turpentine. However, diseases were believed to be caused by the invasion of the body by demons who had to be expelled before healing could follow. Therapy was mainly sought by exorcism and incantation. There was, however, an anonymous Sumerian physician who lived toward the end of the third millennium B.C. and who kept a record of his many valuable prescriptions. For his materia medica, he did not use magical spells or incantations, but rather went to botanical, zoological, and mineralogical sources.

In the Bible, too, there is evidence of a continuation of the concept that illness and plagues are punishment for sin (Ex. 15:25–26; Lev. 26:14–16; Dt. 7:12–16) or due to Satan (Job 1). Yet, the physician was regarded as a messenger of God. "I kill and I make alive; I wound and I heal" (Dt. 32:39). While Israel regarded the Lord as the physician of Israel (Ex. 15:26), human practitioners were countenanced (Ex. 21:18–19). Joseph hired house physicians (Gen. 50:2), and Isaiah refers to a surgeon or wound dresser (3:7).

There were some occasions on which prophets or holy men engaged in diagnostic or healing activities. Elijah revived an apparently dead child (1 Ki. 17:17–22), and his disciple Elisha performed a similar act (2 Ki. 4:18–20, 34–35). A holy man restored the paralyzed hand of King Jeroboam (1 Ki. 13:4–6). Isaiah cured King Hezekiah of an inflammation by applying a poultice made of figs (2 Ki. 20:7).

While the word "physician" is rarely used in the Bible, it

denotes substantially the same meaning as our present-day medical practitioner (Ex. 15:26; Jer. 8:22; Lk. 8:43). Other than the attempts by the priests and prophets to diagnose leprosy, the functions of priests and physicians were distinctly different (1 Ki. 14:1–13; 2 Ki. 1:1–4, 8:8–9; Isa. 38:1, 21; Lev. 13:9–17; Lk. 17:14–15).

The Jews had their own high-level sanitary code in the Mosaic Law which spared them from many a plague. The Law forbade as food pork products and the flesh of animals which had died a natural death. It required the burial of excreta, emphasized the contagious nature of some diseases, enjoined quarantine in case of communicable diseases, and demanded the inspection and selection of food.

The physician's duties are not clearly outlined in the Bible. We can, however, infer what they may have been. For example, in Ezekiel 30:21, there is reference to a primitive form of bone-setting. Surgical operations mentioned in the Bible are circumcision and castration (Dt. 23:1), though they were probably performed by lay persons. There is recognition of inflammation and abscesses (Dt. 28:35), gangrene and discharges (Ps. 38:5; Pro. 12:4, 14:30). Sores are treated with local application (Isa. 1:6; Jer. 8:22, 51:8). The good Samaritan used wine and oil as local treatment (Lk. 10:34). Wine is also mentioned as a medicament and stimulant (Pro. 31:6; 1 Tim. 5:23). The value of therapeutic baths is suggested in 2 Kings 5:10.

In the Talmud (1–500 A.D.), there are references to surgeons (Sanh. 91b), general practitioners, internists, mental therapists (Sanh. 75a), dentists (Kid. 24b), oculists (B.M. 89b), gynecologists (Nid. 47a), and obstetricians (Ar. 7b ff.). There was a physician attached to the ancient Temple to treat the priests (Shek. 51–52). Mar Samuel, an eminent physician, devised techniques to examine the contents of his own stomach (Ned. 50b). Rabbis experimented on fowls (Hul. 57b), ravens (Mid. Lev. 19:1) and on the hoopoe bird (Yer. Ber. 5, 9b).

When performing operations, some surgeons wore a tunic over their garments (Kel. 26:5). Various surgical instruments appear to have been used. Sleeping potions were employed as anesthesia (B.M. 83b). Venesection was widely used on the healthy and the sick (Shab. 129b). Bleeding by means of leeches and cupping was practiced (Ab. Zar. 12b; Shab. 154a). Fractures, amputations (Ker. 66a; Sem. 28; Shab. 66a), and trephining (Ket. 77b) are also mentioned. The spleen appears to have been removed surgically during a human operation (Ab. Zar. 44a). A form of Caesarean operation was also performed (Nid. 40b).

Prosthetics such as crutches and other orthopedic appliances were known (Shab. 65a). A cranial plate was inserted (Ned. 66b). The use of artificial teeth made of wood, gold, or silver is noted (Shab. 65a; Ned. 66b).

Knowledge of pathology is also evident among the physicians of the Talmud, who were among the first to perceive that the symptoms of all diseases were only exterior signs of internal changes in tissues. Each slaughtered animal underwent an autopsy before it could be eaten, a practice still followed by observant Jews. Any pathology of the lungs was studied as to color, growths, consistencies, cavities, etc.

The Jewish court of justice occasionally hired physicians to testify in criminal cases. When corporal punishment was administered, it was done under the supervision of a physician (Mak. 22b). The local judicial council forbade any physician to practice without a license (B.B. 21a; Mak. 20b). Each city was obligated to have at least one physician, and to live in a city lacking a doctor was considered dangerous to one's health (Sanh. 17b).

The physicians of Talmudic times acquired their medical knowledge from tradition, dissection of human bodies, their keen observation of their patients, and experiments upon animals (Hul. 57b). When they made their rounds to their patients, they were accompanied by their apprentices (Dt.R. 10). Many sons of physicians followed their fathers' profession (Yer. R.H. 1:3, 57b).

Attitudes toward physicians seem to have varied. Asa is denounced for having consulted physicians (2 Chr. 16:12), though they may have been pagan magicians. He is condemned for "not having sought the Lord." Job chides his comforters "as physicians of no value" (13:4). Jesus, considered the physician of the soul (Matt. 9:12), mentions physicians twice in the New

Testament (Lk. 4:23, 5:31), while Luke is described by Paul as the "beloved physician" (Col. 4:14). Then there is the woman "who had suffered many things of many physicians" (Mk. 5:26–27). One statement in the Talmud declares "the best of physicians are hell bound" (Kid. 82a). This may reflect the belief that some physicians were irreligious, careless, occasionally killing their patients by bungling, and sometimes refusing to serve the poor.

Later, physicians enjoyed great prestige. Ecclesiasticus 38:1–12 declared, "Honor a physician with the honor due unto him for the uses ye may have of him, for the Lord hath created him." Another Jewish teacher called the physician "God's angel and personification of the word of God" (Alphabet of R. Akiba, 21). Patients were advised against minimizing seemingly mild ailments (Mid. Ab. Zar. 2.2), and told rather to call a physician immediately.

Although the Talmud complains about high medical fees, it also states, "The physician who charges nothing is worth nothing" (B.K. 85a). Umna, another revered physician, charged no specific fee but had a box into which patients dropped whatever fee they could afford.

See *Apothecary, Circumcisor, Midwife, Nurse.*

Plasterer

Excavations in Biblical lands reveal that from very early times, people knew how to secure lime for plastering walls and for other building purposes by burning limestone until it yielded white caustic, alkaline earth. Lime is a calcium oxide made by heating limestone in kilns. There were many kilns in ancient Palestine; the hill country east and west of the Jordan afforded much limestone.

The Bible uses *sid* as signifying plaster, lime, or whitewash (Dt. 27:2; Isa. 33:12; Am. 2:1; Dan. 5:5). Plasterers applied plaster to the interior walls and ceilings to form fire- and rain-resistant surfaces which could also be decorated. In interior work, the plasterer used a square plate of wood or metal to hold small amounts of wet plaster and used a trowel to apply the plaster to the lath. For exterior stuccowork, the plasterer followed the same basic procedure. The Temple walls of Jerusalem were plastered white (Neg. 1.1).

An ancient Egyptian, as now, plastered his buildings inside and out. The poor used clay mixed with straw. Because of the rainy seasons in Palestine and Syria, the coating on the outside walls, if made of clay, had to be replastered often. In these two countries, lime was the basic material for making mortar. For the first coat, lime was mixed with "fat" red sand or with ash from bathhouse fires, while the finishing coat was made of white sand and slaked lime with or without chopped flax straw. The ancients preferred plastering to decorating. Even the best granite was covered with stucco on which decorations were painted or carved (Dt. 27:2; Dan. 5:5). Columns were frequently stuccoed and then painted.

Police Official

In Biblical times, undoubtedly, there was some machinery to maintain public safety and morality. There are a number of terms in the Bible which have been translated as magistrates or police officers, but the accuracy of the translation is often questioned by modern scholars.

Deuteronomy requests the appointment of *shoterim*—officers—and most Jewish commentators translate this as police officers who served to discharge the decisions of the court. The Bible suggests that the duties of the *shoterim* included issuing proclamations to the people, especially in times of war (Dt. 20:5, 8, 9; Jos. 1:10). Since the *shoterim* are usually coupled with the judges (Dt. 16:18; Jos. 8:33), it is believed that the former were attached to courts of justice and carried out the orders of the judges.

The chief of the judicial department organized by Jehoshaphat appears also to have had authority over the police. 2 Chronicles 19:11 and Song of Solomon 3:3, 5, 7 also refer to the watchmen who patrolled the city at night and attacked suspicious persons.

We know that the Temple had its own security force, most of whom were Levites, who were the gatekeepers–*shoarim* (1 Chr. 9:17, 24–27, 26:12–18). These men guarded the entrance of the Temple mount as well as supervised the cleaning of its precincts. Levites were stationed at twenty-one points in the Temple courts. At three of them, priests maintained watch throughout the night. A captain carrying a lantern patrolled to check on the watchmen. If he found one asleep, he was permitted to beat him and set his garments afire (Mid. 1.1.2).

The Talmud mentions various police officials who held office in the Jewish communities of Palestine and Babylon. Most of them derived their authority from the local courts, which appointed them as assistants to the communal organization. Since many bore Greek names, it suggests a later period, after Hellenistic influence became strong among Jews. These officers supervised weights and measures and regulated the market prices of commodities (B.B. 89a, 68a). Watchmen also guarded the city (B.B. 68a). There were mounted and armed guards who maintained law and order in the suburbs (B.B. 8a). Other officers supervised the dispensing of alms (B.B. 8b). These officials were paid by the town treasury, to which all the residents contributed. There were also special officers to test the quality of wine so as to protect the consumer against adulteration (Tos. Kel. B.K. 6:10; Ab. Zar. 58a).

Officials designated by the community administered corporal punishment to law violators. When a judge sentenced a condemned man to be flogged a certain number of times based upon the severity of his crime, the rule was "forty stripes he may give him and not exceed lest if he should exceed and beat him above these with many stripes, then thy brother should seem vile unto thee" (Dt. 25:3). The rabbis commenting on this passage add that "the wicked is still thy brother" (Sifre 286; Mak. 22).

Talmudic law required that three persons be present at a flogging (Maimonides, Yad Sanhedrin 16.2). One ordered the blows to be administered, the second counted them, and the third read the verses of Deuteronomy 28:58–68 as the blows were administered. The flogging was done by a beadle of the congregation. The law required that he be stronger in mind than in body so as not to strike too hard (Mak. 23).

In the New Testament, John the Baptist was imprisoned in Herod's fortress in Peraea, east of the Dead Sea (Jos. Ant. 18. 5.2), where two dungeons were found, one containing evidence of fetters. The chief priests imprisoned the apostles (Acts 5:18). Police guarded Peter when he was in prison, two chained to him and two posted outside the doors (Acts 12:3–6). Paul was also imprisoned at Philippi (Acts 16:23–24) and at Caesarea in Herod's castle (Acts 23:35).

See *Executioner, Jailer, Judge.*

Postal Employee and *Letters*

Mail deliveries of communications written on clay tablets occurred early in Babylonian history. We have samples of clay tablets found in upper Egypt containing letters of state dating to about 1400 B.C. Regular postal service in early times was usually limited to official business. Private correspondence was delivered by friends or merchants (1 Pet. 5:12; Eph. 6:21 ff.). Both official and private correspondence yielded important information to the government on political and social conditions. There are thousands of clay tablets or ancient letters, some still in their unbroken clay envelopes, from Ras Shamra, Tell el-Amarna, Lachish, Nineveh, Babylon, and Mari which illuminate the Biblical period.

Many samples of correspondence are found in the Bible. Splendid examples of Persian and Roman letters are found in Ezra 4:6–24, Acts 23:25–30, and the Maccabean appeal by letter to Rome (1 Mac. 8) and Rome's reply. Most of the New Testament consists of twenty-one letters or Epistles. There are also letters of introduction mentioned in 2 Corinthians 3:1, Acts 18:27, and 1 Corinthians 16:3. The name of the sender, the addressee, and the messenger are found in 2 Samuel 11:14 and 2 Kings 19:14; and the method of delivery was usually by foot or runners, horse, camel, or donkey (2 Chr. 30:6; Est. 3:13–15).

Among the specific letters in the Bible are those of David to Joab delivered by Uriah (2 Sam. 11:14 ff.), Hiram's to Solomon (2 Chr. 2:11), Jezebel's to the elders (1 Ki. 21:8), Jehu's to the rulers (2 Ki. 10:1–7), Elijah's to Jehoram (2 Chr. 21:12–15), Benhadad's to the king of Israel (2 Ki. 5:5–7), Sennacherib's to Hezekiah (2 Ki. 20:12), Jeremiah to the exiles (Jer. 29), and Mordecai and Esther to the Jews (Est. 9:29). In the New Testament, priests were asked to write letters to the Damascus synagogue (Acts 9:2, 28:21); the Jerusalem council wrote to the gentile converts (Acts 15:22–29); and Claudius Lysias to Felix (Acts 23:25–30).

The term "postmaster" or "chancellor," which is found in Ezra 4:8–9, 17, is believed to designate an Assyrian office such as "lord of official intelligence" and, according to some scholars, "postmaster."

With the expansion of commerce during Talmudic times, there was an increase of correspondence which added to the work of the postal messengers. The volume of mail must have been considerable, since almost every town had its official letter writer. The rabbis prohibited scholars from living in a town lacking a letter writer (Sanh. 17a).

The postal workers were the employees of the king or of wealthy individuals, and they probably enjoyed a higher standard of living because of the difficulties and the confidential nature of their work.

See *Letter Writer, Runner, Scribe.*

Potter and *Pottery*

The potter followed one of the world's oldest vocations. Some specimens of pottery found in Palestine date back to the Neolithic or late Stone Age (8000–4500 B.C.) in Jericho. One specimen found at Lachish, south Palestine, was a pot with a two-winged figure, a scroll, and the stamped name indicating that it was made at Hebron during the Jewish monarchy (1000–587 B.C.). Philistine pottery dating back to the time of David and Solomon has been unearthed in the Shephela. It is tan, painted with bands of red and brown spirals or trimmed with painted birds.

Thanks to the enduring nature of pottery, many periods of history which might otherwise be unknown have been illuminated by the archaeologist. From pottery we have gained information on the dating of unearthed tablets, and from the inscriptions and paintings that many of them bear, we have gleaned precious historical data.

The work of the potter was both useful and, as his art developed, aesthetic, for it served a wide range of purposes and a varied clientele. His art and technology, known as ceramics, involved making clay utensils for ordinary families as well as elegant ware for the wealthy and royal families.

His handiwork became so familiar, probably through observation of him at work, that reference to him enriched the language.

> Thou shalt dash them in pieces like a potter's vessel (Ps. 2:9).
>
> I will break this people and this city as one breaketh a potter's vessel that cannot be made whole again (Jer. 19:11).
>
> Shall the clay say to him that fashioneth it, "What makest thou?" (Isa. 45:9).

Tell Beit Mirsim by J. L. Kelso and J. P. Thorley tells how pottery was made in Biblical times. Clay, which was of earthy consistency containing fine sand, foreign animal and vegetable matter, and gravel, was cleansed in a group of vats on descending levels. The lowest vat's contents were strained through cloth to produce the finest clay. A common variety was red clay, which turned this color after firing. In warm weather, the clay was spread out on a hill to "weather" it. Following this, it was made plastic by continued foot stamping (Isa. 41:25) and mixing with water. Then the clay was tossed into the air to expel the air. The potter would then knead it for several hours and throw it onto a wheel which was turned counterclockwise by hand or, subsequently, when the two-wheeled model arrived, by kicking it with his feet.

The potter's wheel greatly added to the skill, speed, and beauty of the potter's craftsmanship. Its use became common in Palestine about 1900 B.C. and in Egypt more than one thousand years earlier. While the wheel revolved, the potter shaped the mass of clay into the desired form (Isa. 64:8; Lam. 4:2; Jer. 18:6). He made the hollow interior by jabbing his forearm into the wet clay. Then the piece was dried in the sun until it became leathery. It was then returned to the wheel for removal of excess clay, for smoothing or for strengthening its bottom to prevent leakage.

Remains of kilns were excavated in Tell en Nasbeh, Gezer, and Megiddo. Pottery seems to have been produced here in wholesale quantities. Hollow cones of clay were shaped on the board and pinched off at the top. Bottoms were smoothed, handles and bases were added, joints sealed, necks molded, and then the products were decorated. The paint was added either before or after the firing in the kiln (for strength and durability). One of the best preserved pottery workshops in Palestine was found at Qumran.

Decorations were made on even inexpensive cooking vessels. A simple design was that of parallel grooves cut into the handle or neck with sharp stones. Also popular were twisted cords pressed around in the wet phase to form a rope design while the clay was still soft. Decorations included zigzag patterns, half-moons, patterns of men and women, keys, scrolls, animal scenes, and circles.

Although the early Palestinian potters did not glaze, they rubbed the piece with shells, a tool, or a pebble. Ancient Egyptian potters knew how to coat their clay pottery with a liquid glass glaze. They became famous for their brilliant blue. Some resourceful potters combined several glazes with great beauty. These glazes were mixed by gathering soda, copper, tin, silver, and lead. A very beautiful specimen is the blue scepter of Amhotep III (*ca.* 1413–1377 B.C.), five inches in diameter and five feet tall.

Objects made of pottery were a wide variety of jars and cooking pots, ladles and dippers, bowls, dishes, cups without handles, immense storage jars for grain, oil, and wine, small lamps, as well as the several-branched candelabra. There were portable clay stoves, primitive jewelry, buttons, spindle whorls, clay bottles, toys, theater tickets, voting ballots, figurines of gods, and statuettes of royalty and other important figures, as well as babies' feeding bottles. Ceramic tiles decorated public buildings. Lachish letters and numerous clay fragments reveal that remains of pottery were used as writing materials.

Pottery centers were located at the outskirts of towns near open fields so that vessels might be dried in the sun and in kilns. Potters field became the burial ground in many cities where the remains of thousands of tombs built through the centuries were found.

See *Artist, Glassmaker.*

Poultry Farmer

The only direct mention of chickens in Scriptures is attributed to Jesus: "How would I have gathered thy children together, even as a hen gathereth her chickens under her wings, and ye would not" (Matt. 23:37; Lk. 13:34). There are Babylonian records from about 600 B.C. that seem to refer to cocks. We know that during Hellenistic times, about the third century B.C., chicken and egg production became important economic activities in Israel. It was a period when the poultry farmer became an important economic figure.

See *Farmer*.

Priest

Priests played very important roles in the religious and social life of the ancient Near East. Sometimes they were so influential that they could dislodge kings and replace them with their own choices. They also changed religious worship as they desired. Thus, during the eighteenth Egyptian dynasty, the priests and officials of the Theban god Amen helped the young Pharaoh Tutankhamen to remove the priesthood of Aten which the monotheistic Akhenaton (*ca.* 1377–1360 B.C.) had instituted at Tell el-Amarna. Throughout the ancient world—Egypt, Assyria, Phoenicia, Greece—the priesthood was a hereditary office with privileges and responsibilities transmitted, thus giving rise to a class system.

In early Sumer, the priests of Ur were also kings. The priests of Canaan and Phoenicia were both numerous and influential. Ahab's Phoenician queen, Jezebel, maintained hundreds of priests at her palace table (1 Ki. 18:19; 2 Ki. 10:11). For over fourteen centuries in Israel, too, its priests exercised more influence than any other group (Dt. 33:8 ff.).

Early in their history, Jewish priests were not consecrated to the service of the sanctuary or the altar; laymen also ministered. Gideon (Jg. 6:26 ff.) and the Danite Manoah, though he was not consecrated (Jg. 13:16–19), sacrificed at the command of God and of the angel of God. Neither David nor Solomon were priests, yet they, too, offered sacrifices: David on the altar on the threshing floor of Araunah (2 Sam. 24:25) and Solomon before the ark in Jerusalem (1 Ki. 3:15). Both continued to minister as priests. Likewise, Elijah offered sacrifices at Mt. Carmel (1 Ki. 6:12 ff.). Even when there was a sanctuary with a priesthood such as at Shiloh, the layman could offer sacrifices without priestly intervention.

The role and functions of the priests seem to have undergone substantial change during the course of the centuries. The early priests performed two main duties: they cared for and guarded the sanctuary, its images and palladia, and they consulted oracles. More important than the shrine were its images. The early priest also carried the sacred ark. Those who consulted the oracle were always of priestly descent; it is believed that the skill of using and interpreting the oracle was probably transmitted from father to son. This may be how a hereditary priesthood arose such as the sons of Eli at Shiloh and Nob, and of Jonathan and his descendants at Dan (1 Sam. 2:23 ff; Jg. 18:30).

Moses apparently organized the priests under the leadership of his brother Aaron, from whom all Aaronides descend (Ex. 29). Following Aaron, the function of the high priest was assumed by his eldest son. The consecration of the high priest required an elaborate ritual lasting seven days (Ex. 29; Lev. 8) of washing, the solemn vesting of his robes, his anointment, and such ceremonies as sprinkling with blood and anointing with oil of various parts of the body.

As for the ordinary priests who belonged to the family of Aaron, they were consecrated by special ceremonies similar to those of the high priest but which were less elaborate (Ex. 29; Lev. 8) with the omission of anointing in later times. They did, however, sprinkle various portions of their body with oil or blood (Ex. 29:20; Lev. 8:30).

From the time of Moses until after the Exile, priests were also known as Levites. The Levites were consecrated by being sprinkled with water, their bodies shaved and their clothes washed. The high priest laid his hands on them and they were required to present two bullocks (Num. 8:5–22). The ceremonies represented a solemn offering up of the Levites to God.

The vestments of the high priest included a blue robe, woven without seam, which reached to his knees and which had an opening for his head. He also wore an ephod—a robe embroidered in gold, purple, scarlet, or the like—which reached from the breast to the hips. His breastplate, which was attached to the ephod and originally contained the mysterious Urim and Thummim, was also embroidered. His headgear was a turban, with the crown or plate bearing the inscription "Holy to Yahweh" (Ex. 28:36).

The duties of the high priest included offering the daily meal offering to God (Lev. 6:19–20) and the ceremonial sprinkling of the entire people when sin offerings were made (Lev. 4:13–21). His most dramatic function was on Yom Kippur when, wearing the linen garb, he entered the Holy of Holies alone and sprinkled the mercy seat with the blood of a bullock and a goat as a sin offering (Lev. 6).

The duties of the ordinary priests included the offering of all sacrifices (2 Ki. 16:15). These included making the fire, washing the inwards and legs, collecting the blood and sprinkling it on the altar, placing the pieces of burnt offering upon the fire, burning them, doing similarly to the memorials of other offerings, and then removing the ashes. They were busiest during the three festivals when tens of thousands of pilgrims brought sacrifices and oblations. They also rendered decisions following examinations concerning suspected leprosy, plagues, molds in garments and houses, and they performed the required rituals (Lev. 13:13–14). Further, they blew the trumpet either as an alarm of war or to announce the new moon, and at the scheduled feasts (Num. 10:10; Lev. 23:24; Ps. 81:3) as well as on the Day of Atonement and the Jubilee Year (Lev. 25:9). Priests also served as army chaplains and participated in battles (Dt. 20:1–4; 1 Chr. 12:23, 27; 2 Chr. 20:21–22).

Down to the close of pre-exilic times, the priests were the authentic interpreters of the Law and the sanctuaries were the seats of judgment. This function of expounding the Torah and of administering justice continued throughout pre-exilic times (Dt. 33:9–10). According to Deuteronomy, all difficult criminal and civil cases were referred to the priests (17:8–11,

21:5). The prophets often allude to these judicial and teaching functions of the priesthood (Am. 3:9; Hos. 4:6; Isa. 28:7; Mic. 3:11; 2 Chr. 15:3, 19:8–11).

Priests were ordained by kings of Israel on the basis of personal preference (1 Ki. 12:31). Thus David invested his own sons and the Jainite Ira of the tribe of Manasseh (2 Sam. 8:18, 20:26).

Priests were forbidden many things. They were forbidden to mourn for their dead except their closest kin, (Lev. 21:1–2) nor were they to make cuttings in their flesh (Lev. 19:28). They were also forbidden to marry prostitutes, dishonored or divorced women. Priests with physical blemishes or disabilities were also barred from service in the Temple though permitted to eat the holy food (Lev. 21:17–23). If they became Levitically unclean, they were barred on penalty of death from priestly service and from partaking of holy food during the period of their impurity (Lev. 22:2–7). Before officiating, priests washed their hands and feet (Ex. 40:30–32) and refrained from wine or strong drink (Lev. 10:9).

Levites assumed their duties variously at ages twenty, twenty-five, and thirty (Num. 4:3, 8:24; 1 Chr. 23:24, 27) and were to be regarded as servants of the priests. Thus, they fetched and carried the Tabernacle and its furniture in the wilderness. They "kept the charge," which meant the protection and cleaning of the vessels and furniture and other duties connected with the service not mandatory for the priest (Num. 18:2–7, 3:5–39).

The priests and the Levites were later divided into twenty-four guilds, each of which was believed to be a separate family. At a very early date, the priests became a hereditary guild. Each guild or group was assigned a period when it served in the Temple.

Since the Bible often links the Levite with the slave, widow, and the fatherless (Dt. 12:12, 16:11), we may infer that his economic status was low. There is supporting evidence of this in Judges 17–19 where Levites are found wandering about in search of a living.

The income of priests and Levites consisted largely of the

shoulder, the cheeks, and the maw of sacrificed animals as well as the first fruit of the field and garden produce. They also shared in the feasts of the firstling (first born of an animal) and farewell offerings (Num. 18:1–8, 12:17–19).

The priests also supported themselves partly by the "tithes of the tithes" which they received from the Levites (Num. 18:26), partly by the redemption money for men and unclean beasts (Num. 18:12–18; Lev. 7:30–34), and partly by sacrificial dues of various sorts. Among the latter were mostly meal offerings (Num. 18:9), the breast and the thigh of peace offerings (Lev. 5:13, 10:16–20; Num. 18:1; Lev. 7:30–34), the skin of burnt offerings (Lev. 7:8), the shewbread, and several special offerings such as that of the leper (Lev. 14, 24:9; Mk. 2:26). On their settlement in Canaan, priestly families had thirteen cities assigned to them with pasture grounds for their flocks (Jos. 21:13–19).

During the captivity (587–538 B.C.), many priests perished or preferred to remain in exile with their people. Under Ezra, they renounced their foreign wives (Ez. 10:18–19). There were periods of spiritual decline, especially among the upper-class priests (Mal. 1:6–14, 2), when corruption and lethargy set in. The prophetic group may have emerged from the priestly class. The spiritual sterility of some priests was denounced by Hosea (4:4–9) and Isaiah (1:10–17). The priests earned the disdain of the populace when the high priesthood, no longer hereditary, was often bought and sold to the highest bidder. Nevertheless, Ezekiel envisaged the revival of a holy priesthood and the ideal sanctuary (40–48). After the first return from the Exile and the resumption of the Temple worship, the power of the priesthood returned. The prophets Zechariah and Haggai urged the building of the Temple and praised Joshua, the high priest.

In rabbinical literature, the status of the priesthood was consonant with the priestly code. The main purpose of the altar and priesthood was to atone for sin. Subsequently, there was rigid enforcement of laws relating to the pedigree of priests which repeated the earlier laws. Only men of unblemished purity were permitted to the priestly service. Similar rules were established regarding the women they married. Before a priest married a woman of uncertain pedigree (if she were not of priestly descent), he was expected to investigate her lineage for five generations. Priests were forbidden to marry proselytes or freed women.

In the New Testament there is a continuation of the classical distinction between priests and Levites as shown by the parable of the good Samaritan (Lk. 10:31–32) and the Jewish ambassadors sent to John the Baptist (Jn. 1:19). The missionary Barnabas was also a Levite (Acts 4:36).

See *Judge, Rabbi, Synagogue Functionary, Teacher.*

Proconsul

This refers to a Roman governor or commander of a province or region. In the New Testament (Acts 18:12), Gallio was proconsul of Achaia and Acts 13:7 mentions another. As a high official, the proconsul's duties included carrying out the policies of the Roman senate, maintaining peace and order, serving as judge, and, in general, attempting to promote the interests of his government. Many who could not resist the temptation of serving their own interests acquired considerable wealth during their term of office.

See *Ambassador, Governor, Procurator.*

Procurator

The procurator was a steward or bailiff of a private estate or a financial agent with the power of attorney. Later he became an imperial officer. Still later, procurators functioned in the capacity of viceroys (Matt. 27:2, 11, 14; Lk. 3:1, 20:20; Acts 23:24). Procurators had auxiliary troops and were responsible for military and financial administration, but they were under the superior authority of the imperial legate of Syria. Procurators governed from Caesarea.

In Roman imperial government, the word "procurator" signified the financial officer of a province, but it was also employed as the title of the governor of a province, such as Judea, designated third class by the central government at Rome. In the New Testament, the most famous procurator was Pontius Pilate, 26–36 A.D. (Matt. 27:2). Others were Antonius Felix, 52–59 A.D. (Acts 23:24) and Porcius Festus, 59–62 A.D. (Acts 24:27).

See *Ambassador, Governor, Procurator, Steward.*

Prophet

This term usually refers to the extraordinary spiritual leaders and counselors of Israel whose moral courage, inspiring insights, and ethical teachings have been unsurpassed. Some prophets were supported by rulers; others earned their livelihood from secular pursuits.

The prophetic age consisted of three periods. Before Samuel, the period of the *hozeh* or seer (1 Sam. 9:11), mainly known for his ecstatic visions, contained sporadic manifestations of prophecy. Then came the rise and growth of prophecy from Samuel to Amos; finally, the major canonical prophetic writings extending from the eighth to the fourth century B.C. formed the third period.

Though the prophets predicted future events, they were not fortunetellers. The events which they predicted usually dealt with the social, political, economic, and national affairs of Israel. Their message was religious and ethical, and they emphasized spiritual rather than mechanical adherence to law and cult.

They denounced all forms of evil, luxury, self-indulgence, and oppression.

The prophet was viewed as the man to whom God revealed Himself, usually by dreams or visions, and who therefore felt an irresistible compulsion to speak the message (Am. 3:7; Ex. 4:16, 7:1). He often came from humble callings. Elisha was a farmer (1 Ki. 19:19–21); Amos was a herdsman (Am. 1:1, 7:14); Moses was a shepherd. The prophet did not have to receive a formal call to prophesy—many who were trained in the schools never became prophets. Some, like Amos, had no formal preparation. Some received the divine spirit occasionally and others, often. Their main idea of prophecy was revelation rather than mystery mongering (Am. 3:7).

The prophets immersed themselves in contemporary problems and strove to correct the social evils of their time. They proclaimed God's holiness and interpreted His demands as requiring that they and the people lead more ethical and moral lives. They castigated the hypocritical observance of sacrifices and ritual, especially when accompanied by corrupt behavior. They demanded that justice, mercy, and righteousness be practiced (Am. 4:6, 5:22–25; Hos. 6:6; Isa. 1:10–21; Mic. 2). They advocated "hate the evil and love the good" (Am. 5:15).

Although some of the lesser-known prophets isolated themselves in distant areas and led austere and detached lives (2 Ki. 9:1), the well-known literary prophets lived among the people and shared their problems. They boldly denounced kings and the selfish rich (Am. 4:1, 6:4–6). Nathan rebuked David (2 Sam. 12); Jeremiah castigated the princes of Judah (Jer. 26).

While denouncing the leaders of their country and others for their transgressions, they were nonetheless patriotic. They interpreted the events of the day as God's purpose working through their nation's history. While they often foresaw gloomy events, they also pictured a bright future for the "righteous remnant" who would survive (Isa. 10:20, 22, 37:32; Ezek. 6:8).

They conveyed their teachings through oral utterances, as did Samuel and Elijah, and by the written word which they or their disciples recorded. Later, these notes were edited and augmented. They also conveyed their message by symbolic acts such as Ahijah rending his garments into twelve pieces (1 Ki. 11:29–32), Elijah casting his mantle on Elisha (2 Ki. 2:13), or by using symbolic names (Jer. 27:2; 1 Ki. 22:11). Many of the prophets employed symbols in preaching their message. Moses used the uplifted hand (Ex. 17:11) and the uplifted serpent (Num. 21:8). They also interceded for their people (Dt. 9:18; 2 Ki. 13:4). Some clothed their oracles in parables and allegories (Isa. 5:7; 2 Sam. 12:1–7; Ezek. 16).

Besides the literary prophets, there were schools of prophets known as "sons of the prophets" or guilds or schools of ecstatic persons (mentioned in 1 Sam. 10:5, 10, 19:20) who were wonder workers and soothsayers similar to the prophets of the Ba'alim (Dt. 13:1). They appear to have had much in common with the dervishes of the Near East of later times. These prophets sometimes bore marks branded on their foreheads or wore distinctive tonsures. They also used music (1 Sam. 10:5) for inspiration. Some became so emotionally aroused that they were known as "mad fellows" (2 Ki. 9:11; Hos. 9:7). Occasionally, these religious leaders traveled as wandering counselors or settled in remote parts such as the hot Jordan Valley where they led ascetic lives.

There were centers for prophets at such places as Bethel, Gibeah, Gilgal, Mt. Ephraim, and Ramah. At Ramah, Samuel lived and ran a "school of the prophets." There they worshiped, trained themselves for their prophetic roles, and gave counsel (1 Sam. 19:20–23).

The dedicated prophets of Israel decried the material motives of many of the sons of the prophets, who accepted fees for their services (1 Sam. 9:7–9; 2 Ki. 8:7–9). Elisha refused to accept payment for the counsel that had led to the cure of Naaman's leprosy (2 Ki. 5:16). Amos even asserted that he was not a professional prophet (Am. 7:14). A substantial number of the prophets of integrity preferred to be called men of God.

An example of both priest and prophet was Samuel, who was highly regarded throughout all Israel (1 Sam. 3:20, 7:3). He toured the country ministering to his people, offering counsel, and settling disputes. The prophet Gad influenced King David and is accredited with having established the musical ritual of the sanctuary (2 Chr. 29:25) and with having recorded, along with Nathan, David's reign (1 Chr. 29:29). Both Gad and Nathan were important court chaplains. The main and best-known literary prophets were Isaiah, Jeremiah, and Ezekiel. The minor prophets were Amos, Hosea, Micah, Zephaniah, Nahum, Habakkuk, Haggai, Zechariah, Malachi, Obadiah, Joel, and Jonah. Some authentic prophets were also court prophets. At every sanctuary in Biblical times, the prophet worked alongside the priests. There were prophets who declared God's word publicly for the nation or privately for individuals. It was customary to visit the prophets on holy occasions (2 Ki. 4:23); there were prophetic quarters within the Temple (Jer. 35:4).

Among the women prophets mentioned in the Bible are Miriam, sister of Moses and Aaron (Ex. 15:20; Num. 12:2); Deborah, wife of Lapidoth (Jg. 4:4–5); Huldah, wife of Shallum (2 Ki. 22:14); Noadiah (Neh. 6:14); and the prophetess mentioned in Isaiah 8:3. In the New Testament, there are Anna of the tribe of Asher (Lk. 2:36) and the four daughters of Philip (Acts 21:9).

Jesus, who referred to himself as a prophet (Lk. 13:33), quoted the prophets and considered John the Baptist the "greatest prophet of the former age" (Matt. 11:9–13). In the New Testament, the work of prophets was described as exhortation (Acts 15:32), edification, and consolation (1 Cor. 14:3).

There were also false prophets mentioned in the Bible. Pashur arrested Jeremiah (Jer. 21:1–6). Four hundred false prophets were defied by Micaiah, son of Imlah (1 Ki. 22:8–27). Micah 3 denounced mercenary prophets who were more concerned about their fees than with religious teachings. False prophets also prophesied cheerful events such as security and prosperity. Ezekiel 3:17 speaks of false prophetesses. In Jeremiah 23 there is bitter denunciation of false prophets.

In Deuteronomy there are laws dealing with the false prophet who is called a dreamer of dreams. The ordinary person who tempts people to idolatry is known as either a *mesit* or *maddiah,* depending on whether his followers were individuals or communities (Sanh. 7.10.67a). Such a person according to the Talmud is presumed to speak in God's name unbidden. An example was Zedekiah, son of Chenaanah, who predicted that Ahab would vanquish the Syrians at Ramath-Gilead (1 Ki. 22:11). Another example is one who pretended to have been commissioned to prophesy that which was the mission of another, namely, Hananiah, son of Azur. Also considered false is he who speaks in the name of other gods (Dt. 13:3, 18:20). The story of Balaam, however (Num. 22–24), indicates that the prophetic gift was also acknowledged among non-Jews.

Additional examples of false prophets, according to the Talmud, are those who refrain from enforcing basic doctrines thus leading to the violation or the changing of the Mosaic Law, or those who refrain from correcting sinners. If it were found that the suspect's attempt to mislead was a development of presumption (Dt. 18:20, 22), he was to be tried by the Sanhedrin (Sanh. 1.5), and if found guilty, he was to die by strangulation.

Another class of prophets who were considered false but not subject to human punishment were those who suppressed the divine message, such as Jonah (1:3) or those who disobeyed a revelation (1 Ki. 13:9–24; Sanh. 1).

In the New Testament there are a number of false prophets mentioned. In Revelation 16:13 they are denounced. A false prophetess named Jezebel is also listed (Rev. 2:20).

The Talmudic authorities offer no systematic view of prophecy. However, among their many references to the subject are: "The prophetic gift is granted only to those who are physically strong, mentally wise, and rich" (Shab. 92a). Moses is described as having seen truth as if reflected by a clear mirror; all others as by a dull glass (Yeb. 49b). "The holy spirit" that descended upon individual prophets was not the same in each case (Lev. Rab. 15). "All written prophecies begin with words of censure but end with words of consolation" (Yer. Ber. 8d). The Talmud recognized seven non-Jews as prophets (B.B. 15b).

See *Magician, Priest, Rabbi, Teacher*

Prostitute and *Prostitution*

Prostitution as an occupation was practiced as early as the third millennium B.C. and was both a regular part of the temple rites as well as of private enterprise. The ancients worshiped the generative forces of nature and visualized their gods as male and female who cohabited.

Intimacy with the temple prostitutes was neither illicit nor an act of private indulgence. Sexual relations with these women was regarded as means of inducing fertility among humans, crops, and animals, and such activity was common in Babylon, Egypt, Syria, Canaan, Arabia, and Phoenicia. In Biblical times, there were permanent *hierdouloi* (male and female prostitutes) dedicated to the service of the goddess.

Herodotus speaks of the Babylonian custom which required that every woman, rich or poor, sit in the temple of Ishtar and copulate with a stranger, who indicated his choice by throwing a silver coin into her lap. She was required to accept the coin and his sexual advances. Once the rite was performed, she was freed from the obligation to the goddess. Unattractive women sometimes waited long before they were selected. During the period when prostitution was practiced as a religious rite, much of the money paid to the women by their clients was turned over to the priests, many of whom eventually became financial experts.

Male prostitutes, along with females, offered their bodies for ritual purposes (1 Sam. 2:22; 2 Ki. 23:7; Ezek. 8:14; Hos. 4:13). King Asa is said to have ended male prostitution (1 Ki. 14:24, 15:12, 22:46), and houses of cult prostitutes were broken down (2 Ki. 23:13). They were condemned for their wailing (Hos. 7:14), and their earnings were termed the "wages of a dog" (Dt. 23:18).

To the Hebrews, these attitudes and practices were an abomination against which their religious teachers thundered (Am.

2:7; Isa. 47:3; Hos. 4:2). Priests were forbidden to marry prostitutes (Lev. 21:7). No vice except idolatry drew as frequent and as powerful censure from Israel's prophets. Consorting with the sacred prostitute represented worship of a foreign deity. Hebrew fathers are forbidden to turn their daughters into prostitutes under threat of the death penalty (Lev. 19:29; Dt. 23:17). It was forbidden to use income from prostitution to pay vows in the Temple (Dt. 23:18). The expression "playing the harlot" symbolized infidelity to God (Num. 25:1–2; Jg. 2:12, 17, 8:27, 33; Jer. 3:6).

Notwithstanding the opposition to all forms of immoral and deviant sexual behavior, prostitutes functioned freely. In fact, besides the cultic prostitute, the commercial prostitute who offered her favors in return for a fee in money or in kind flourished. Her patrons paid for her services in money, grain, and wine (Hos. 9:2). The widow Tamar served temporarily in that capacity when her father-in-law Judah failed to provide her with another husband (Gen. 38:14–15). While sitting at the gate in Enaim on the road to Timnath, she veiled herself and solicited him, thus suggesting the existence of an easier set of morals for men. The references to venereal diseases (Lev. 15) suggests there was considerable sexual congress with prostitutes. Eli's two sons were condemned for their immorality (1 Sam. 2:22). Destruction was believed to have befallen Judah during the reign of Rehoboam because immorality was rife (1 Ki. 14:24).

In the Old Testament, however, there are also indications of a neutral or even kindly attitude toward prostitutes. Thus Rahab was esteemed because of her aid to the Hebrew spies, and tradition claims that she later married Joshua (Jos. 2:3–21; Heb. 11:31). Hosea is said to have married a prostitute (Hos. 1:2).

The prostitute was probably easily recognized by her coiffure, by a special mark on her brow, or by head ornaments. She customarily wore gay garments and fine ornaments. (Ezek. 16:10). She exercised her persuasive powers and appealed to the carnal impulses of her clients (Pro. 7:16). She may also have sung to them. She attracted her clientele by waiting in public places

(Gen. 38:14). Sometimes, like Rahab, she was employed as an innkeeper serving food and giving lodging as well as sex.

In the Talmud, there are many references to unchastity. One of the alleged reasons for the destruction of Jerusalem was the prevalence of shamelessness, or unchastity (Shab. 119b). To forestall immorality during Talmudic times, Jews instituted marriage at the age of eighteen for males, and even earlier for females (Ab. 5:21; Kid. 29b). During much of the first five Christian centuries, severe economic conditions led to a decline in morality, and prostitution grew so alarmingly that harlots had their own market place (Pes. 113b). At the time of the destruction of the Temple, adultery became so common that the administration of the bitter waters (trial by ordeal) was discontinued.

The early Christian church denounced prostitution (Acts 15:20, 29) and preached against it in large communities by teaching that the body is the temple of the holy spirit (1 Cor. 6:12–20). Harlots and tax collectors were grouped together in the New Testament (Matt. 21:32). However, Jesus declared that prostitutes would enter the Kingdom before some priests and elders (Matt. 21:31), and advocated clemency toward the woman condemned by sinners (Jn. 8:3–11) as well as toward the harlot who was repentant (Lk. 7:37–50).

See *Dancer*

Publisher and *Books*

"Of making many books there is no end" (Eccl. 12:12) implies the occupation of author. On papyrus or parchment, authors wrote books of poems (Num. 21:14), prophecies, and wise sayings. It is, however, unlikely that the Biblical author was paid for his literary efforts.

During New Testament times, book merchants trained teams of expert slaves to write and copy books, which were sold at high prices, thereby making their publishers rich. Books of verse, a common product, were sent all over the world (J. Carcopino, *Daily Life in Ancient Rome,* p. 194). Books were written both on papyrus and on parchment. Parchment books were in scrolls which were unrolled for reading. Some books were illustrated with ink drawings. First editions were generally a thousand copies. Books included poems, pamphlets, histories, memoirs, textbooks, and biographies. The Roman philosopher Seneca laughed at the new rich who bought books in ornamental sets but never read them.

See *Historian, Librarian, Scribe.*

Quartermaster

Solomon's quartermasters assembled their supplies from the governors of the twelve administrative provinces in Israel, each of whom had to supply a month's provisions a year for Solomon's court. One day's supply consisted of about ninety pints of meal, thirty cattle, a hundred sheep, venison, and fowl as well as provender for the royal stables (1 Ki. 4:7, 22–23, 27–28).

See *Steward.*

Queen

There are only a few queens mentioned in the Bible as having ruled as sovereigns of their country. They were Athaliah, a usurper, who ruled over Judah for six years (2 Ki. 11:3; 2 Chr. 22:12), the queen of Sheba (1 Ki. 10:1–13; 2 Chr. 9:1; Matt. 12:42), and Candace, queen of Ethiopia. Women rulers generally had to deal with the same national and domestic problems that faced male monarchs.

Queen consorts or wives of reigning monarchs were Vashti and Esther, queens of Ahasuerus (Est. 1:9, 2:17), Jezebel (2 Ki. 21:5), Maachah (1 Ki. 15:13), and Nehushta (Jer. 13:18, 29:2), but they had no discernible official status among the Jews. In Persia, they were expected to render complete homage to their spouses (Est. 1:13). Bath-sheba, one of David's wives, bowed and prostrated herself before David (1 Ki. 1:16, 31), but Michal, another of his wives, ridiculed and berated him with immunity (2 Sam. 6:20–23).

Since marriages of diplomacy occurred in Biblical times, the queen's influence depended on the political influence of her family. Athaliah's usurpation of the throne and her retention of it for seven years revealed her influence (2 Ki. 11:1–3). Some consorts such as Jezebel seem to have exercised considerable influence over their mates. It was she who influenced the frame-up of Naboth and his eventual execution for failing to sell his plot to Ahab (1 Ki. 21:5–16). Normally, the queen consort sat at the right of her husband (Ps. 45:9).

The queen mother in Israel had an official status, as illustrated by Asa of Judah who removed Maachah, his mother, as queen mother because of her cultic sins (1 Ki. 15:13). Most of the names of the queen mothers are found in the Bible (1 Ki. 14:21, 15:2). Solomon arose and bowed before his mother, Bath-sheba, who generally sat on a throne beside him (1 Ki. 2:19) and apparently also wore a crown (Jer. 13:18).

See *King*.

Rabbi

The word "rabbi" as an honorific title is not found in the Old Testament. In the New Testament, however, it designates teachers of the Law in general (Matt. 23:7–8); even John the Baptist is called rabbi by his disciples (Jn. 3:26). In all other cases in the New Testament, both rabbi and *rabboni* (my master) refer to Jews and were used in addressing Jesus.

Rabbi derives from the Hebrew *rabi,* meaning "my master." *Rab* designated a master who was schooled in Jewish law or a teacher of the Law. While rabbis were ordained from the time of the Mishnah (about 200 A.D.), the term *rabbi* was Palestinian and given to the sages who were ordained by the Sanhedrin during the first century. *Rab* was the title conferred upon those who were ordained in Babylon. Either title authorized them to judge penal cases. Earlier sages, however, like the prophets, bore no honorary title.

Rabbi became the title of the learned sages who were authoritative teachers of the Law and the appointed spiritual heads of the community. Anyone, regardless of his antecedents, could become a rabbi by virtue of his learning.

The role of the ancient rabbi was radically different from that of his modern counterpart, who is elected by a congregation and paid a salary. The ancient rabbi taught the members of the community the Bible and oral and traditional laws. He could ultimately occupy one of three positions—the presidency of the community with the title *nasi;* the head of the judiciary, *ab beth din;* or an ordinary master of civil and ritual laws who was a leader in charitable work and moral conduct.

For the first position he had to be selected by the leaders of the community; for the second, by the leaders of the judiciary; and the third was a duty imposed by the Torah. All of these posts were nonsalaried, although there was provision for expenses to compensate for the loss of income sustained while engaged in voluntary religious work.

Though much time was spent in religious work and in studying and teaching the Law, strictly speaking, the rabbinate was not a vocation. The rabbi earned his living from the pursuit of other, usually humbler, secular careers. He considered it sacrilegious to derive material benefit from the Law. Among the approximately one hundred secular careers which rabbis pursued were: blacksmith, woodchopper, laundryman, water carrier, shoemaker, builder, winetaster, tailor, smith, carpenter, brewer, merchant, and farmer.

Although he received no salary for his religious activities, the rabbi enjoyed some economic benefits; he was exempt from taxes (Ez. 7:24) and was often given preference in trades and enterprises. Unlike others, he was not required to provide substitutes as laborers on public works, but he was required to help dig street wells.

The ancient rabbi worked at a gainful occupation one-third of the day and studied or performed his rabbinical functions of teaching the remainder of the time. Some rabbi-farmers worked during the summer and studied during the winter (Eccl. Rab. 7).

In performing his rabbinical function, the rabbi lectured to his students at the academy. He preached or lectured to the general public only infrequently except on certain stipulated occasions when he explained the laws and customs pertaining to the forthcoming festivals. Some rabbis were preachers of homilies which they expressed after the Scriptural reading of the week (Sot. 41a; Bez. 38b).

The rabbi was expected to be tidy in appearance and to command respect. He usually dressed in a long, flowing white robe and occasionally wore a gold-trimmed official cloak (Git. 73a). He was venerated and the honor due him was considered greater than that due to parents because "parents bring one into this world while the teachings of the rabbi aid one to enter the future world."

See *Judge, Lawyer, Priest, Scribe, Synagogue Functionary, Teacher.*

Realtor

There is evidence in the Bible that at various times property was sold and the sale recorded. Well-known examples of dealings in realty are mentioned in connection with Abraham (Gen. 23), Jeremiah (32), and Ananias and his wife Sapphira who sold property (Acts 5:1).

There were probably persons who specialized in finding buyers and who acted as agents for property owners. They emphasized the selling points calculated to appeal to prospective buyers and were undoubtedly skilled in the art of bargaining, which to this day is characteristic of the Near East and other parts of the world. These realtors probably received a commission for their services.

Refiner and *Smelterman*

Smeltermen were persons engaged in smelting ores to separate and recover the metals they contained. They then refined these metals to a state of purity required for commercial use. The smelting and refining plant of Ezion-geber (Tell el Kheleifah) was one of the largest in the Near East. According to the American archaeologist Nelson Glueck, smelting operations were conducted in a narrow valley, located so that the strong north wind, which blows almost constantly, supplied adequate draft for the furnaces and compensated for the inadequate wood fuel used. Scholars differ on whether bellows were used to heat the furnaces (Jer. 6:27–30; Ezek. 22:20–22; Job 28:1).

Evidence of the work of smeltermen is found in the heaps of copper slag in the area. Smeltermen were mainly slaves, probably supervised by hired Phoenicians who were experienced in copper smelting in Cyprus. These slaves were housed in walled encampments, traces of which are still discernible near the working area.

The earliest smelting was done by bonfires, the ore being placed on fuel. This was followed by the shaft furnace, fed from the top with the product removed from the bottom. The next development was a furnace with a natural forced draft to produce the higher temperatures necessary for iron-ore smelting.

In Biblical times there were two different processes of refining, denoted by the words *zakak* and *zarof*. The former means "to filter" and refers to the physical process of transforming metal from a solid to a liquid, while *zarof* means "smelting" (1 Chr. 28:18, 29:4; Job 28:1; Ps. 12:6).

Any worker who refined material such as silver or gold to a state of purity was known as a finer or refiner. The finer usually used a fining utensil to refine silver or gold (Pro. 17:3). Bending over his fining pot, he tested precious metals for jewelry. In the silver markets of Jerusalem and Damascus, refiners may still be seen operating in this manner.

Refining is a very ancient art practiced by the Egyptians, who purified gold by placing it in earthen crucibles with lead, salt, a little tin, and barley bran. They then sealed the crucible with clay and exposed the materials to the heat of a furnace for five days and nights. Similarly, refining silver by cupellation was a very old process. The silver mixed with lead was placed into a crucible of bone and earth and then inserted into a reverberatory furnace, one in which the heat is reflected from the roof to the material. The oxide that was formed was blown off by bellows, and toward the end of the process the thin covering of oxide became iridescent and soon disappeared. This process is mentioned in Jeremiah 6:29.

Different techniques were used with different metals: to refine gold and tin, only simple melting was necessary. To refine copper required the most advanced methods as used in Solomon's copper mine at Ezion-geber. The copper came from his mines in Arabah. Evidences of silver-lead refining ore found in Jeremiah 6:27–30 and Ezekiel 22:20–22 describe a jeweler melting scraps to recover silver. Three iron refineries found at Tell Jemmeh are dated to the twelfth century B.C.

See *Jeweler, Metalworker, Miner.*

Ritual Slaughterer (Shohet)

When animals were slaughtered for private or family use, the male of the family probably performed this task. But when animals were dispatched in great numbers, as in the Temple or in royal households, specialists probably arose. The Jews developed a prescribed manner of slaughtering animals known as *shehitah,* the purpose of which was to slay the animal as painlessly as possible.

These specialists are not expressly mentioned in the Bible but rather indirectly, such as: "We are counted as sheep for the slaughter" (Ps. 44:22) and "He is brought as a lamb to the slaughter" (Isa. 53:7; Jer. 11:19). These functionaries, who originally were probably priests, not only slaughtered animals and fowl but helped to prepare them for cooking or for the sacrificial ritual.

Though the Bible uses the word *shahat,* "slaughtered" (Lev. 1:5, 11, 3:28, 13), to refer to the act or preparation of the animal for sacrifice, there is no definite manner of slaughter mentioned in the Bible. It is believed, however, that early in Biblical times, prescribed methods of slaughter developed, and, eventually, the authorized practitioner became known as a *shohet.* He had to possess a certain degree of manual dexterity, be thoroughly familiar with the prescribed rules and be a pious person as well as learned in the Law.

According to the Talmud, those barred from this occupation

were the mentally incompetent, minors, the intoxicated, those with unsteady hands, non-Jews (Hul. 13a), Jews who deliberately flouted the Law, and women (though there were some women in later times who were permitted to slaughter poultry).

To become a shohet, one had to pass a rigid test in all the laws of *shehitah,* "slaughtering," as well as in the laws of *trefah,* "dealing with ritually unfit foods," particularly those laws relating to the examination of the lungs. To function as a shohet, the candidate had to receive a certificate testifying to his knowledge of the laws, his piety, experience, the condition of his knife, and his skill in slaughtering. He had to review the laws of *shehitah* every thirty days so as to be thoroughly versed in them.

The slaughter knife had to be sharp, smooth, and with no noticeable notch. Before and after slaughtering, the shohet examined his knife thoroughly (Hul. 17b). If, after slaughtering, he discovered a notch in it, the animal was declared unfit for Jewish consumption. He was required to submit his knife to the rabbi's examination periodically.

Before slaughtering, the shohet recited a prayer following which no irrelevant conversation was allowed (Hul. 86b). After the slaughtering, he examined the throat of bird or animal to determine whether the windpipe or gullet had or had not been cut through according to the Law. When birds and certain wild beasts were slain, some of the blood lost had to be covered with earth or ashes (Lev. 17:13) and another blessing recited (Yoreh De'ah 28).

See *Butcher.*

Road Builder

There are numerous references in Scriptures to roads and ways, as well as suggestions on how to improve roads (Isa. 40:3; Jn. 1:23), that imply the existence of road builders.

Ancient roads in Biblical times were originally paths trodden by men and animals. They were commonly strewn with boulders and pebbles and overgrown with reeds, which made it difficult for chariots to traverse. Some scholars believe that road building may have started to aid traffic and to facilitate troop movements. Others hold that it started with Solomon's construction of cities for chariots and horsemen (1 Ki. 9:19).

Further evidence of road construction in Biblical times are references to casting up of a trodden path for passenger and vehicular traffic (1 Sam. 27:10), and Deuteronomy 19:3, which refers to the preparation of roads to cities of refuge where persons who had innocently committed homicide might find haven. Jeremiah (31:21) also advised the exiles to erect road signs. The Romans, who were noted as excellent road builders, built and maintained roads to serve their military and commercial purposes. Their police power helped to keep their roads safer.

See *Slave, Stoneworker.*

Robber

Despite Israel's Law code prohibiting robbery (Lev. 19:13) and the prophets' denunciation (Isa. 10:2; Ezek. 39:10) of robbery, especially of the poor (Pro. 22:22), thieves existed and even flourished. In the New Testament, even in the time of Jesus, robberies were rife. A story is told of a road robbery in a Jericho wilderness (Lk. 10:30–37). Jesus also denounced robbers of sheepfolds (Jn. 10:7–10) and house burglars (Matt. 6:20). Paul, too, refers to many robberies he had witnessed (2 Cor. 11:26). Barabbas is recalled as the thief who was released at Passover in place of Jesus (Jn. 18:40).

Thieves who made robbery a career were found in pre-Biblical as well as Biblical times. When roads and communications were poor, robbers would lurk at important junctions to attack and despoil their victims. In Abimelech's time, they crouched on hilltops to rob caravans (Jg. 9:25). Leaving home alone after nightfall was hazardous, and at night, families bolted their heavy doors until dawn. During the time of the Judges (5:6) and Hosea (6:9), men feared to walk on public roads, and commerce was paralyzed. This condition continued for many centuries.

Ropemaker

The art of ropemaking is very old. A number of Hebrew words such as *hebel* and *abot* are translated as "cord" or "rope" (Jos. 2:15; 1 Ki. 20:31; Job 39:10; Jg. 15:13–14; Ps. 118:27), but the Bible does not differentiate between the two. Ropemaking antedates spinning and weaving. Egyptian and Mesopotamian art reveals that rope was used for many purposes.

Ropemakers usually used twisted hair or strips of skin to make their products (Ex. 35:18; Jg. 16:7; Ps. 11:2). Rope was inexpensive in Israel and to wear it as a part of one's garment signified poverty (Isa. 3:24) or submission (1 Ki. 20:31).

The Bible does not reveal the process of ropemaking but discloses its varied uses: raising or lowering weights (Jos. 2:15; Jer. 38:11), harnessing or leading animals (Job 41:2; Isa. 5:18), holding a tent ("cords," Isa. 33:20), hauling stones and throwing down fortifications (2 Sam. 17:13), making snares and traps (Job 18:10), tying prisoners (Jg. 15:13, 16:11–12; Ps. 129:4; Ezek. 3:25), ships' tackle (Isa. 33:23), and as a measuring line or cord (2 Sam. 8:2).

In the New Testament, the rope is referred to in connection with the tackling of a ship (Acts 27:32, 40).

Runner

In ancient times, there were fleet-footed persons employed by royalty and by wealthy persons to transmit messages swiftly. They may have been used especially in areas where roads were impassable or unsafe and other means of transportation were not available or were much slower.

The royal runners apparently also served as the king's guards. In 1 Samuel 22:17, King Saul orders his guards to slay Ahimelech and his fellow priests for having harbored David. "The king said to the runners [guards] 'Turn and slay.'" In another passage, King Rehoboam entrusted brass shields to the captain of the runners, or guards (1 Ki. 14:27).

The word *razim* is translated "runners" or "guards" or "post-messenger." Thus in Esther 3:15, "the posts went forth in haste" suggests that they delivered their message on foot; in Esther 8:10 is found: "and sent letters by post [runners] riding on swift steeds that were used in the king's service, bred of the stud."

See *Bodyguard, Executioner, Postal Employee.*

Saddle Maker

There is no direct reference to this occupation in the Bible but there are references to saddles: "Thy servant said, I will saddle me an ass" (2 Sam. 19:26); "And he said unto his sons, Saddle me the ass" (1 Ki. 13:13); "Abraham rose early and saddled his ass" (Gen. 22:3); as well as Balaam (Num. 22:21) and others (Jg. 19:10; 2 Ki. 4:24). There were saddle makers in New Testament times.

The saddler cut, assembled, and joined leather parts and other materials to make his saddles. He was governed by the size he desired, the color and grain of leather, and the type of saddle. After cutting out parts of leather according to specifications, he joined the edges of parts to form the saddletree cover, using needle and thread. He then inserted covering and cushioning material such as cotton batting over the saddletree, using cement, needle and thread, and nails. He attached ornamentation or accessories to the saddle with needle and thread. Saddlers often applied paint to the saddle to give it a glossy finish. Some even incised decorative designs into the leather.

See *Harness Maker, Tanner.*

Sailmaker

Sailmaking is a very ancient occupation. Early man discovered that it was simple to move a boat without rowing in the same direction as the wind if he hoisted a portion of skin, cloth, or other material on a stick. It took many centuries, however, before he also learned to sail against the wind, and ancient Egyptian vessels depicted on carvings or drawings show both oars and sails.

The sailmaker was supplied with the dimensions of the mast and yards and the sail plan. He would then determine the dimensions for each sail, making allowance for stretching. This procedure was followed by a casting or determining the shape and length of each individual cloth in the sail. The cloth was joined by double flat seams sewn with specially prepared twine. Strengthening pieces were also affixed to stress and other essential areas.

Sailcloth was made from flax or cotton. It was plain woven fabric of heavy construction, usually of plied warp and filling yarns. The number of warp ends per inch varied from 26 to 48 and may have been 2- to 5-ply, and from 16 to 34 filling picks per inch 2- to 8-ply.

Among the references to sails in the Bible are: "they could not spread the sail" (Isa. 33:23) and "fearing lest they should fall into the quicksands, stroke sail and so were driven" (Acts 27:17).

See *Shipbuilder*.

Sailor

Sailors and mariners are mentioned only six times in the Bible. We are told that the inhabitants of Zidon or Sidon, an ancient Phoenician city, the modern Saida in Lebanon, were mariners. Earlier, the Tell el-Amarna letters of 1400–1370 B.C. also refer to them. Merchants and mariners are also mentioned in Isaiah 23:12, 14 and Ezekiel 27:8, and in Jonah 1:5 the storm causes the mariners to "become frightened and cry." In Revelation 18:17 there is a reference to "all company in ships and sailors stood afar off." Sailors are also mentioned in Acts 27:27. When

Paul's ship approached Malta, the sailors lowered a boat, but the soldiers cut its ropes. According to Acts 27:30, the sailors were bent on escaping the ship. Revelation 18:19 describes John's vision of the mourning of shipmasters and sailors over the destruction of Rome, since all who had ships at sea grew rich by her wealth.

The crew's quarters were undoubtedly close and primitive and the sailor's work hard and, in times of storms, dangerous. The food, in the absence of refrigeration, was necessarily limited and bare. Crew and officers were paid for their services, although often the sailors were slaves. Frequently, the owner of the vessel was also its captain.

The sailor's ordinary duties included standing watch to observe obstructions in the water and measuring the depth in shallow or unfamiliar waters. He also used rigs and repaired and stowed cargo-handling gear as well as other gear. He probably painted and chipped rust on the deck or superstructure of the ship.

See *Shipper*.

Saltworker and *Salt*

Saltworkers probably availed themselves of the enormous deposits of salt in the Dead (Salt) Sea (Dt. 3:17) and the deposits of Jebel Usdum in the southwestern extremity of the Dead Sea. It is said that one hundred pounds of water from this sea can produce about twenty-five pounds of salt as compared to about six pounds from the Atlantic. Salt was obtained from the water by a process of evaporation. A residue of salt remained when the water placed in pans had evaporated.

Salt was also available in its natural or rock form and was usable without purification. The outer portion was usually discarded; inferior varieties were used as manure to the soil or as aids to speed the decomposition of dung (Matt. 5:13; Lk. 14:35). Another method of obtaining salt was from salt pits (Zeph.

2:9; 1 Mac. 11:35). To extract the salt from the pits, a bucket was lowered and the salt dissolved by water was drawn to the surface and evaporated by the sun. The residue was crystal salt.

In Palestine, under the Seleucidae, salt was a government monopoly (1 Mac. 10:29, 11:35) and provided important revenue to the rulers of the country (Jos. Ant. 13.4.9). Antiochus presented Jerusalem with a valuable gift of 375 bushels of salt for the Temple service (Ant. 12.3.3).

Salt was so valued because it was regarded as an almost indispensable commodity. Besides its daily use as a condiment in preparing food (Job 6:6) and its important role in sacrifices (Lev. 2:13), salt was widely used in other ways. The Mishnah 6:5 refers to its use in preserving fish and pickling olives and vegetables. It was also used for salting meat in accordance with dietary laws so as to drain the blood. A further use was as an antiseptic. Newborn infants were rubbed with salt (Ezek. 16:4), and salt was used to cure toothaches.

The extensive use of salt in offering sacrifices such as the sacred incense, the shewbread, and the animal and meal offerings was probably based on the belief that since salt was an essential element in man's diet, it should also serve as the "food of God," namely, for sacrifices (Lev. 21:8, 17).

In the priestly legislation, salt took on a symbolical meaning, a sign of permanence. Therefore, a covenant of salt (Num. 18:19) suggests perpetuity and an unbreakable alliance between friends (Lev. 2:13; 2 Chr. 13:5). Salt also represented desolation, barrenness and death (Dt. 29:23). Abimelech destroyed the city and sowed it with salt (Jg. 9:45), suggesting its complete dedication to God and forbidding its resettlement for all time.

Scale Maker

Since scales were extensively used in Biblical times, it is reasonable to deduce that some artisan specialized in making scales. The balances of the ancient Hebrews were similar to those used by the Egyptians, that is, a horizontal bar either pivoted on a perpendicular rod or suspended from a cord and held in the hand. At the ends of the bar were pans or hooks from which the objects weighed were suspended, occasionally in bags. One container held the object to be weighed while the other was the counterpoise or weight. Early weights were of stone (Dt. 25:13).

Weights were often faked by dishonest merchants, and the Bible sternly denounced these tricks, terming a "false balance an abomination of the Lord" (Pro. 11:1; Lev. 19:36; Am. 8:5, etc.).

See *Weigher, Weights and Measures Inspector.*

Scribe

Scribes were known in Sumer as early as 3000 B.C. By the middle of the third millennium, there are believed to have existed a number of schools where writing was formally taught. There were thousands of junior and senior scribes, royal and temple scribes, some of whom specialized in certain administrative duties. Throughout Sumer there were scribal schools which were originally established to provide for the needs of the temple, the palace, and the rich.

Scribes seem to have been maintained by the revenue received from tuition. Most of the students came from wealthy families and from urban communities. There do not seem to have been female students.

Among the Babylonians, scribes supervised the temple archives of sacred literature and served as royal secretaries, recording on clay tablets land boundaries and business transactions. Among the Egyptians, the scribes kept account of the contents of royal granaries, recorded the Nile flood tides, and wrote religious texts such as the *Book of the Dead* and wisdom writings. Their equipment, which is illustrated on wall reliefs near Memphis (2750–2652 B.C.), included a palette with a groove for reed brushes and two depressions for red and black ink.

In ancient Israel, the vocation of the scribe was highly regarded. His duties and employment varied. He worked as a public secretary transcribing legal contracts (Jer. 32:12), wrote letters, and kept accounts, usually from dictation (Jer. 36:26). The king's scribes (2 Chr. 24:11) were governmental officials attached to the royal household. The chief scribe functioned as secretary of state and as one of the royal counselors (1 Chr. 27:32; 2 Ki. 18:18; Isa. 36:3). Some scribes specialized in military duties, which included drawing up a list of those conscripted for war (Jg. 5:14) or a catalogue of the spoils.

The scribes both composed and edited such sacred books as Chronicles, Jubilees, the Aramaic Ahikar, the early Apocalypse, and expositions of original work of a semi-Biblical nature. In theology, they edited, fixed, and transmitted the Hebrew text in an authoritative manner. Beginning with Ezra, the scribes were also busy in reviving Hebrew, which had almost been forgotten during the Babylonian exile.

Senior scribes were assigned their own quarters in the palace (Jer. 36:12) or the temple (36:10). Their chief official was called "principal scribe of the host" (2 Ki. 25:19; Jer. 52:25). Whole families were often scribes (1 Chr. 2:55) and functioned in the manner of guilds.

In pre-exilic times, the scribe was often wealthy. He wore fine garments and his vocation was easily recognized by his pen case or inkhorn, which dangled from his girdle (Ezek. 9:2). His equipment consisted of reed pens (Jer. 8:8), a small knife for erasures and for cutting papyrus (Jer. 36:23), and occasionally styli for writing cuneiform. Papyrus is the pith of a plant, sliced and pressed into writing materials. A stylus is a hard pointed instrument for pressing cuneiform on clay.

A turning point in the development of the scribe was the Maccabean reaction against Hellenism when their vocation became even more important. The materialism of the aristocratic priesthood amid widespread poverty led the masses to lose confidence in the priests. The scribes identified themselves with the poor and opposed the aristocratic and materialistic priesthood. The study of the law was no longer limited to the wealthy (Neh. 8:9). Scribes recruited from the common folk, accustomed to menial labor, became the new religious leaders. They spurned payment for their religious labors, preferring to support themselves by pursuing humble vocations. Henceforth, the scribes played an enormous role in the perpetuation of Judaism, having assumed the religious functions formerly performed by aristocratic priests.

Amid difficult social and economic conditions, they sought to make Judaism viable. To achieve this, they served as preachers, lawyers, secretaries, magistrates, and scholars. They taught in the synagogue, in private homes, in the open air, and in the Temple. Moreover, they elaborated and codified traditional law and interpreted the written Torah. They gave Hebrew a more useful script known as *ketab ashuri* or uniform writing (Yer. Meg. 1.71b). They reached the common people and trained disciples in their own vocation. As for jurisprudence, the scribe supplied members to the Sanhedrin, the Supreme Court in Jerusalem, which formally ratified their interpretation as binding. They had the power to determine the legality of marriage and divorce. With the fall of Jerusalem, their judicial power waned.

In liturgy, they are credited with having instituted many prayers. Their revision of the Bible text is known as *tikkune soferim.* The dots above certain Hebrew words in the Bible are believed to be the original marks of the scribes.

One type of scribe transcribed the Pentateuchal Torah, the contents of phylacteries and mezuzoth. While writing Torah scrolls and other documents, the scribe exercised great care. His ink had to be black and indelible; the parchment had to be especially prepared from an animal permitted to the Jews as food. He traced and squared his lines so that his writing would be straight and uniform. The tracing was done with a ruler and style (Git. 6b) and the writing was done with a quill. When the Alexandrian scribes gilded the names of God in the Pentateuch, the rabbis forbade reading from such scrolls, preferring simplicity (Masseket Soferim, Shab. 103b).

Exactness in spelling, crowning certain letters, dotting others, and following prescribed regulations as to spacing for sections was mandatory. Rabbi Ishmael cautioned a *sofer,* "My son, be careful in thy work as it is a heavenly work, lest thou err in omitting or adding one iota and so cause destruction of the whole universe" (Er. 13a).

Before writing the names of God, he recited a prayer. An error in writing God's sacred name required discarding of the entire sheet; erasures were forbidden. If three or more errors were found on one page, the scroll was not to be used (Men. 29b), and even a loose sheet made the scroll unfit for public reading.

Another type of scribe was a notary public and court secretary. He specialized in preparing divorces and served as public notary and recording clerk in the court house. Later, he became the scribe of the community or recording secretary and notary for legal documents. His fees were individually negotiated and were paid only in lieu of the time he lost from his own personal activities. Generally, he was paid by the person who stood to gain the most by the transaction. Otherwise, his fee was paid by both parties (Hoshen Mishpat 13). His fees were apparently modest, since he usually also pursued other trades.

Sirach (Ecclus.) 38:24, 39:11 (*ca.* 180 B.C.) gives a description of the ideal scribe and his threefold aim: to seek (study) the Law of the Lord, to practice it, and to teach rules and duties in Israel (Ez. 7:10).

They counted among their ranks many noble persons such as Hillel, Shammai, and Gemaliel (Acts 22:3), who spoke against the persecuting zeal of the Sadducees (Acts 5:34). By the first century, they had made their way into the aristocratic society of the Sanhedrin (Acts 5).

The New Testament denunciation of the scribes and the Pharisees (Matt. 3) as a group has been found wanting by such scholars as G. F. Moore, R. Herford, and L. Finkelstein. In the New Testament, Jesus declared that many scribes had been scourged in synagogues, persecuted, crucified, and killed (Matt. 23:34). The scribes, along with the Pharisees, opposed Jesus because he occasionally violated their traditions (Matt. 7:29). Scribes are unfavorably portrayed in the New Testament because of their alleged role in the crucifixion (Mk. 14:43; Lk. 23:10) and because they sided with the rulers and elders against Peter,

John (Acts 4:5), and Stephen (Acts 6:12). However, Jesus, their severest critic, owned, "The scribes and Pharisees sit in the seat of Moses, so do whatever they tell you, obey them" (Matt. 23:2 ff.).

See *Accountant, Counselor, Historian, Judge, Lawyer, Letter Writer, Publisher, Priest, Teacher, Writing Materials Producer.*

Seal Maker

An essential art in ancient times dating back to about 3200 B.C. was seal making. The Mesopotamian seals, which look like small spools about four-fifths of an inch long and two-fifths of an inch in diameter, are engraved with religious symbols and scenes, social customs, pictures of trades, apparel, and animals. They include winged, human-headed lions, cherubs, horned snakes, lotus flowers, scenes of worship, seated gods, and birds.

Seals were used from the end of the fourth millennium B.C. to about 700 B.C. when the stamp type was found in Mesopotamia, though the Hittites and Palestinians always preferred stamp seals. These stamp seals were engraved in hard semiprecious stones which were thought to possess magical properties: silicate, hematite, carnelian, crystal, chalcedony, copper coated with silver, gold and silver jasper, limonite, magnetite, steatite, and glazed clay.

The early Hebrews appear to have developed this art to a high degree (Ex. 28–29). The engravers in Biblical times were able to cut letters, figures, etc., on stone, wood, and metal. They developed what became known as glyptic art or the art of engraving on hard and fine stones. The engraver along with Bezaleel (Ex. 31:1) was believed to be endowed with a divine spirit of wisdom and understanding. Seal engravers were deemed so essential in ancient times that they were exempt from military service.

The instruments employed by the engraver were *ayt barzel*, an iron style tipped with a diamond point (Jer. 17:1), and *heret*, a graving tool to make incisions (Ex. 32:4). Most seals were engraved by an experienced seal cutter who employed copper gravers, a cutting wheel, and, occasionally, a small bow drill to work semiprecious stones. Engravers apparently made both relief engraving such as the cherubs, and intaglio engraving for gems and signet rings. From Job 19:24, it is inferred that along with an "iron pen," lead was used for inscriptions. Though the Decalogue forbade the reproduction of human beings or animals, it was permitted to produce relief work for objects used in sacerdotal service. Engravers became so large and influential a group that they established their own guilds for mutual benefits.

Seals were the sign of authority used to affix what was the equivalent of written signatures to documents. An example was the written document of Nehemiah, which was sealed in the presence of many princes, priests, and Levites (9:38; 10:21). Because seals could be passed around among deputies, they were superior to signatures.

As early as the patriarchal period in Palestine, men like Judah wore their personal seals on a cord or about their wrists. Tamar asked her father-in-law a pledge in the form of his signet and his cord (Gen. 38:18). The first Biblical reference to a seal is the ring, his scarab seal, which Pharaoh gave to Joseph (Gen. 41:42). The seals were pierced longitudinally so that they could be worn easily (Jer. 22:24), or on a pin which could be attached to a dress. The scarab seals were set in a ring to be worn either on the hand or on the arm (Est. 3:12).

Israel's seals, unlike those of other nations, bore symbols but no images. They were used as ornaments and as protection for bales, jars, wine, olive oil, and for tombs. The Hebrew signets were seal stamps, not cylinders (Hag. 2:20–23; Jer. 22:24). We know that in the ninth century Jezebel wrote letters in Ahab's name and sealed them with his seal (1 Ki. 21:8). The book of Esther records that King Ahasuerus signed his documents with the king's ring and that its contents were irrevocable (3:12, 8:2, 10). The seal of Darius shows him in his chariot between two date palms with bow and arrow aimed at a lion.

To seal jars, a stopper was placed in the mouth of the jar and tied in place with cord or linen bands. It was then covered with a lump of clay upon which an inspector's cylinder seal was rolled or a stamp seal pressed down. Then the jar top was covered with plaster and stamped with the royal seal. The same process of sealing was followed with bales (Job 14:17).

In the Apocrypha, the redeemed are described as having seals stamped on their foreheads (Rev. 7:3). The "Book of the Lamb" was sealed with seven seals which no man could break open until the lamb opened them (Rev. 6:1, 8:6). Solomon's seal is more commonly known as the Star of David, the most popular symbol today.

Many seals survive in various museums and libraries throughout the world. Since many seals give the name of their owner and overlord, as well as occasionally his occupation, they shed considerable light on their period.

See *Artist, Ivory Carver, Jeweler.*

Servant

Among the ancient Hebrews, there were two kinds of servants: Hebrew and non-Hebrew. All slaves were servants but not all servants were slaves. There was the *sahir,* the worker who was paid at the end of the day.

The Jewish master was enjoined not to treat his Hebrew servant harshly (Lev. 25:43). This was later interpreted by the rabbis to mean that he was not to be assigned to perform needless duties simply to keep him in line. If practicable, Maimonides later declared, the servant should be assigned to the same work which he had performed as a freeman. A master who discharged a servant could not send him away empty-handed but had to give him a gift. Rabbinical law declared that the master of a Hebrew manservant or maidservant must place him on an equal basis, provide him with food and drink, lodging and bedclothes, and treat him in a brotherly manner since Scriptures refers to him as "thy brother." Consequently, the Talmud (Kid. 20a) stated, "whoever buys a Hebrew servant buys a master for himself." The Ten Commandments declare that all domestics are to be allowed to rest on the Sabbath (Ex. 20:10).

When a maidservant reached puberty, her master usually either married her or betrothed her to his son. In either case, she was treated as any free Jewish woman. The master could not sell her later to an outsider either as a worker or a wife (Ex. 21:7–11).

As for the non-Hebrew servants, some were strangers either bought or captured during war. They were either kept by their masters, sold, or exchanged (Lev. 25:44). When the Bible refers to real slaves rather than servants, the English versions usually state "bondman" for the Hebrew *ebed* and "bondwoman" for *shifhah.*

The word "servant" is also employed in the Bible in the sense of a disciple. Thus, Joshua was the servant of Moses, Elisha of Elijah, Gehazi of Elisha, and the apostles were the servants of Jesus. A further meaning of servant is as the subject of a ruler and as a mere domestic (2 Sam. 11:11; 1 Chr. 21:3). Finally, all creatures are *servants of God* (Ps. 119:65). Moses is the *servant of God* (Dt. 34:5). Such *servants* are those who are faithful and godly. Royal examples were Cyrus, who was called the *servant of God, His shepherd and anointed* (Isa. 44:28), and Nebuchadnezzar, who was similarly described (Jer. 25:9). "Servant" was also a pejorative term referring to ignoble persons (Eccl. 10:7; Jn. 8:34).

See *Armor-Bearer, Bodyguard, Cupbearer, Doorkeeper, Eunuch, Nursemaid, Overseer, Runner, Slave, Taskmaster, Waiter, Wine Steward,* APPENDIX III AND APPENDIX IV.

Sharecropper

In Genesis 47:19–26 we have a clear picture of the practice of sharecropping. The Egyptians are described as having sold their land to Pharaoh and becoming sharecroppers. They planted, cultivated, and harvested their crops, one-fifth of which went to Pharaoh, who provided the seed.

See *Farmer.*

Sheepshearer

Sheepshearing is an occupation dating back to the time when man first learned to use the wool of sheep. Sheepshearing (Gen. 38:12, 31:19; 1 Sam. 25:2; 2 Sam. 13:24) was performed in shearing houses (2 Ki. 10:12, 14) after the spring lambing season (Isa. 53:7; Acts 8:32). The firstlings of the flocks were considered sacred to God and were not to be shorn (Dt. 15:19). Sheepshearing time was a gala occasion when friends came to participate in the offering of new wool (Dt. 18:4) and to eat the communal meal. A substantial income was derived from the shorn wool in addition to the articles of clothing made from it for the use of the family.

See *Shepherd.*

Shepherd

This was one of the oldest and most important occupations among the ancient Hebrews, and there are many references to it in Scriptures. There were two kinds of shepherds: nomads who, after their flocks had thoroughly grazed one area, led them elsewhere, and shepherds who lived in villages such as the shepherd's village, Beit Sahur, below Bethlehem (Lk. 2:8–20). The Hebrew patriarchs were nomad chiefs who, with their retinue, led their flocks from Ur around the Fertile Crescent into Canaan or down to Egypt and then returned to Palestine.

The duties of the shepherd were manifold and often demanding. He was often exposed to frosty and inclement weather, and his hours were very long. He was required to protect his flock from the cold, from predatory animals, and from robbers (Am. 3:12). Each morning and evening, he counted his flock (Jer. 33:13; Ezek. 20:37), since he had to make restitution for missing animals (Gen. 31:39; Ezek. 34:8; Matt. 18:12). His only protection against thieves and wild animals were his staff and sling (1 Sam. 17:40), although later he also used dogs (Job 30:1). Sometimes he carried a thick club about three feet long, studded with metal, which he used on attackers of his flock. He often drew water for his sheep or other livestock (Gen. 24:20, 29:8–10). He sheared the wool, which was used not only to make domestic clothing, but also to export in bulk and as manufactured goods. He probably also aided in lambing.

During the summer, the flocks remained outdoors at night, and the shepherd slept beside them, waking at intervals to see that all were safe (Nah. 3:18). During inclement weather, he slept in a tent (Isa. 38:12) or in a special tower (Gen. 35:21). Some shepherds gathered their flocks in caves (1 Sam. 24:3) or in sheepfolds built of stones (Jg. 5:16; Zeph. 2:6).

His clothing consisted of a rough whole animal skin with the wool retained (Matt. 7:15), which he also slept in (Jer. 43:12). Later, for additional protection, he added an undertunic or outer mantle or cloak, often a seamless garment. These garments, usually woven with gray and black stripes by his wife or daughter, were long-lasting. He also wore a fabric girdle with folds in which he placed his money and pebbles that he threw at sheep when he sought to draw their attention. He commonly wore a veil, which was a yard-square piece of material folded into a triangle and kept in place by a black ring of twisted goat's hair.

The ancient shepherd had long hair and a beard. He normally

carried a bag with several days' supply of food consisting of bread, cheese, olives, and dried raisins.

During the afternoon, when he was able to relax, he either stretched out or whiled away his time playing his reed pipe. He was usually devoted to his flocks and at times was even willing to sacrifice his life to save them (Jn. 10:11). His integrity is mentioned in Psalms 78:70–72, and, symbolic of this quality, the prophets reminded the kings that they were shepherds of their subjects (Jer. 23:4, 25:34; Ezek. 34:2; Zec. 10:2).

The Bible required that the shepherd as well as others show kindness toward animals by, among other considerations, allowing them to rest on the Sabbath (Ex. 20:10, 23:12; Dt. 5:14). During the Sabbatical year, they were allowed to wander through the fields feeding on the products that grew spontaneously (Lev. 25:7; Ex. 23:11). Castration of animals or cohabitation with them was forbidden (Lev. 18:23).

Though shepherds were often praised for faithfulness and integrity, the attitude toward them varied at different times from high esteem to disdain. Examples of the former are the revered Moses who, from being a shepherd employed by his father-in-law, rose to the leadership of his people; and David, who was also a shepherd and advanced to the throne. In the Old Testament God is depicted as the faithful shepherd (Ps. 23:1) of His people. In the New Testament (Jn. 10:11; 1 Pet. 2:25) Jesus is called a shepherd. Similarly, religious ministers (Jer. 3:15; Eph. 4:11) and civil and political rulers are called pastors or shepherds (Jer. 12:10, 25:35).

Shepherds were looked down upon (Ex. 2:17) for, among other reasons, neglecting their duty (Nah. 3:16; Isa. 56:11). Such faithless shepherds were sharply denounced in Ezekiel 34; Jeremiah 23:1–4, 25:32–38. As agriculture advanced, the status of the shepherd continued to decline.

In the Talmud, too, the rabbis disapproved of shepherds because many were guilty of grazing their flocks on other persons' property. Consequently, they viewed them as dishonest and uncouth (Sanh. 25a).

See *Cattleman, Sheepshearer.*

Shipbuilder and *Ships*

Egypt and Mesopotamia engaged in maritime traffic as far back as 4000 B.C. when the Egyptian boats were mere wooden dugouts. There were boatbuilders in prehistoric Egypt who bound bundles of papyrus reeds together to make boats with upturned prows. Isaiah 18:2 speaks of bulrush boats. Some Egyptian ships were one hundred feet long, had eight-foot cabins, were sheltered by awnings, and were propelled by sixty oarsmen. These boats were used to trade in the Aegean Islands for gold and obsidian.

Boatbuilders built sailboats that were used in lively maritime commerce between Egypt and Phoenician Byblos. These boats unloaded Nile reeds for the papyrus papermaking of the Phoenician coast.

Ship carpenters also built flat-bottomed Nile boats which carried heavy stone for obelisks and temples while the Hebrews were in Egypt. Round boats were made of bitumen-calked basketwork. By 2130 B.C. Egyptian shipbuilders were building ships 180 feet long with sixty-foot beams. They had single masts with a crow's nest at the top and a large rectangular sail. The pilot stood on the prow holding a long sounding pole. By the Amarna period (1490–1437 B.C.), the Egyptian carpenters were building large sailing vessels with center keels.

Solomon built his own port on the Gulf of Aqaba where, with the aid of the Phoenicians, he also built his large, seagoing vessels, the "ships of Tarshish" (1 Ki. 9:26–28; Ezek. 27:25). Some believe that Solomon's ships used thirty to sixty double-banked oars. These early merchant ships had rounded bows while warships had long, protruding bows. Another common Phoenician type of boat was the *hippos* with a carved wooden horse's head at the prow, though this is not mentioned in the Bible. The Assyrians, too, had seacraft dating from about 721 B.C. (Sargon II). Their ships featured high, horse-headed prows of carved wood, and lofty sterns. They were propelled by both oars and by sails which could be attached to the center mast that was crowned with a crow's nest.

Although the Bible mentions ships, it does not clearly distinguish what kind they were. *Oniya* is mentioned (Jon. 1:3) but without specification. The *sefinah* was a large vessel with a deck (Jon. 1:5) manned by sailors and headed by a pilot (Jon 1:6). *Onishayit* (Isa. 33:21) could be either a small or a large ship manned by many oarsmen (Ezek. 28:8). The *abara* (2 Sam. 19:18) may have been a ferry or a flat-bottomed skiff.

Ships built for the Sea of Galilee were generally small and were used mainly for fishing (Matt. 4:21; Mk. 1:10; Jn. 21:3), although they were used for transport as well (Matt. 8:23). Ships sailing the Mediterranean were usually between fifteen and seventy-five tons and had sails, but they frequently carried up to twenty oars for emergencies. However, a large merchant ship is said to have carried Paul to Rome (Acts 27:41), and Josephus mentions traveling on a ship carrying six hundred passengers (Vita 3).

In New Testament times, the bows of ships were swept up to a carved or painted figure to represent the name of the ship (Acts 28:11); and, on the raised stern sculptured into a swan-neck shape, was a statue of the patron god of the vessel's home port. In the stern were two large oars that served as rudders. The anchors were also made of wood, with lead arms on which small marker buoys were attached.

A relief in the Vatican is believed to represent one of the ships used by Agrippa in the Battle of Actium, 31 B.C. It shows part of a bireme (two banks of oars), though craft with as many as five banks are known to have existed. The bireme had eighteen oars on each side and is estimated to have had 108 rowers, 25 mariners, and 80 soldiers, making a total crew of 213. It had three levels of fighting men, an outside gangway, a main deck, and raised platforms. It was about 103 feet long with a seventeen-foot beam, had a cargo weight of about 61,770 pounds, and a displacement of eighty-one tons.

Each vessel carried at least three anchors. When the ship was in port, several of these anchors would be lowered from the bows with moving cables from the stern attached to the shore. Because of severe winter storms common from mid-November to mid-February, ships were usually dismasted and put in dry-dock (Acts 28:11).

Probably a master ship's carpenter laid out the design of a ship, and he and his assistants used such tools as planes, saws, scrapers, hammers, nails, and so forth. Shipbuilders were highly skilled persons who probably acquired their skills through apprenticeships. While many of the workers were slaves or convict labor, the masters were probably well paid for their services.

See *Sailmaker, Shipper.*

Shipper and *Shipping*

In antiquity, the Mediterranean and the northern part of the Indian Ocean were the scenes of the most intensive maritime activity. Navigation in the Red Sea, the Persian Gulf, and the Indian Ocean is believed to have originated before 3000 B.C. Egyptian annals from about 2650 B.C. reveal the existence of boats over 170 feet long with sixty-foot beams. Cretans also developed extensive commerce including trade with Egypt, Syria, and Greece. Following their decline in power in 1400 B.C., the Phoenicians rose to prominence. Inhabiting the coastal regions of Lebanon, they naturally engaged in Mediterranean trade. The Phoenician merchants exported luxury goods to Greece and to the west from about 1100 B.C. to 700 B.C. Their ships roamed the Mediterranean and they established a chain of trading posts and colonies from the Levant to the Straits of Gibraltar.

During Bible times the Jews were not a seafaring people. They had few ports since their coastline was occupied by the Phoenicians and the Philistines. The seacoast of Palestine south of Mount Carmel was very poor in natural harbors and even their interior waterway, the Jordan River, was unsuited for maritime commerce because of its quick descent and many rapids.

The tribes of Zebulun (Gen. 49:13; Jg. 5:18) and Issachar fronted the Mediterranean (Dt. 33:19), as did for a while Dan and Asher. They may have sailed the Mediterranean, but there is no record of their having engaged in active trade. The Hebrews were not active in maritime commerce prior to Solomon, but because of their relationship with the Phoenicians, they knew about ships and shipping.

It was only in Solomon's reign that the Jews engaged in shipping from the Gulf of Aqaba. With the aid of Hiram of Tyre, to whom he exported wheat and oil (1 Ki. 5:11), Solomon built a fleet of ships at Ezion-geber (1 Ki. 9:26; 2 Chr. 8:17–18). Once every three years they brought back gold, silver, ivory, apes, and peacocks (1 Ki. 10:22) from distant lands. When the Jews concluded a commercial treaty with Hiram (2 Sam. 5:11), the Phoenicians floated cedar logs down the rivers from the Lebanon mountains and along the coast to Joppa. This route was also used when the supplies for the Second Temple were transported (Ez. 3:7).

During the second century B.C. Simon Maccabeus (1 Mac. 14:5) developed Joppa as a port to receive large vessels.

After Solomon, Israel's maritime trade apparently halted. During Jehoshaphat's reign an effort was made to reactivate the trade in Ophir gold somewhere in Somaliland by using the "ships of Tarshish," but they were wrecked at Ezion-geber (1 Ki. 22:48). These ships were large ocean-going vessels capable of carrying substantial cargo (Ezek. 27:25). Ezekiel describes this commerce of Tyre which included wood, ivory, fine linen with embroidered work, blue and purple dyes, silver, gold, iron, tin, lead, copper, chamois, ebony, balm, wine, silken goods, cassia, calamus, emeralds, coral, rubies, wheat, balsam, honey, and oil. Animals traded included lambs, castrated rams, and he-goats. Other items were spices, ornamental wares, blue cloaks, and chests of damask cloth. After Tyre fell to Alexander in 332 B.C., its commerce was dwarfed by that of Alexandria, Corinth, Ephesus, and Rome. All of these ports became the main trading centers during the Hellenistic period. Caesarea also became a famous port (Acts 18:22).

In the New Testament we read of Paul sailing on a large

merchant ship (Acts 27:41). From the wreckage of a ship found near the Riviera, we learn much concerning the cargoes of ships during the first century B.C., which may have been characteristic of earlier periods. The sunken vessel was over one hundred feet long and carried grain in bags as well as many other articles for export.

Freighters also carried passengers (Acts 27:37). Josephus asserted that he once sailed on a ship carrying six hundred passengers (Vita 3). Rates were about $1.20 from Athens to Alexandria with the passengers supplying their own food.

Shipwrecks were frequent in ancient times. Paul survived three before his trip to Rome (2 Cor. 11:25). Another hazard was pirates. Josephus refers to pirates during the time of Pompeii as well as during the period of the war with Rome (Ant. 14.3; B.J. 39). Nevertheless, a successful voyage could yield a large profit. The Talmud mentions a form of marine insurance (B.K. 116b).

See *Sailor*, APPENDIX I.

Shoemaker and *Shoes*

We do not know exactly when the craft of shoemaking began, but it clearly dates far back in history. Syrian and Mesopotamian monuments reveal that sandals were worn very early in Palestinian history. The earliest reference to footgear is the fourth millennium B.C. The Beni Hasan panel (early nineteenth century B.C.) shows an Asiatic group in Egypt with the men wearing soles fastened by ankle straps, while women are depicted wearing a low, brown boot which reaches above the ankle and is trimmed with a white band around the top. Egyptians wore their soles turned up at the toes like ice skates, while the Hebrews preferred rounded or pointed shapes. The Assyrian bootmakers made sandals with heelcaps, and for their warriors, laced boots (Isa. 5:27).

Terra cotta or clay shoes dating from about 900 B.C. were discovered in the Athenian agora. These shoes looked like modern snow boots with two eyelets at each side of the front openings provided for laces. The thickness of the sole suggests that they were designed for walking.

In antiquity, the main purpose of shoes was utilitarian. Cobblers made shoes to protect the wearer against cold, damp soil, hot sands, or sharp stones. Shoes were highly useful to the shepherd when he had to traverse rough terrain in tending his flock. Among the Hebrews, too, a shoe was mainly a sole of leather, or occasionally of wood, supported around the ankles by leather bands. Most shoes were made of leather. Later, wood was also used, but leather bands or strings were usually supplied with them (Matt. 3:11, 10:10). Still later, efforts were made to beautify women's shoes. These more elaborate shoes for women covered their entire feet (Cant. 7:1; Ezek. 16:10).

With increasing urbanization, the wearing of sandals became common and the work of the shoemaker increased. The wealthy also became more style-conscious, a fact which added to the income of the cobbler. In Talmudic times, shoemakers made sandals for summer use as well as for winter (B.B. 58a). For lime workers, they made wooden sandals since lime burned through leather (Eduy. 28).

The occupation of shoemaking was not considered demeaning in Talmudic times. The eminent Rabbi Johanan followed this vocation. In later times, however, it was generally pursued by the unlearned and held in low esteem.

Shoemakers used hand tools such as knives, shears, and awls and thread. They cut out parts of leather with shears and knife and sewed them together to form the uppers. Then they marked eyelets and punched them out. After they had assembled the last and attached it to a stand, they tacked the insole on the last and drew the upper over the last, tacking it into place, and trimmed it with a knife. When they had sewed on the welt, they sewed and hammered the outer sole to the lasted upper. Finally, they trimmed the edges of sole and heel with a knife.

The Biblical shoemaker also repaired shoes by restitching defective portions or by replacing worn portions with new leather (Jos. 9:5, 13).

Ordinary people generally went barefooted except when traveling (Jos. 9:5). It was also customary to go barefooted during periods of mourning (2 Sam. 15:30; Ezek. 24:17; Isa. 20:2) and on certain religious occasions. Moses removed his shoes during the theophany at the burning bush (Ex. 3:5). Shoes were also removed by priests during religious ceremonies at which they officiated and while they were present at shrines (Jos. 5:15; Acts 7:33). As the Hebrew entered his home, he removed his shoes. (1 Kings 23:8, 44). On the other hand, to be unsandaled meant to be dispossessed (Dt. 25:5–10; Ru. 4:7–8). When sandals were cast on someone's property, this action signified taking possession (Ps. 60:8, 108:9). Thus, when the ancient Hebrew bought property, he customarily removed his shoes and handed them to the seller as a symbolical expression of transference (Ru. 4:7). The shoe was also removed from the foot of the near kinsman who refused to marry the widow (Dt. 25:5–10; Ru. 4:7–8).

See *Clothier, Tanner.*

Silk Manufacturer

The silk industry is believed to have started in 2640 B.C. in China under the encouragement of Si Ling-chi, wife of Emperor Huang-ti. She is reported to have dedicated herself to the care of silkworms as well as to have invented the loom. Royal and noble families continued the activity but carefully guarded the secret of its manufacture.

Other references in Sanskrit literature suggest that the silk industry may have flourished as early as 4000 B.C. in India. From India, the silkworm was slowly carried westward to Persia, Khotan, and Central Asia.

Silk is a fibrous matter produced by many insects, mainly in the form of a cocoon or covering which encloses the creatures and protects them during the time of their main changes. The fibers essential for manufacturing purposes are made only by the Chinese mulberry silk moth and by a few other kindred moths. To get the raw silk, cocoons were steeped in warm water, causing the gum or glue which held the filaments together to soften. The continuous filaments were then unreeled by hand. The fine thread was sometimes one thousand yards long, although more usually it was five hundred yards long.

The juice of the mulberries is mentioned in 1 Maccabees 6:34, while in Ezekiel's oracle, silk (*meshe*) is mentioned as the clothing of the maiden: "I covered thee with silk" (16:10, 13). Silk was also an important article of Roman trade. Toward the end of the first century A.D., raw silk became worth its weight in gold. Silk weaving flourished during that period in Upper Galilee; the township of Gischala was famous for its fabricated silk, which was sold in the markets of Tyre.

See *Clothier, Dyer, Weaver.*

Slave and *Slavery*

Although references to slaves are found in many parts of the Bible, the economy of Biblical Palestine and ancient Mesopotamia was based on free labor. Slave labor was utilized mainly by royal and wealthy families. The slave was usually a domestic servant rather than an agricultural or industrial worker.

Laws regarding slaves are found in Exodus 21; Leviticus 25, and Deuteronomy 15. The only contemporary extra-Biblical reference to Jewish slavery in ancient times is the Aramaic papyri dating from the fifth century B.C. from the Jewish colony of Elephantine, Egypt.

Near Eastern Slavery

There is, however, much extra-Biblical evidence regarding slavery in the Near East, dating from the Ur-Namu code about

2500 B.C. to the beginning of the Christian era. In ancient times, commerce in slaves was important business. There was a lively traffic in exporting and importing slaves to and from various parts of Mesopotamia. There were also some foreign slaves imported into Palestine (Lev. 25:44–46). There were two laws dealing directly with the export of Hebrew slaves (Ex. 21:16; Dt. 24:7) in which the death penalty is ordered for the kidnaping and sale of free-born persons. The law in Deuteronomy 23:15–16 prohibits the extradition of fugitive slaves and probably refers to Hebrew slaves who fled from a foreign country seeking refuge in a new land.

Causes of Slavery

Indigent persons became slaves because of their inability to pay debts. Impoverished parents sometimes sold their children. References to this may be found in Exodus 21:7–11 and in Nehemiah 5:1–5, which refer to the sale of a young girl by her father.

A major factor leading to insolvency and subsequent slavery was the extortionate interest rate on loans. In Babylonia and Syria, the average rate was 20 to 25 per cent on silver and 33⅓ per cent on grain. Israelites were warned against charging interest to their coreligionists (Ex. 22:25; Lev. 25:35–36; Dt. 23:19–20).

The Palestinian creditor could seize his debtor and enslave him if he failed to meet his obligation. Some of David's followers in the cave of Adullam were defaulting debtors who fled their creditors (1 Sam. 22:2). In 2 Kings 4:1 a creditor is described as having seized the orphans of a debtor, whereupon his widow appealed to Elijah for aid. Another reference to an impoverished debtor is Isaiah 50:1.

Status of Slaves

In Biblical times, a slave was considered chattel who could be bought, sold, leased, exchanged, or inherited. Literally nameless, he was usually marked by a sign or a tag. In ancient Egypt, slaves were branded and stamped with the king's name. Privately owned slaves had their heads shaved, sometimes with pigtails left dangling.

The slave was not without rights; he could claim justice (Job 3:19) or go to law, but he could also be abandoned by an indifferent master such as the sick Egyptian who was spared by David (1 Sam. 30:11). Sometimes a childless master adopted a house slave (Gen. 15:3).

Biblical law required that if after his sixth year of servitude, a slave elected to remain with his master permanently, his ear was to be pierced with an awl (Ex. 21:6; Dt. 15:17), presumably as a stigma because he had rejected the freedom proffered him.

Female Slaves

Female slaves were also regarded as a commodity and were leased for work, given as a pledge, and handed over as a part of dowry. They were not only utilized for their physical capacities, but, by the male members of the master's household, for their sexual attractions and the highest status they could attain was that of childbearing concubines to their masters. They also bred slave children. The lowest status was to be used as professional prostitutes. They could not, however, be sold, which was also the law in the Hammurabi code.

Sources of Slaves

The supply of slaves was augmented by capture, especially prisoners of war (Gen. 14:12; Num. 31:9; Dt. 20:14), by purchase from other owners (Gen. 17:12; Eccl. 2:7; Ezek. 27:13; Jl. 3:4–8), by birth, such as those born to slave parents (Gen. 15:3; Jer. 2:14), as restitution, for if a thief could not pay his fine or damages, he was sold as a slave (Ex. 22:3), by self-sale to escape poverty (Lev. 25:39), through default on debts (2 Ki. 4:1; Neh. 5:5, 8), and by abduction (Gen. 37:27; Ex. 21:16; Dt. 24:7).

Types of Slavery

Two other types of slavery were state and temple slavery. State slavery was practiced on a limited scale. David subjected the conquered Ammonites to forced labor (2 Sam. 12:31) and Solomon drafted the descendants of the Canaanites into a state labor force (1 Ki. 9:15, 21–22) which served as burden bearers and quarriers (2 Chr. 2:18). Israelites, too, were among the drafted state laborers who served in Lebanon, but only on a rotating basis (1 Ki. 5:13).

As for temple slaves, after the war with Midian, Moses requested from the warriors and Israel "one in five hundred, and one in fifty" respectively of their booty both in persons as well as in material for service in the Tabernacle. The slaves served as menials in the Tabernacle (Num. 31:28, 30, 47). Later, the Gibeonites who were spared by Joshua were added to the number of menials and became "hewers of wood and drawers of water" (Jos. 9:3–27) for the house and altar of the Lord. David and his officers employed the Nethinim for similar menial service with the Levites in the Temple. Solomon's servants appear to have served on a similar basis (Ez. 2:58).

Price of Slaves

The price of slaves fluctuated but was always related to their sex, age, physical condition, appearance, and to the supply and demand. The average price rose steadily. The female slave of childbearing age was always considered more valuable than the male. The average price of a slave in the third millennium B.C. in Mesopotamia was 10 to 15 shekels while during the Persian Empire it rose to 90 to 120 shekels. Joseph was sold (about 1700 B.C.) for 20 shekels (Gen. 37:28), while in Assyrian times (about 725 B.C.) Israelites tried to pay the Assyrians 50 shekels each, their value as slaves, presumably to prevent their deportation to Assyria (2 Ki. 15:20).

In the Roman world of Jesus' time, slaves constituted a large portion of the average city population. Many were intellectuals who had fallen upon lean days. Jesus knew Roman slaves and ministered to them (Matt. 8:6).

Unlike classical Greece and imperial Rome, the economy of Israel was never based mainly or even largely on slave labor. This may partially account for the kinder spirit manifested in the Old Testament toward slaves than in classical literature. Moreover, the prevailing attitude toward the poor and underprivileged has always been markedly benevolent, and Job (31:13–15) anticipates the idea of the equality of men regardless of their economic situation.

See *Servant*, APPENDIX III and APPENDIX IV.

Snake Charmer

This ancient vocation reached its highest development in Egypt and India. The equipment usually consisted of a shrill pipe and a basket or bags in which a trained snake or snakes were kept. Some of the snakes were venomous while others were harmless. The dangerous snakes had their fangs extracted or their lower jaw sewn to the upper one with silk thread or silver wire. When the piper played a shrill air, as he still does, the snakes crawled out, coiled the tail end of their bodies, erected their heads and swayed back and forth. The charmer probably also wound some of the snakes around his body, arms, and legs. Sometimes, he grasped a serpent behind its head and bit pieces out of the head.

The Bible (Jer. 8:17; Ps. 58:4) refers to this vocation in the passage, "I will send serpents, cockatrices, among you which will not be charmed and they shall bite you."

See *Magician.*

Soldier

It is not known when the first professional soldier appeared, but it was probably some time after the rise of the city-states in Mesopotamia and Egypt, where there was a constant struggle for arable land and water rights. The use of fortifications and the development of city-states into kingdoms is believed to have led to armed forces.

Types of Military Forces

In the early history of the Fertile Crescent and Nile Valley, there were four types of military forces. Foremost was an elite corps of warriors who constituted the king's bodyguard and "ate before the king," in other words, those who were his close intimates. Second were the provincial troops who served outside the capital under a royal governor or prince. Third were the mercenaries who were sometimes slaves such as the Nubians who defended the first Pharaohs; sometimes they were freebooters such as the Philistines who were found in various armies in the ancient Near East. Fourth were the men from the ordinary population who, from earliest times, were drafted into service. While the men from this forced levy were often used for public works, in wartime they were pressed into service. They were lightly armed and, when not in combat, probably carried burdens, built earthworks during sieges, and buried the dead.

Early Weapons

There were also soldiers during the fourth millennium B.C. in Sumer who were regular members of the infantry. These men were armed with short spears and wore conical copper helmets and thick cloaks for body protection. Later, the Sumerian soldier carried a large rectangular shield and heavy pike and battle-ax. He also used the bow and javelin.

Ancient Recruitment

At the beginning of the second millennium B.C., we know from the code of Hammurabi, soldiers in the regular army were recruited from a military class and were granted hereditary land rights by the king. The middle class also had to serve in the armed forces as light-armed archers or as service groups. Eventually, they were able to purchase exemption from military service.

In Egypt, the soldiers were usually Nubians who were drafted to build huge monuments. Soldiers were the first free landowners. Then a standing army arose, recruited from the free middle class and called "citizens of the army." These fought with copper battle-axes and bows and used the quiver. Wings and center, flanking movements, recruit training, and the cadence step were introduced. During the thirteenth century B.C. the Egyptian army reached its highest level of organization.

Archers

The main military strength of Assyria during the ninth century B.C. was its archers and mounted lancers who fought from horseback without saddles. A corps of archers may have existed among the Hebrews. They were found among Israel's enemies, for Saul was wounded by Philistine archers on Mount Gilboa (1 Sam. 31:3; 1 Chr. 10:3). Uriah, the Hittite, was killed by Ammonite archers (2 Sam. 11:24) and King Josiah was slain by Egyptian archers (2 Chr. 35:23). The tribe of Joseph is also described as having been attacked by archers (Gen. 49:23).

The archer's weapons were bows and arrows (Gen. 21:20; Jer. 50:29). The arrow was a shaft made of reed or light wood, notched at one end with a head or tip either socketed or with a tong. Tips were made of bone, bronze, or flint and often had barbs or were dipped in poison to render them deadlier (Job 6:4). The bow was made of a strip of wood or of other elastic material with a cord to link the two ends. When the cord was bent, the arrow could be propelled. To improve their marksmanship, archers undoubtedly practiced shooting at targets.

From Israel's Irregulars to a Standing Army

There was no regular Israelite army before Saul. Previously, when an emergency arose, a leader of the clan or tribe would summon the able-bodied men who served as volunteers in the battle. Saul's standing army consisted of a corps of privately chosen permanent warriors.

David did likewise and increased his country's armed forces (2 Sam. 15:18). Whereas previously soldiers were forced to live off the land or were brought provisions by their families (1 Sam. 17:17–18) or clans (1 Sam. 25:18; 2 Sam. 17:27–29), with the establishment of a regular army during David's reign, a commissariat was established and the soldiers were paid regular wages (1 Ki. 4:27).

Military Morale

The majority of King David's forces consisted of Jewish soldiers, although he had some foreign mercenaries, mainly Philistines (2 Sam. 8:18). The Jewish soldiers were taught that they were engaged in a holy war that was solemnized by the support of priests and the cultus (Dt. 20:2–4). Since, as soldiers, they were also offering service to Yahweh, their activity took on a priestly quality. Before a decision to launch military actions occurred, priestly oracles were usually consulted and inquiry was made before the Ark (Jg. 20:27, 28), the ephod (1 Sam. 30:7–8), or the Urim and Thummim (1 Sam. 28:6). Priests and the Ark accompanied the army (Num. 4:5–15, 31:6; 2 Sam. 11:11). During the Maccabean wars, Jewish soldiers carried charms as protection (2 Mac. 12:10).

During Solomon's rule, levies were made to provide food for the "king and his household" (1 Ki. 4:7, 27–28). Soldiers also benefited from the booty, which was divided after victory by the precedent established in 1 Samuel 30:24 with special shares allotted to the officers (Jg. 8:24ff.).

Military Draft

There were military exemptions in Biblical times. Besides the priests (Num. 2:33), exempted were the fearful, those married less than one year, and those possessing newly purchased property which, if neglected, might cause severe economic loss (Dt. 20:1–9). Men were eligible for military service from the age of twenty (Num. 1:3; 1 Chr. 23:27) until their fiftieth year (Jos. Ant. 3.12.4). Soldiers were called to arms by messengers sent throughout the country (Jg. 6:35, 7:24) or by the sound of the shofar (Jg. 3:27; 1 Sam. 13:3). Later, during the monarchy, a trumpet was blown and a mast raised on a hill to rally the people (Isa. 5:26; Jer. 51:12).

Infantry and Cavalry

Infantry was the basic corps of the Jewish army throughout its history, and infantrymen are mentioned in a number of places (Jg. 20:2; 2 Sam. 8:4; 1 Chr. 18:4, 19:18). Solomon introduced cavalry (1 Ki. 4:26, 10:26), although it was cumbersome and impractical in the hilly terrain of Palestine. Later kings abandoned it. Shalmaneser II of Assyria, who fought against Ahab in 854 B.C., claimed that the latter had two thousand chariots. Hezekiah of Judah was taunted by an Assyrian official because he lacked war horses and riders (2 Ki. 18:23).

Mercenaries

Under the Hasmonaean rule, a regular army was formed, and the soldiers were paid for their services. Jews also served as mercenaries in the Syrian army (1 Mac. 10:36). According to Josephus (Ant. 13.8.4), Hyrcanus I was the first to maintain foreign mercenaries.

Fighting on the Sabbath

The Jewish soldier was seriously disadvantaged at the beginning of the Hasmonaean uprising against the Syrian-Greeks because of his refusal to carry arms on the Sabbath. After a number were ruthlessly slaughtered, the rabbis decreed that during defensive wars and especially during sieges, fighting on the Sabbath would be permitted (Shab. 19a).

Jewish Military Camp

The camp of the Hebrew soldier was probably in the shape of a circle or square (Num. 2); it was constantly guarded (Jg. 7:19). The entire camp was surrounded by a barricade (1 Sam. 17:20, 26:5), but during battles some forces remained behind to guard the base (1 Sam. 25:13). Camps were kept clean in deference to the "presence of God" (Dt. 23:14). The soldiers slept in tents or booths (2 Sam. 11:11).

Israel's Military Strategy and Tactics

The signal to attack or retreat came with a blast of the trumpet (2 Chr. 13:12). The first line of defense was a solid line of shield-bearing spearsmen, and in the rear were archers who carried a sword and buckler as well as their bows and arrows (1 Chr. 5:18). When the battle was joined, hand-to-hand combat followed.

Siege warfare was fought by cutting off the enemy's food and water supplies, and for this purpose chariots were used for mobility. Slingers, who constituted the light infantry (2 Chr. 26:14), were also used, as well as equipment to catapult fire (Jos. 8:8). Military tactics included sieges, ambushes (Jg. 9:34–45, 20:29), raids (1 Sam. 14), and surprise night attacks (2 Sam. 4:7). As throughout history, wars were fought for plunder, captives, and territorial expansion.

War in antiquity was very brutal. Cities, temples, and homes were often burnt to the ground, and soldiers frequently slew captured kings and leaders and mutilated or enslaved the males

(1 Ki. 11:15; Jg. 1:6; Dt. 20:11). Women and children were taken as spoils of war. Pregnant women were disemboweled (2 Ki. 8:12, 15:10; Am. 1:13), and infants were dashed to pieces (Ps. 137:9). Survivors were fortunate to be deported (2 Ki. 17:6).

See *Armor-Bearer, Armorer, Captain, Charioteer, Quartermaster, Spy.*

Spice Dealer and *Spices*

A significant number of Levites, priests, and others were engaged in growing, obtaining, blending, and selling spices that occupied an important role in the ancient world (Ex. 30). First, spices were essential for sacrifices. The use of many spices in the Temple service for the holy anointing oil and the fragrant incense is mentioned in Exodus 30:23–24. Spices were also used in cosmetics (Est. 2:12) and in preparing corpses for burial as in the interments of King Asa (2 Chr. 16:14) and Jesus (Mk. 16:1; Lk. 23:56, 24:1; Jn. 19:40).

Among the spices used for religious, cosmetic, and other purposes were aloes, balm, calamus, cane, cassia, cinnamon, dill, frankincense, galbanum, gum, henna, myrrh, nard, saffron, and stacte. Spices used in the preparation of food and in the flavoring of wine were cinnamon, cumin, dill, and mint (Ezek. 24:10; Cant. 8:2).

Because of their rarity, spices were very costly in antiquity. They were prized as gifts and were among the expensive gifts Solomon received from the Queen of Sheba (1 Ki. 10:2, 10; 2 Chr. 9:9). Much wealth accrued to the land of Sheba through its control of the spice trade route across southern Arabia.

Solomon had spice gardens near Jericho, and Hezekiah later revealed his store of spices to the envoys of Merodach-baladan of Babylon (2 Ki. 20:13; Isa. 39:2). Alexandria was the center of the spice trade, and spice was also exported from Rhodes. Because it was so essential and lucrative a commodity, it was a royal monopoly and was supervised by an official to whom all spices entering Egypt had to be delivered.

One especially prized spice was frankincense, which was burnt on Jewish, Greek, and barbarian altars. Grown in the coastal district of south Arabia, its trees were considered sacred and only men of selected families were allowed to tap them. This tapping was performed with religious rites since they were drawing the lifeblood of a divine creature. To appease the trees during tapping, styrax incense was burnt to them as to gods. When the factory workers who handled frankincense in Alexandria left the plant at the end of their workday, they were stripped and searched lest they had secreted the precious material on their persons. When the commodity reached the Aegean, it brought per pound about a week's salary of a skilled worker (W. W. Tarn, *Hellenistic Civilization*, pp. 260–261).

See *Apothecary, Merchant,* APPENDIX I.

Spinner and *Spinning*

Spinning was known among the early Egyptians and was practiced by both men and women. Among the Hebrews, however, it was solely a woman's occupation (Ex. 35:25). Spinning is the production of yarn from short fibers by means of the spindle or distaff (Pro. 31:19). This is a wooden shank about a foot long hooked at one end to hold the yarn. The rotating spindle is speeded by a disk or shaft of stone, clay, or other heavy material on the shank. The fingers and the thumb of the right hand operate the spindle, while the left hand holds the distaff on which the unspun fibers are wound. The spun yarn is wound around the spindle shank. Yarn was thus produced in linen and wool (Lev. 13:47) and in byssus, a fine Egyptian linen (Pro. 31:22), in goats' hair (Ex. 35:26) and in camels' hair (Matt. 3:4).

See *Weaver*.

Spy

In early times, rulers who felt threatened by surrounding peoples or who had designs on other territories employed intelligence agents for reconnaissance. The agents were expected to provide essentially the same kind of information which their modern counterparts seek—the enemy's strengths and weaknesses (Gen. 42:9, 12). Moses dispatched twelve spies to the Negev and hill country to report on the terrain, its fortifications and inhabitants, and on the fertility of the soil (Num. 13:17–20). Later, Joshua sent two men on reconnaissance to Jericho who would have been apprehended by the king's officers had they not been concealed by Rahab the harlot (Jos. 2).

Another function of spies was to spread rumors designed to undermine the enemy's morale. This occurred during Absalom's revolt (2 Sam. 15:10). In the New Testament, two references to spies are to those sent by Jesus' enemies, the scribes and the high priest (Lk. 20:20), and praise to Rahab for receiving the spies (Heb. 11:31).

Though the Bible gives no information about the training of spies they were undoubtedly given some instructions.

See *Soldier.*

Stableman

There are references to horses in the Bible which clearly imply the existence of stablemen. Egypt had horses from the eighteenth dynasty onward (Gen. 47:17, 49:17; Ex. 14:9). Horses were used with chariots (Ps. 76:6), by the cavalry (Pro. 21:31), and by other horsemen. David (2 Sam. 8:4) and Solomon (1 Ki. 4:26, 22:4) had chariots that required stablemen.

The stableman watered and fed the horses while they were in stables. He groomed, brushed, curried, washed the horses and trimmed their manes and tails. He swept refuse and old bedding from the stalls and spread fresh bedding and straw.

See *Charioteer, Driver, Harness Maker, Horse Breeder, Saddle Maker.*

Stevedore

There are references in the Bible implying the presence of stevedores. We know also from other sources that they were found at various ports in Biblical times. They loaded and unloaded cargo to facilitate transfer to and from ships. They also carried cargo to the ships' holds and stacked it so as to prevent shifting during the voyage (Ezek. 27:25; 1 Chr. 9:21; Jon. 1:5; Acts 27).

Stevedores worked at Tyre, Gebal, and elsewhere, as well as at Rome. The Talmud reports (Sot. 48a) that stevedores sang while they worked.

Steward

Stewards were officials who supervised the affairs of royal and wealthy households. Eleazar of Damascus held this position in the employ of Abraham (Gen. 15:2), and Joseph under Potiphar. Among the kings of Israel, there were stewards over their palace affairs (1 Ki. 15:18; 1 Chr. 27:31; Isa. 22:15).

In the New Testament the stewards are all Christians who are referred to as "stewards of God's mysteries," while bishops are described as "stewards of the affairs of God" (Tit. 1:7;

1 Cor. 4:1). One steward was a royal treasurer (Acts 8:27). The ruler at the wedding party in Cana was a steward (Jn. 2:8–9), as was the master of the vineyard (Matt. 20:8). Chuza is mentioned as Herod's steward (Lk. 8:3).

The duties of the steward were probably broad. He was in charge of the servants, ran the finances, supervised the preparation of the meals for the family, and in general served as a major-domo.

See *Cupbearer, Paymaster, Wine Steward*

Stoneworker

Stoneworkers quarried stones in remote antiquity from which were built palaces, shrines, roads, walls, cisterns, idols, and homes. The evidence of quarries in ancient times are the stripped caves east and west of the Jordan. The marks left by masons using picks, as well as extant wall decorations and inscriptions, are further proof. There may also be a reference to quarries in Judges 3:19, 26.

Solomon's quarry is a huge cavern adjacent to the Dome of the Rock. The former Temple area, whose mouth is 350 feet across, may have supplied stone for Herod's Temple, which was snow-white. Some of its stones are still in position (1 Ki. 6:7). There are other quarries near Zarephath or the modern Sarafand (1 Ki. 17:9 ff.), close to Sidon, and at Caesarea.

Marble Worker

While the purest form of marble is white, there are also many colored varieties. Marble was one of the materials that David prepared for the Temple (1 Chr. 29:2). Josephus asserts that Solomon's Temple was built from the Lebanon quarry although surviving stones from the Wailing Wall seem to derive from the neighborhood of Jerusalem. Masons who built the Jerusalem Temple are said to have been paid in cash. Additional references to marble are Song of Solomon 5:15 and in Revelation 18:12 to the merchandise of Babylon.

Stone Carver

Stone carvers were ancient letterers who employed chisels and square blades to chisel into stone laws, decrees, notices, treaties, honors conferred on certain persons, and other facts they were instructed to memorialize. Early inscriptions were usually the work of amateurs and were cut unevenly. Later, however, professional carvers took over, and their work reveals definite styles, methods, and different places and periods. In Egypt, hieroglyphics were delicately wrought but later became less finished. In Greece, the best lettering occurred during the fifth and fourth centuries B.C. when strokes were made with equal thickness. In Egypt, inscriptions were inscribed or painted on the inner walls of tombs and were intended for the dead rather than for the living. Inscriptions designed for the attention of the public at large were prominently displayed on temple walls or within its precincts. The signature of the artists was usually found only on potters' lamps and on other vessels.

Stonecutter

The Biblical stonecutter, *harash* (1 Chr. 22:15), either quarried or cut stone for buildings. Solomon had eighty thousand such workers quarrying stone for the Temple (1 Ki. 5:15). In New Babylonian times (*ca.* 600 B.C.) when stonecutters who were working on a Temple building project had not been paid for several months, they refused to continue working and called one of the first known strikes.

See *Marble Setter, Mason.*

Surveyor

Surveyors were active in Biblical times surveying the land's contours and supervising workers engaged in determining the exact location and measurement points, elevations, and lines for construction purposes.

The Biblical surveyor first surveyed with a measuring line consisting of a rope or cord (Jer. 31:39; Zec. 2:1), a string (1 Ki. 7:15), or twisted linen thread (Ezek. 40:3) marked in cubits (1 Ki. 7:15, 23). During Hellenistic times, a reed rod marked in furlongs was used (Rev. 11:1, 21:15). The site was marked by more than one line (2 Sam. 8:2), and the survey was noted in plan and in writing. The progress of the building was checked by the surveyor or chief of construction, who used a plumb line or cord weighted with lead or tin (Am. 7:7–8), a stone (Zec. 4:10), or a plummet (2 Ki. 21:13) to test the structure.

The work of the surveyor was considered a symbol of God's judgment (Jer. 31:39).

See *Architect, Mason.*

Synagogue Functionary

The origin of the synagogue is obscure, but it is generally believed to have arisen among the Hebrew exiles in Babylonia. Gatherings for worship occurred in the house of Ezekiel (8:1, 20:1–3) and these may be the origins of the synagogue. The closing century of the Persian rule, 430–330 B.C., is considered the period of the rise and development of the synagogue. The only mention of the synagogue in the Bible is Psalms 74:8.

During the religious reforms instituted by Ezra and Nehemiah, the Law of Moses became the norm of faith, and systematic instruction in the Torah became common (Neh. 8:7).

The synagogue in a Jewish town was also a court of Justice, a school, and a place of assembly, but it had no regular minister. An official was appointed as *ruler* of the synagogue, responsible for its physical care (Mk. 5:22; Lk. 8:41).

Rosh Hakenesset was the highest officer of the synagogue. Initially, he was the highest officer of the assemblies and was responsible for maintaining order during the meetings as well as for eliminating disturbances (Lk. 4:20). He distributed the honors, such as calling persons up for the reading of the Torah on Mondays, Thursdays, Sabbaths, and Holy Days (Acts 13:15; M. Sot. 7:7–8). Formerly, he read the entire prescribed Scriptural portion alone. It is believed that he later became the head of the synagogue building, jointly administering it with the head of the council of the community. He could be elected annually or for life.

Hazzan—minister, servant, or officer—is mentioned in Luke 1:2 and in Acts 13:5. Earlier rabbinical sources cite the *hazzan* as assistant to the archsynagogos or *Rosh Hakenesset*. He removed the Torah from the ark during services and handed it over to the archsynagogos, who handed it to the captain or to the high priest or to the king (Sot. 7.7.8). He also handed the Torah and the prophetic scroll to the reader (Lk. 4:20) and received them after they were read. He summoned the priests to pronounce the benediction (Sifre Num. 39) and accompanied the archsynagogos at funerals and mourning feasts, reciting eulogies or benedictions. He was in charge of the Temple utensils and aided the priests to disrobe (Tamid v.3; Yoma 7:1). Later, he also taught children reading and other skills (Yeb. 13a).

Earlier sources describe the *hazzan* as accompanying members of the synagogue in their processions when they brought the firstlings to Jerusalem (Tos. Bik. 11:8). He was a reader and an officer of the law court who carried out the sentence of scourging (M. Mak. 3:12). Early Friday afternoon before sunset, he announced the approach of the Sabbath from the roof of the synagogue by blowing the shofar (ram's horn) thrice as a signal to discontinue work (Tos. Suk. 4:199). This practice still continues in Jerusalem.

See *Priest, Rabbi.*

Tanner and *Tanning*

Leatherworkers or tanners were common in Biblical Palestine. They were engaged in converting hides of animals such as goats, sheep, camels, and calves into leather for a wide variety of articles, including such items as leather containers for water (Gen. 21:14), milk (Jg. 4:19), wine (Matt. 9:17ff.), and oil. For such containers, entire hides of small animals were used.

Tanners also prepared leather for footwear (Ezek. 16:10) and for military articles such as shields, helmets, girdles, chariot fittings, quivers, and slings (Gen. 3:21; Lev. 13:48; 2 Ki. 1:8; 2 Sam. 1:21; Mk. 1:6). There were also leather coverings for the Tabernacle (Ex. 26:14) and for its furnishings (Num. 4:6). Treated leather served as parchment for writing materials. It is also believed that, as in Assyria and Egypt, the Palestinian tanner used fine leather for beds, chair covers, and other furnishings.

The usual process of the tanner was to remove the hairs of the skin by smearing or soaking it in lime or some other substance, and then to treat the sun-dried hides with sumac pads, oak bark, pine bark, or leaves. Occasionally, skins were dyed and tanned with mineral salts, usually alum, or treated like parchment.

Because of the odorous nature of his work and the need for water to treat the hides, the working quarters of the tanner were usually located outside of the town or a considerable distance from other residents. Simon, the tanner, lived on the shore of Joppa (Acts 10:6). The Talmud calls tanning an "odious" trade (Kid. 82a).

Taskmaster

Taskmasters assigned tasks to their staffs and enforced strict performance, often by administering corporal punishment (Ex. 1:11). Egyptian reliefs depict them with rods for disciplining workers. "They were cruel taskmasters" (Ex. 3:7, 5:6–14; Job 3:18). David and Solomon employed them (2 Sam. 20:24; 1 Ki. 4:6, 12:18; 2 Chr. 10:10), the latter to build the Temple.

Drivers were considered "taskmasters" of their animals (Job 39:7); foreign rulers were also so considered by the prophets (Isa. 3:12; Zec. 10:4).

See *Driver, Overseer.*

Tattooer and *Tattooing*

It is believed that tattooing and similar mutilations date back to prehistoric times. Explanations offered include the possibilities that it was a tribal convention, a means of adornment, an initiation ceremony, a religious rite, a punishment, or possibly a health measure.

The tattooer pressed a charcoal-coated stencil, drew a design, or traced the pattern of the design on the skin of the patron. He then dipped his needle into colored pigment and pressed the needle into the skin to impregnate it with the indelible pigment following the outline he had made.

In the Bible, tattooing is called "writing of incision" (Lev. 19:28) and was forbidden to the Hebrews, probably because it was a pagan rite.

Tavern Keeper

There were so many wine taverns during the first Christian century in Rome that to the poet Martial the city seemed like one huge saloon (L. Friedlander, *Roman Life and Manners under the Roman Empire,* I, 5). The Three Taverns was a station on the Appian Road which has been translated "three shops." Many people walked there to greet Paul on his arrival in Italy (Acts 28:15). Probably, as a group, tavern keepers were gregarious and skilled in catering to the preferences of their patrons.

See *Innkeeper.*

Tax Collector

Early in history, governments found it necessary to meet expenses by obtaining revenue in money or in kind. To ensure a steady flow, various systems of taxation such as land or poll taxes were introduced. Some taxes were paid in money, others in produce or cattle, and still others were paid in labor. Such revenue was used not only for domestic needs, but also for tribute to foreign rulers and even to allies. References to such tribute are found in Sumerian, Egyptian, and Assyrian literature as early as the eighteenth century B.C. There are also references to the payment of foreign tribute in the Bible (2 Ki. 15:17–30, 16:7–18).

When the Egyptians ruled Palestine, we are told by Josephus (Ant. 12.4) that the taxation of each city was leased annually to the highest bidder and that the stipulated sum was paid to the royal treasury. If his collection fell below this sum, the tax collector had to make good the difference. However, he could retain whatever he collected above this sum.

He usually made sure he came out ahead. Josephus charges that one named Joseph beheaded twenty leading citizens of Ashkelon and Scythopolis when they refused to pay their taxes and confiscated their possessions. Under the Syrian rulers, state officials collected taxes.

Solomon was the first Jewish king to impose a regular system of taxation by demanding taxes from caravan merchants who passed through his land (1 Ki. 10:15). He probably also imposed taxes on ordinary citizens (1 Ki. 12:4). Later, during times of war, money taxes were demanded to pay for reparations to the enemy (2 Ki. 15:20, 23:35). Every male Jew was also expected to pay half a shekel for the support of the Temple (Ex. 30:13; 2 Ki. 12:9–16). The Persian kings and the Pharaohs (Gen. 47:22) exempted priests and Levites from taxes (Ez. 4:13; Neh. 5:4), an exemption that was common practice in antiquity.

From the very beginning the tax collector was an unpopular person. Undoubtedly, then as now, many sought to deceive him or to dodge him. To perform his duty, he was often forced to resort to either cunning or stringent methods.

So great was public hostility toward him that he sometimes suffered physical violence and, in one instance—that of Adoniram, a tax collector for King Rehoboam—was stoned to death. The Ptolemaic and the Seleucidan rulers employed tax farmers who collected the king's due plus a sizable bonus for their labors (1 Mac. 11:28, 13:15). Josephus (Ant. 12.4) cites Joseph, son of Tobias, who, though required to pay the staggering sum of sixteen thousand talents (a talent was about $960) to King Evergetes, yet remained nonetheless a rich man.

Matthew 22:17 speaks of the introduction of the census into Judea. While we don't know the exact amount of the tax demanded, it was believed to be high. Refusal to pay was tantamount to rebellion against Rome and was subject to drastic retribution.

In New Testament times, Roman officials in Palestine were responsible for collecting poll and land taxes. Tolls were exacted from those transporting articles by land or sea, and imposts were levied on pearls (Kel. 17:15), on slaves (B.B. 127b), and on boats (Ab. Zar. 10b). The collection of taxes was farmed out, usually for a period of five years, to private contractors who paid a stipulated sum for this privilege. Then, the contractors proceeded to extort as much as they could. These collectors were chiefly Romans, although occasionally they were Jews who earned the contempt of their coreligionists by trying to extort taxes from them and for serving the hated enemy, Rome.

The rabbis regarded tax collectors as akin to robbers, and barred them from serving as judges or even as witnesses (Sanh. 25b). They were excluded from holding any communal office. It was permissible to deceive them as it was to deceive a highwayman (M. Ned. 3:4). The New Testament associates tax collectors with sinners (Matt. 9:10–11; Mk. 2:15–16; Lk. 5:30), and they were considered along with prostitutes (Matt. 21:3) as offenders against morality. Even exchanging money with them was disapproved because they were suspected of possessing stolen currency. If one member of the family was a publican, he tainted the reputation of the entire family (Sheb. 39a).

Nevertheless, rabbis and Jesus believed that the tax collector might eventually reform. Matthew Leo surrendered his job as tax collector to become a disciple of Jesus, and the rich Zacchaeus resolved to restore fourfold his deceitful gains and to donate half of his capital to charity (Lk. 19:1–10).

See *Accountant, Appraiser, Census Taker, Treasurer.*

Teacher and *Schools*

The Jewish reverence for teachers was unsurpassed in antiquity. Teachers were held in such high esteem that "reverence for one's teacher should be as reverence for God" (Ab. 4:12). Teaching was not to be interrupted even for the establishment of the Sanctuary (Shab. 119b).

The Hebrews viewed learning as a lifelong process. The man

of wisdom and understanding should increase his knowledge and understanding (Pro. 1:5). In Psalms 1:2, the thought is expressed that "study, besides other benefits, can provide intellectual delight."

Schools and professional teachers date back to the third millennium B.C. At Mari in the middle Euphrates, two well-built schoolrooms have been excavated. School texts dating from about 2500 B.C. reveal a knowledge of botanical, geological, mineralogical, and mathematical problems and solutions. Many grammatical and lexicographical texts survive. Classes were held from sunrise to sunset, and discipline was strict.

Many schools for the training of scribes flourished throughout ancient Sumer. Textbooks that survive contain copying exercises along with the pupil's copies and their teacher's corrections. Their essays shed light on school life and surroundings. At these schools, the literary work of the past was copied and studied by the older students. The purpose of the school was to train professional scribes for the many needs of the temples, palaces, and courts and to serve other administrative and economic functions of the time.

Egypt, too, has furnished us with early records of schools from about 1570–1185 B.C. Papyri, writing books, and ostraca (clay tablets) served as school texts.

Originally, among the Hebrews, parents were the child's teachers (Pro. 1:8, 4:1, 6:20). The daily recital of chapters in Deuteronomy (6:4–9, 11, 13–21) reminded each Jewish parent of his duty to teach his children to lead a moral, ethical, and useful life. The child was taught reverence for parents and compassion for the aged, the handicapped, and the stranger. He was exhorted to refrain from any dishonest and oppressive act. Josephus (Contra Apion 1:12, 2:18–25) and Philo (Legatio ad Caium 16, 31) refer with pride to the fact that Jewish children were taught the law and traditions of their people. Besides religious and ethical instruction, parents taught their children such everyday duties as pasturing the sheep (1 Sam. 16:11) and working in the fields (2 Ki. 4:18). Some, like David, were taught the lyre (1 Sam. 16:15–18). Girls were taught by their mothers or by other females such domestic arts as baking and cooking (2 Sam. 13:8), spinning and weaving (Ex. 35:25–6). The Talmud (first to fifth century A.D.) declares that a father is obligated to teach his son a trade to prevent him from turning to thievery (Kid. 29a), and the sage added that he should also teach him swimming (Kid. 1c).

Naturally, parents varied in their effectiveness as teachers, and children in their aptitude for learning. Although the use of the rod is urged (Pro. 13:24, 19:18, 22:15), for the intelligent, reproof was deemed better than a hundred stripes (Pro. 12:10). The Bible urges that the child be taught at the right age (Pro. 22:6) without specifying when this is. It probably refers to the child's readiness. Many children began their formal studies after they were weaned (Isa. 28:9). Josephus says they began at the first glimmerings of consciousness.

The parents were followed by the prophets as teachers. Prophets taught small groups of disciples. The priests and Levites also taught students their religious duties. The Levites traveled throughout the cities of Judah to teach the people at large, using the book of the Law as a text (2 Chr. 17:8–9, 35:3). They visited the towns regularly, gathered both Israelites and non-Israelites, and explained the Law (Dt. 31:10–13; 2 Chr. 17:8–9). The Levites continued this method of teaching after the return, in 538 B.C. (Neh. 8:7–9).

During the Persian period, the Jews of Elephantine, Egypt, used a manual of instruction similar to the Book of Proverbs. When the Jews returned from Babylonia, for the first time an organized body of professional teachers arose. Synagogue schools were operated throughout Palestine. Students memorized portions of the Bible and learned Deuteronomy, Psalms, and Proverbs. Later, some teachers taught in their own homes. The Temple porticoes were also used for instruction (Matt. 4:23).

Several years before the destruction of the Temple (70 A.D.), Joshua ben Gamala (B.B. 21a) decreed that teachers of children be appointed in every province and in every town, and that children be enrolled in school at the age of six or seven.

A system of compulsory formal education for children was launched by the Pharisees under the leadership of Simon ben Shetah during the first century of the Christian era. Simon ordained (Jer. Ker. 8, 11) that children should attend elementary school where the Torah was the basic text supplemented by explanations and interpretations based on the oral law which was later recorded in the form of the Mishnah.

The first of these elementary Pharisaic schools was opened in Jerusalem, but other schools sprang up in other urban centers. Instruction was also provided on a secondary and higher level for adolescents and for young persons of ability. Moreover, there were adult education classes.

Pupils were given small wooden tablets covered with wax upon which they wrote passages from scrolls of sacred writings. Subjects of instruction probably included reading, writing, and arithmetic. The main book and possibly the only textbook was the Scriptures.

Ordinary Jewish education did not include the study of a foreign language. Besides Hebrew, most children learned to speak Aramaic and Greek in the cities of Palestine, and a knowledge of Greek was essential for membership in the Sanhedrin. The basic method of instruction was constant repetition.

In Talmudic times, Oriental customs of teaching prevailed. The teacher, who was always a male, sat on a raised platform surrounded by his students, who sat in a semicircle on the ground. Instruction was oral. A verse of the Bible was learned daily and the text was explained and, wherever possible, given an application. Discipline was strict, for the school was considered more sacred than the house of worship (Sanh. 71a).

At the age of five, the student began to study the Bible; at ten, the Mishnah; at fifteen, the Talmud. Students were supplied with large and small tablets. Even the alphabet was taught moralistically. In teaching the Talmud, because of the wide range of Jewish law, other subjects such as anatomy, arithmetic, astronomy, and history were introduced.

The school day began early in the morning (Isa. 50:4; Jer. 32:33). A little was taught at a time (Isa. 28:10) and most instruction was oral (Isa. 50:4; Pro. 1:8). Mnemonic devices were used (Pro. 3:10–31). The parables, a technique widely used in the New Testament, were also used for moral instruction. Since there is no reference to trade schools, it is likely that skilled artisans learned their trade by apprenticing themselves to masters. This may also have been true of musicians.

Teachers were referred to under various names in the Bible. Some religious leaders, such as the prophets who taught, were not specifically referred to as teachers. Among the references signifying teachers are "the wise" (Pro. 13:20). Public teachers were *mevinim,* meaning those who make understand (Neh. 8:7; 1 Chr. 15:22, 25:8); and *maskilim,* meaning enlighteners (Dan. 11:35, 12:3). A teacher of higher subjects was called *moreh* (Isa. 30:20), while *mellammed* meant teacher of lower subjects for younger children. *Melitz* is sometimes translated "teacher," but also as "intercessor"; *rab,* which originally meant master, came to mean teacher (Lk. 2:46; Jn. 3:10). In the Pharisaic schools, he was known as *hazzan,* a name later used to refer to a cantor. The *hazzan* taught the children reading as well as other skills and duties.

Gifted teachers arose among the Jews from the time of the prophets down through the period of the Talmud. These men contributed enormously to the advancement of Jewish learning and of Jewish consciousness.

Commenting on the desired characteristics of teachers, the following Talmudic statements are illuminating:

> Only the pure may be entrusted with the pure.
>
> Before you correct others, rid yourself of your own faults.
>
> An intemperate person may not teach.
>
> The teacher should be humble.
>
> Hospitality toward teachers is like giving to God.

Elementary school teachers were paid by the parents. For other teachers, it was a duty to teach in the academies without salary: "'As I have taught you without pay,' said God, 'so must you likewise'" (Ned. 36a). These unpaid teachers earned their living pursuing the humblest vocations such as farming, tailoring, and shoemaking.

Teachers were exempted from paying taxes. Unlike other vocations, they could settle wherever they liked without objection from other teachers who were already settled in that location since "the more teachers, the more teaching zeal" (B.B. 21b). The rabbis favored students' learning from a variety of teachers "so as to go deeper into the meaning of the Law."

In Talmudic times, a teacher was employed for every twenty-five students. Sessions were held throughout the day and part of the evening. Friday was review day. Vacations were given on days prior to Pentecost, half-days of Hannukah, the new moon, and on the fifteenth day of Ab.

Teachers were advised to study the temperament of their children (Er. 54b). When a student was persistently inattentive, a strap of reeds was utilized. A three-day absence was considered reprehensible. Teachers were urged to be stricter after the child reached the age of twelve since "from then on the youngster showed mature mental capacity and acumen." Repeated reviews and changing of the material to be learned was believed to strengthen the memory. Reading aloud was encouraged. Parents helped review at home (Ab. Zar. 120a).

Mainly because of poverty, there were no Christian schools during the early days of the Church, but children were a part of the church fellowship and probably received their training both there and in the home. Jesus is regarded as an outstanding teacher.

See *Custodian, Philosopher, Rabbi.*

Tentmaker

The most eminent tentmaker in history was Paul (Acts 18:3). Tents were probably first simply sewn for personal use. In time, however, specialists arose who made them more elaborate and more effective. Tentmakers in Biblical times included men and women who wove tent cloth on homemade looms. The narrow loomed strips were sewn together. The material, a goat's-hair cloth that mainly came from Cilicia (Cant. 1:5), shrank taut when wet. Goat's hair and woven reed cloth were the first fabrics the Hebrews used. These strips were supported by poles, usually nine in number, arranged in three rows of three, six to seven feet high, which were kept in position by ropes. The larger the tent, the longer the cords and the stronger the stakes (Isa. 54:2). The cloth used was dark brown or black (Cant. 1:5). When the sun baked the original material to a golden brown, the addition of new materials added a striped effect.

The tent was probably divided into two parts by a curtain hanging from the three middle poles along the length of the tent. The front portion was open and free to all, while the rear was closed and reserved for women and the privacy of home life (Jg. 15:1; Cant. 3:4) and for storage. Rich wives enjoyed separate tents (Gen. 18:10, 24:67, 31:33). The limited space of most tents offered scant privacy, so tent dwellers conducted many of their affairs near or outside the tent door. The floor was earthen or covered by hand-woven matting. The rich sat on hand-woven carpets.

Tents were pitched in Biblical times as they are today. The top was spread smoothly on the ground, the ropes straightened, the pegs driven into the ground firmly for support (Ex. 35:18; Isa. 54:2; Jer. 10:20). Then, one person ducked underneath the cloth to lift it onto the poles. Women made, pitched, patched, and loaded nomad's tents and continue to do so today.

During wartime, both tents and booths were used (2 Sam. 11:11). Special tents were pitched for newlyweds (2 Sam. 16:22; Ps. 19:5; Jl. 2:16), a practice still continued among the Arabs. The canopy, known as the chuppah, under which traditional Jews are wed, is a survival of the ancient bridal tent.

After their settlement in Palestine, Jews lived in tents with simple furnishings. A few coarse mats covering a portion of the floor were used both to sit and sleep on. A round piece of leather spread on the floor served as a table. Bags of goatskin held water, milk, or grain. Heating equipment was a sheet of metal that was heated with charcoal until hot enough to bake loaves. There were some earthen pots, bowls, a stone grain mill of mortar, and a pestle. A vivid picture of tent life is found in the eighteenth chapter of Genesis. After the Hebrews began to live in villages, they still returned to live in tents during the summer harvest season.

See *Weaver.*

Tool Grinder

The ancient tool grinder sharpened shears, scissors, knives, farm equipment, and other fine-edged tools. He used a grinding and polishing wheel and then honed the tools on the whetstone.

In the Bible, the Philistines (about 1100 B.C.) exercised a monopoly on tool grinding and charged high fees for their service (1 Sam. 13:19–23).

See *Toolmaker.*

Toolmaker

Toolmakers functioned early in history. They laid out, fitted, and assembled parts to make and repair cutting tools, jigs (contrivances to guide tools), and other fixtures essential for military and agricultural needs.

The toolmaker heated the metal stock in a furnace, hammered the stock into the desired shape on an anvil, and then forged metal parts by heating and hammering them together. He also devised jigs and forged special hand tools such as hammers and chisels, and tempered or annealed forged articles. He also cut, assembled, and welded metal parts, using fire to do so. In the Bible, Tubal-cain is mentioned as "the instructor of every artificer of brass and iron" (Gen. 4:22).

See *Metalworker, Tool Grinder.*

Town Clerk

In Greco-Asiatic cities under the Roman empire, there was the *grammateus* or town clerk whose job was to provide the finished text for the decrees approved by the senate and assembly. He also disbursed doles or gifts from the public treasury or directed the erection of statues decreed by the senate and people in honor of the emperor or other distinguished persons. At Ephesus the clerk was fearful that he would be held responsible for the irregularly constituted assembly (Acts 19:35).

Town Crier

Some scholars believe that the passage "she [wisdom] crieth in chief places of the concourse" (Pro. 1:21; Jn. 1:23) points to the presence of a town crier. Even today virtually every village in the Orient has a town crier who proclaims public announcements.

See *Herald.*

Treasurer

Treasurers were very important persons in Biblical times. They were in charge of royal or sacred treasures, which usually consisted of money, jewels, goods, and documents. Azmaveth was David's treasurer (1 Chr. 27:25). Possibly under him in rank was Jehonathan, son of Uzziah, who managed the treasuries throughout the kingdom. He may have supervised the royal tax collections and royal lands (1 Chr. 27:31). Ahijah is mentioned as treasurer of the House of the Lord under David (1 Chr. 26:20). During Solomon's reign, Jehiel held the same position (1 Chr. 29:7–8). Isaiah speaks of Shebna as a steward (Isa. 22:15). Nebuchadnezzar also had treasurers among his officers (Dan. 3:2). Mithredath was treasurer to Cyrus and supervised the booty captured and then restored to the original people (Ez. 1:8). Nehemiah appointed several treasurers to manage contributions (Neh. 12:44; 1 Chr. 9:26). In the New Testament, the Ethiopean eunuch managed the treasury of Candace, the queen (Acts 8:27). Erastus was the chamberlain of Corinth who headed the city's finances (Rom. 16:23). These men were probably familiar with various forms of bookkeeping.

Temple treasuries included basins of silver and gold, bowls of silver and gold, miscellaneous vessels, money, priestly garments, the decoration and trim, candlesticks, altars, etc. (Ez. 1:9–11, 2:69–70; Neh. 7:70). Royal treasuries included silver, gold, precious stones, spices, shields, and costly vessels, as well as grain, wine, oil, cattle, and sheep (2 Chr. 32:27–29; 2 Ki. 20:13; Eccl. 2:8).

See *Accountant, Banker, Census Taker, Priest, Steward, Tax Collector.*

Tree Surgeon

There were many jobs in agriculture. Amos 7:14 refers to himself as a practitioner of tree surgery (dresser of sycamore trees) rather than as a professional prophet. The process involved pruning or nipping back the trees to improve the fruit yield.

See *Farmer, Forester, Fruit Farmer, Gardener.*

Vintner and *Wine*

The vine was cultivated in predynastic Egypt (before 2000 B.C.) as well as in early Palestine, where it became one of the basic crops, noted for both its quality and quantity (Num. 13:21–27). It was generally cultivated on hills (Ps. 80:10; Isa. 5:7; Am. 9:13), although occasionally vineyards were attached to homes (1 Ki. 21:1). Vineyards were cultivated by their owners or by hired laborers (Matt. 21:1–6). Many landowners rented their vineyards to tenants (Cant. 8:11; Matt. 21:33–43), from whose harvest they received a share.

Vines were usually planted in rows from eight to ten feet apart. Stems were allowed to trail on the ground, but the clusters of grapes were propped up with forked sticks. Sometimes the vine was allowed to climb a newly planted tree (Ezek. 19:11) whose branches allowed a man to sit under its vine (1 Ki. 4:25). After the plants budded and the blossoms turned into ripening grapes, the vine dressers cut off the barren branches (Isa. 18:5). This pruning strengthened the remaining branches and made them more productive. Grapes were harvested in August and September. Fully ripe ones were eaten in their natural state or were dried, made into raisins, boiled into a thick grape syrup, or made into wine. Each was worth a shekel.

After the grapes were harvested, they were spread in the sun before being pressed into wine by the bare feet of the vintagers. Usually several men trod on the grapes together (Neh. 13:15; Jer. 25:30, 48:33; Isa. 63:3). Because of its quality and consistency, wine produced by the pressure of bare feet has continued to be preferred despite the invention of mechanical wine presses. While the wine was being produced the vintagers shouted joyfully or sang (Isa. 16:10; Jer. 25:30, 48:33), and it is believed that several psalms are these former vintage songs (8, 81, 84).

Both in Old Testament and New Testament times, vats were chiseled out of the rocky ground. The vat (*gat*) where the grapes were trodden was higher than its counterpart, *yekev,* and was linked to it by a channel so that one flowed into the other. The upper vat was generally about twice the size of the lower, though the latter was deeper.

Six hours after the pressing of the wine in the lower vat, fermentation began. The liquid was then transferred to jars (Jer. 13:12, 48:11) or skins for further fermentation and storage. The skins were usually whole goat hides with the neck and feet tied. An opening allowed for the escape of gases formed by fermentation. The freshly made wine was transferred to new wineskins since the old ones would burst under the pressure (Matt. 9:17; Mk. 2:22; Lk. 5:37–38).

Wine Districts

In Biblical times, a number of areas were famous for wine. In Judah, the area surrounding Hebron was famous. Abel-Keramim, Anab, Beth-ha Kerem, Eshkol, and Transjordan were also notable. Isaiah speaks of the wine of Sibmah (16:8). Syrian wines were internationally known. Damascus exported to Tyre wine of Helbon and Uzal (Ezek. 27:18–19). Gibeon was also the site of an extensive wine-making industry in the seventh century B.C.

Wine Production

In early post-Biblical (rabbinical) times, the production of wine started with gathering the grapes into a vat, of which there were various types. Some were hewn out of stone, cemented, or made by a potter, while others were wooden (Ab. Zar. 5:11). Near the vat was a cistern (*bor*) into which the juice rose through a connecting trough or pipe. Occasionally, two vats were linked with one cistern (B.K. 2:2). The freshly pressed wine was strained through a filter, sometimes funnel-shaped, or through a linen cloth, to remove impurities. Then a wooden roller attached to a socket in the wall was lowered to squeeze the grapes into the vat (Shab. 1:9; Toh. 10:8).

A ladle or dipper known as *mahaz* (Toh. 10:7) was used to convey the wine to larger containers known as *kad, garab, kan-kan,* or *habit*. All were rounded earthen vessels, tightly sealed with pitch. New wine had to be at least forty days old before it could be offered as a drink offering (Eduy. 6.1; B.B. 97a). After the wine had settled, it was drawn off into bottles, which were then stored in cellars and thence transported into storerooms or shelves in the wineshop or pantry. Bottles from the storeroom were put on sale in baskets in front of the counter (Ab. Zar. 27, 39b).

Types of Wine

Yayin referred to wine in general, matured and fermented. This is used in the Hebrew Bible more often than any other word. *Tirosh,* new wine, refers to freshly pressed wine (Pro. 3:10). At first, it denoted an intoxicating beverage, but later it signified ritual wine. *Tirosh* is often grouped with grain (*dagan*), oil (*yitzhor*), and juice (*asis*), derived from the Hebrew word meaning "to press" or "to crush." *Homer* was also an intoxicating beverage derived from the Hebrew word meaning "to foam." Wine was also called "blood of the grape." *Shakar* was an aged, powerful wine. The vine of the field (2 Ki. 4:39) was a wild, uncultivated variety. *Sorek* (Isa. 5:2) was an excellent vine, producing dark, colored grapes.

The quality of wine was recognized by its color, taste, and origin. Red wine was preferred over white. The best wine came from Keruhim (Men. 8.6). Then followed the red wine of Phrygia (Shab. 147b), the light red wine of Sharon (Shab. 77a), and *Yayin Kushi,* Ethiopian wine (B.B. 97b).

Among the special mixtures of wine were *aluntit,* old wine, mixed with very clear water and balsam, a drink especially popular after bathing (Tos. Dem. 1:24; Ab. Zar. 30a), as well as the following:

yen zimmukin: raisin wine
kafrisin: Cyprus wine used in the sacred incense
inomilin: wine mixed with honey and pepper
meushan: a product of the juice of smoked or fumigated sweet grapes
ilyoston: sweet wine from grapes dried in the sun for three days and then gathered and trodden in midday heat (B.B. 97a)
enogeron: wine mixed with a sauce of oil and garum
apiktewizin: wine emetic taken before a meal (Shab. 12a)
yen tappuhin: made from apples
kunditon: a spiced wine
yen temarim: date wine

Wine that had become sour was called *yayin koses* (Yer. Peah 2 end). When it became matured, it was called *homez* or vinegar. Good vinegar was produced by placing barley in the wine. One rabbi, Raba, declared that ordinary fermented wine should be strong enough to take one-third water. If not, it should not be considered wine (Shab. 77a).

The Romans often mixed wine with water. 2 Maccabees 15:39 says that such a mixture is "sweet and delicious and enhances one's enjoyment." Isaiah, however, viewed such a mixture as an adulteration (1:22). Wine was often mixed with spices (a common practice in the Near East) to produce a very intoxicating concoction (Ps. 75:8). Although it was deemed suitable for a banquet (Pro. 9:2, 5; Cant. 8:2), austere persons considered it as leading to woe, sorrow, contention, and complaining (Pro. 23:29–30). When mixed with myrrh or gall, wine was used as a drug. It was this potion the soldiers offered to Jesus when he was crucified (Matt. 27:34; Mk. 15, 23).

Besides the persons who were engaged in producing wine, there were a number of persons who sold it. Still others worked in various aspects of delivering it. Solomon, for example, exported wine to Hiram (2 Chr. 2:10, 15), which required persons to transport it.

Attitudes toward Wine

In rabbinical literature, there is a very positive attitude shown toward wine, which is often used figuratively to represent goodness, the Torah, Israel, Jerusalem, the righteous, and Messiah. All are compared to wine, while the wicked are compared to vinegar (Ber. 34b).

Talmudic passages revealing this are:

> Wine is the greatest of all medicines; when wine is lacking, then drugs are necessary (B.B. 58b).
>
> Wine helps to open the heart to reasoning (B.B. 12b).
>
> Three things reduce the feces: wine, white bread and fat meat.
>
> They help one to carry himself erect and strengthen the sight. Very old wines benefit the whole body. (Pes. 42b).
>
> Until the age of forty, generous eating is beneficial, but after forty, it is better to drink more and eat less. (Shab. 152a)
>
> Ordinary wine is harmful to the intestines, but old wine is beneficial (Ber. 51a).
>
> Wine creates an appetite, cheers the body and satisfies the stomach. (Ber. 35b).

Drinking Customs

In conformance with the Scriptural passage, "Give strong drink unto them that are ready to perish and wine to those of heavy heart" (Pro. 31:6), the rabbis ordered ten cups of wine to be served with the meal of consolation at the home of mourners, three cups to be drunk before the meal "to open the bowels," three cups between courses to aid the digestion, and four cups after grace was recited. Later four cups were added in honor of various individuals and the Temple. This naturally led to intoxication, so the last four cups were later eliminated (Ket. 8b), but the custom is said to have lasted over five hundred years.

Alcoholism

In Biblical times, alcoholism was more a social than a serious economic problem. While temperance and moderation in satisfying one's natural appetites were fostered by the Bible, the use of wine was not forbidden except to priests while officiating (Lev. 10:8–9). Wine was lauded for its pleasureful and cheering qualities (Jg. 9:13; Ps. 104:15; Pro. 31:6–7) and was used in the sacrificial meal (Dt. 14:23, 26; 1 Sam. 1:24; Am. 2:8). From Talmudic times to the present, the Sabbath and holy days have been ushered in and out with blessings over wine.

Although the Bible and later literature approved the moderate use of wine, its abuse was strongly condemned. Few persons denounced intoxication, gluttony, and unrestrained luxury as did the prophets of Israel (Isa. 5:11–12; Am. 6:6; Pro. 31:4–6). Many Biblical references deplore the folly of intoxication (Pro. 23:29–35). References abound on the ill effects of alcoholism: staggering, dizziness, reeling, stupor, incoherent speech, vomiting, red eyes, insensibility to blows, excessive jollity, insatiable desire for drink, poor thinking processes, loss of good judgment, blabbing secrets, desire to forget one's misery in drink, quarrelsomeness, shamelessness, inability to recall events during drunken condition.

Some Biblical characters who might be called "problem drinkers" were Noah (Gen. 9:21), Lot (19:31–38), Nabal (1 Sam. 25:36), Benhadad (1 Ki. 20:16), Ahasuerus, who engaged in a drinking contest (Est. 1:1), Holofernes (Jud. 12:20, 13:2), the Ephraimites (Isa. 28:1), and the wicked people of Samaria.

From the Bible, we learn that alcoholism seems to have been mainly a problem of the wealthy, who could afford to spend their time and means carousing. The poor are not mentioned as having suffered from the abuse of drink. Alcoholism does not seem to have been the universal economic, social, and health problem it has become today. Some scholars believe, however, that the existence of the austere Nazarites and the Rechabites, who renounced any product of the grape vine (including raisins), might have been a reaction against excessive drinking that had prevailed after the settlement in Canaan. Amos complained that the people of his time forced the Nazarites to drink wine (Am. 2:12). Sirach (Wisdom of Solomon), too, deplored the evils of drunkenness.

In the New Testament, drunkenness is also condemned (Rom. 13:13) as connected with debauchery and depravity. A bishop was forbidden to be intemperate (Tim. 3:3; Tit. 1:7). Drunkards were denied inheritance of the Kingdom of God (1 Cor. 6:10; Gal. 5:21) and were to be discountenanced by the Christian community (1 Cor. 5:11–13).

Although the Talmud recognizes that alcoholism often leads to sin, there are few comments about it, suggesting that the Jews, then as now, were an unusually temperate people.

There is a revealing story recorded in Talmudic literature (Tanh. Noah 13) concerning Noah. Satan is described as having helped Noah to plant the first vine over which he successively slew a lamb, a lion, a pig, and a monkey to demonstrate that when a person takes one drink, he feels like a lamb, after two drinks he feels like a lion, after three drinks he acts like a pig, while four drinks make him act like a monkey.

Miscellaneous

Immoderate use of wine was condemned by the rabbis. Some drank wine only at religious occasions. One, Abba Saul, a grave-digger, studied bones and discovered that those who had drunk natural or unmixed wine, had dry and transparent bones. Those who had drunk moderately had bones which retained their marrow (Nid. 24b).

Priests were forbidden to drink wine while performing their religious duties (Lev. 10:9; Ezek. 44:21). Proverbs denounces drunkenness (20:1); the Nazarites shunned wine entirely (Num. 6:3; Jer. 35:6).

Besides its use with daily meals, wine was consumed in generous quantities at banquets. Wine was given as gifts; Abigail and Ziba gave wine to David (1 Sam. 25:18; 2 Sam. 16:1). It was used as a tonic to revive persons who fainted

(2 Sam. 16:2), for medicinal purposes (1 Tim. 5:23), and to dress wounds (Lk. 10:34).

Rabbi Hanan advanced one interesting notion that "wine was created for the sole purpose of consoling the bereaved and rewarding the wicked for whatever good they may perform in this world so that they may have no claim upon the world to come" (Sanh. 70a).

On pilgrimages to the Temple in Jerusalem, worshipers brought a skin of wine (1 Sam. 1:24, 10:3), which was poured out at the base of the altar (Num. 28:7). Wine was always accompanied by a lamb, fine flour, oil, or a combination of these (Ex. 29:40; Lev. 23:13; Num. 15:7, 10, 28:14). Even in offering libations to false gods, wine was used (Dt. 32:37–38; Isa. 57:6; Jer. 7:18).

Christianity and Wine

Five parables of Jesus pertain to vines and their culture. They are the fig in the vineyard (Lk. 13:6–9), laborers in the vineyard (Matt. 20:1–6), new wine in old wineskins (Matt. 9:17), the two sons (Matt. 21:28–32), and the wicked husbandmen (Matt. 21:33; Mk. 12:1–11; Lk. 20:9–18). Christ described himself as the true vine (Jn. 15:1), to whom all believers are related. In Christian art the fruitful vine has often represented the union of Christ and his followers.

See *Farmer.*

Wagonsmith

The wagonsmith was an early specialist in building vehicles to transport people and baggage. With the invention of the wheel, carts became common in Babylonia, Egypt (Gen. 45:19–21, 46:5), and particularly in the low-lying Shephala of Palestine. They were used mainly to transport the more bulky harvests in the rural areas (Am. 2:13), and were made of wood (1 Sam. 6:7). Some were covered (Num. 7:3).

The wagonsmith made two types of vehicles in ancient Palestine: *agalah* and *merkabah*. The *agalah* was used for heavy loads and general work, while the *merkabah* was a chariot of war or state. Originally, the wheels of these ancient vehicles were solid disks, but in time a more ornamental type with hub fellies (exterior of the rim) and spokes developed. The wheels usually had six spokes, although later Assyrian wheels had eight. The normal height of the wheels was waist-high, but sometimes they were as tall as a man. Occasionally, wheels were made with metal treads (Isa. 28:27–28).

The wagonsmith's early chariots were heavily wheeled vehicles drawn by asses for military purposes as early as the third millennium B.C. The more familiar chariot that appeared during the second millennium B.C. was of lighter construction, namely, wood and leather, though its fittings were bronze and iron. The wagonsmith usually made his chariot open at the back; fittings for shields and receptacles for spears were placed on the outside of the front or side panels.

These ancient chariots were originally drawn by two oxen

(Num. 7:6–7; 1 Sam. 6:10), though later they were drawn by two horses. During the reign of Ashurnasirpal II, however, the Assyrians had three horses. The third was used as a reserve.

The many references to chariots and horses in Scriptures suggests that there were a considerable number of them. David captured chariots and horses while fighting the Syrians but did not use them (2 Sam. 8:4). Solomon introduced war chariots and stationed them both in Jerusalem and other cities (1 Ki. 9:19). The price of a chariot imported from Egypt during the time of Solomon was six hundred shekels. From the time of Solomon on, chariots are mentioned in the armies of both the southern and northern kingdoms (1 Ki. 16:9; 2 Ki. 8:21; Mic. 5:10). In the New Testament references to chariots include Acts 8:28; Revelation 9, 18:13.

See *Charioteer, Wheelwright.*

Waiter

Waiter, meaning deacon, derived from the Greek word *diakonos*. Most of the many references indicate a servant, typically a table servant or waiter. In the New Testament, it usually refers to a waiter (Rom. 15:25; 2 Cor. 8:4; Jn. 2:5, 9). Luke 10:40 speaks of the table-waiting of Martha. Peter's mother-in-law (Mk. 1:31) is *diakonia.*

In Hellenistic times, *deacon* also signified certain cult and temple officials, anticipating the Christian technical usage as assistants in evangelical work. Deacons were responsible for finances and for the administration of the church. They attended the sick. Any servant of Christ was called by the church a "deacon." The deaconess (Rom. 16; 1 Tim. 3:10–13) was charged with precise duties, as was her male counterpart.

The qualifications for deacons were sobriety, straightforwardness, freedom from excess and greed, probity (1 Tim. 3).

Despite these additional meanings and duties, the general and basic meaning of "table waiter" remained.

See *Cupbearer, Nurse, Physician, Servant.*

Wardrobe Keeper

The wealthy, royalty, and the high priests owned many expensive garments that they used for state and religious occasions. The garments were both guarded and kept in condition by the wardrobe keeper (2 Ki. 10:22). A direct reference to this occupation is found in 2 Kings 22:14. Huldah the prophetess was the wife of Shallum, the keeper of the wardrobe (2 Chr. 34:22).

Elegant garments were not only worn by the wealthy, but were also given as gifts (Gen. 45:22; 1 Sam. 18:4; 2 Ki. 5:5).

See *Clothier.*

Warehouseman

There is no specific mention of this occupation in Scriptures, but we know that Solomon built cities for storage purposes (2 Chr. 8:4) and that Jonathan was in charge of the storehouse (1 Chr. 27:25). Probably, there were warehousemen even earlier in antiquity.

There are many excavated sites of storage houses where surpluses were stored in times of prosperity to tide the population over during lean times, as recorded in the story of Joseph (Gen. 41:35–36, 56). David also built storage centers for oil, grain, and wine acquired from tribute and taxes (1 Chr. 27:25,

31). Solomon built store centers such as Tadmor and Beth-horon (1 Ki. 9:17, 10:26). The Temple staff at Jerusalem also had storage space for surplus offerings (2 Chr. 31:10).

The duties of the warehouseman probably included keeping a record of his supplies as well as protecting them.

Water Carrier

When the Israelites discovered the fraud which the Gibeonites had perpetrated by pretending that they had come from a distant land to sue for peace, they punished them by assigning them the job of drawing the water and cutting and gathering wood for the Tabernacle and later for the Temple service. The water was drawn from a well, poured into goatskins, and carried to the desired location (Jos. 9:21, 23, 27). This occupation is still pursued in the Orient. Water carriers in the Bible are usually linked with "hewers of wood."

See *Water Seller.*

Water Seller

Some believe that the passage from Isaiah 55:1, "Ho, everyone that thirsteth come ye to the waters" suggests the cry of a water seller peddling his merchandise as his modern counterpart in the East still does. The water was probably contained in goatskins and carried on the back of a donkey. The water merchant either drew his supply from a well or from a fresh spring or other body of water.

See *Water Carrier.*

Weather Forecaster

Scores of centuries before scientific methods were developed, there were among the ancients shrewd observers of nature who were able to make plausible weather predictions. Among the people of the Near East, weather was believed to be controlled by the gods and the stars. The Babylonians, especially, believed that weather was determined by the stars. Among the Greeks and Romans, however, the notion of the external control of weather weakened.

In the Bible, the *meonen* was believed to be a divinely inspired weather forecaster who studied the formation of the clouds and their dispersal. He was considered to be a master of thunder and rain as demonstrated by Samuel and Elijah (Jg. 9:37; Isa. 2:6; Mic. 5:12).

Because Biblical man was overwhelmingly engaged in agricultural pursuits and rain was so important in his life, the weather forecaster played a very important role. He probably received fees or gifts for his services and was held in high esteem.

See *Magician.*

Weaver and *Weaving*

There are many references to weaving in Scriptures. The shaft of Goliath's spear is compared to a weaver's beam (1 Sam. 17:7; 2 Sam. 21:19). Job comments that his days are "swifter than a loom" (7:6), alluding to the speed of the shuttle that carried the woof from one edge of the cloth to the other between the threads of the warp. The woof threads were then beaten together with the reed or stick (Jg. 16:14) to make a firm cloth.

The weaver examined the cloth he wove for defects, which he removed by cutting and pulling out filling. He then adjusted the pattern chain to resume weaving. He repaired warp breaks by tying a piece of yarn to the broken end and by threading yarn, and repaired filling breaks by pulling out broken filling and pushing the shuttle through the shed to insert a new pick.

There were three kinds of looms used in Biblical times. The Egyptian vertical had two beams: a warp beam at the top and a cloth beam at the bottom. Two weavers stood on each side of the loom and passed the shuttle back and forth, alternating sheds beating the weft down. Gravity helped to pack the wefts tightly, thus producing strong fabrics.

The Greek vertical loom was used widely to weave wool. It had the cloth beam at the top and loom weights on the bottom of the warps. The weaver stood in front of the loom and bent the weft upward. Because he moved about, the weaver could make wide fabrics. Although the weaving process was slow because the weft moved only a short distance at a time, it led to the weaving of color patterns, and it was easy to substitute a new color for a space.

Horizontal looms, the third type, were easily transported by nomadic peoples and consisted of two beams held secure by four pegs driven into the ground. The weaver sat in front of the loom, which was usually narrower than those previously mentioned. Such a loom was probably used by Delilah (Jg. 16:13).

Since linen yarns were much finer than most wool, several linen warps were grouped together to approximate the size and spacing of woolen warps. Otherwise, the pattern would not be flat. It was possible to weave both narrow and wider fabrics on this loom.

A standard width for both woolen and linen materials seems to have been four cubits or six feet (Ex. 26:2). It could be as long as the amount of warp placed on the loom. The hangings for the court were fifty yards long (Ex. 27:9), and were made of plain linen. The goat's-hair curtain was also plain. The veil (Ex. 26:3), the screens of the door of the tent which were embroidered (Ex. 26:36), and the gate of the court were of linen (Ex. 27:16).

Weavers produced the hangings of the Tabernacle in linen and in goat's hair (Ex. 26:1, 7), the hangings of pagan shrines (2 Ki. 23:7), priestly robes (Ex. 39:1), and Christ's seamless robe (Jn. 19:2). Other nations known for their weaving were the Egyptians, who were described as combing flax and weaving white cloth (Isa. 19:9), and the Babylonians, which we may infer from the value which Achan attached to a Babylonian cloak (Jos. 7:21).

Weaving was practiced by both men (Ex. 35:35) and women (2 Ki. 23:7). Priscilla, along with Aquila and Paul, was a tentmaker (Acts 18:3). Although originally weaving was practiced to meet the needs of the family, eventually it developed to serve the needs of all of society. In time, weavers became so numerous that they formed a guild (1 Chr. 4:21).

See *Clothier, Spinner, Tentmaker.*

Weigher and *Counter*

There were persons in Biblical times who were assigned to count or to weigh merchandise such as corn, oil, and cattle. They were employed by either merchants, rulers, or priests to see that the taxes or religious obligations were properly fulfilled. There is a passage in Isaiah 33:18 that seems to point to these occupations: "Where is he that counted, where is he that weighed?" Even in ancient times, unscrupulous persons were known to cheat in weighing and measuring. The Torah prescribed that the Hebrews maintain a just weight, measure, and balance (Lev. 19:35, 36; Ezek. 45:10).

In New Testament times, there were *mensores* in the Italian and other ports who weighed sacks of grain that were either imported or exported.

See *Appraiser, Tax Collector, Weights and Measures Inspector.*

Weights and Measures Inspector

As early as 2050 B.C. Ur-Nammu, founder of the third dynasty of Ur, sought to combat crooked merchants by establishing official weights and measures. In the two millennia prior to the appearance of the Hebrews, there were weights and measures among the peoples residing in the eastern portion of the Mediterranean that probably influenced the Hebrew standards. References to dishonest merchants and their punishment in the code of Hammurabi suggest that the vocation of weights and measures inspector is very old. Common offenses that they sought to eliminate were short weights, false measures, and adulteration of products.

Ancient weights were stones carved into shapes usually with a flat bottom, which made them easier to hold or to recognize. They were often inscribed with their weight. Weights were also carried in wallets or pouches (Dt. 25:13; Mic. 6:11; Pro. 16:11). In the ancient Near East, standards differed between cities and between countries so that at best we can only approximate weights and measures in Biblical times.

While there is no reference to an inspector of weights and measures in Scriptures, such a person may well have existed. The Hebrews insisted on just weights, measures, and balances (Lev. 19:35–36; Dt. 25:13–15; Ezek. 45:10). During New Testament times, Rome's aedile (a public official) was an inspector of weights and measures, to protect consumers. (Roman merchants were noted for their cheating with false or tipped scales.)

See *Scale Maker.*

Wheelwright

The age of this occupation may be discerned from the fact that there are clay models of chariot wheels dating back to the fourth millennium B.C. (C. L. Woolley, *Ur Excavations*, 1956, page 28). Carts and four-wheeled wagons were used in Mesopotamia in the third millennium B.C. Hearses with solid copper-bound wheels have been found in the cemetery at Kish dating to about 3000 B.C. There were ox-drawn high-backed four-wheeled wagons of small chassis.

The ancient wheelwrights made wheels from wooden planks pegged together. When horses came into common use about 1500 B.C., the wheelwright began to make lighter spoked wheels.

In Solomon's Temple there were miniature chariot wheels with axles, spokes, rims, and hubs (1 Ki. 7:33). Wheels were not only made for vehicles (Ezek. 23:24, 26:10), but also for equipment to draw water (Eccl. 12:6).

See *Carpenter, Wagonsmith.*

Wine Steward

The wine steward in Biblical times probably selected, ordered, stored, and served wine to the royal family. He probably also kept inventory. To prevent the poisoning of the monarch, the wine steward customarily tasted the wine before it was served (Gen. 40).

See *Cupbearer, Vintner, Waiter.*

Wood Carver

The ancient Egyptians, from about 2000 to 500 B.C., were extraordinarily gifted wood carvers. Their superb talents are believed to have been rivaled only by the artists of the Renaissance. The Hebrews also learned and practiced this art. At the Amorite tombs at Jericho were found beautiful carved furniture and other wooden objects.

The wood carvers mentioned in the Bible (Ex. 31:5, 35:33) were Bezaleel and his assistant, Aholiab, who directed the wood-cutting in the Tabernacle including pillars with curved capitals (Ex. 36:2, 38) and a recessed horned altar (Ex. 38:2–4).

Solomon's Temple had a pine roof with appliqué palmettes and guilloche borders (2 Chr. 3:5) that were paneled in cedar (1 Ki. 6:15–16). Its walls and doors were carved in bas relief with lotus birds and fleurs-de-lis feathers that formed a triple flower ("knops and open flowers"), palm designs, and figures of cherubs (1 Ki. 6:18, 29). Comparable designs were drawn in the olivewood doors and in the intaglio work (1 Ki. 6:32–35). The whole was overlaid with gold.

Ezekiel's Temple was visualized as possessing carved panels of two-faced cherubs alternating with palm trees and young lions. Its outer doors were veneered with wood (Ezek. 41:16–26).

Sandalwood and ebony were not native to Palestine and had to be imported (1 Ki. 10:11). There were few skilled wood carvers, so the use of paneling, elaborate woodwork, and carved windows was considered by the prophets as a vulgar display of wealth (Jer. 22:14; Hag. 1:4). Wood carvers used knives, chisels, hammers, and scrapers.

See *Carpenter, Ivory Carver.*

Wrestler and *Wrestling*

Wrestling is one of the oldest and most popular sports. It was practiced at least three thousand years before Christ. On the walls of the temple tombs of Beni Hasan near the Nile are found sculptured hundreds of scenes from wrestling matches illustrating virtually all the holds and falls known in wrestling today.

C. H. Gordon, the Orientalist, believes that in very early Biblical times, there was a form of wrestling, which he calls "belt wrestling," wherein participants wore special belts upon which special holds were made. In the University Museum of the University of Pennsylvania, there is a bronze cast dating from the first part of the third millennium B.C. that depicts two crouching men with their hands on each other's belts. The most familiar illustration of this was Jacob wrestling with an angel (Gen. 32:24–27). The belt was called *patil* and was one of the three articles of identification Judah offered to his daughter-in-law Tamar (Gen. 38:18). Gordon believes that almost every important man of the period owned a wrestling belt. We do not know whether wrestling was an athletic activity or a vocation. In New Testament times, it seems to have been both; this is implied in the passage, "Our wrestling is not against flesh and blood" (Eph. 6:12; 2 Mac. 4:14).

See *Athlete.*

Writing Materials Producer

After man learned the art of writing, he needed materials on which to record his experiences and ideas. In different periods, he used stone, metal, papyrus, wood, leather, or parchment; men were needed to prepare these materials. A favorite material for inscriptions in all ages was stone, especially when the author desired to convey an enduring message. In ancient Egypt, there was an abundance of stone. The walls of tombs and temples, which were built to last forever, were covered with hieroglyphic texts. Occasionally, discarded flakes of limestone were used as cheap writing materials and were inscribed with ink.

Since stone was rather scarce in Mesopotamia, cuneiform inscriptions on this material were usually limited to royal texts or public stelas. In Syrian Palestine, too, stone was used for public inscriptions in Aramaic or Canaanite. Examples are the Moabite stone and the Siloam inscription. Famous writers on stone were Moses and his tablets of stone (Ex. 24:12, 34:1; Dt. 4:13; Jos. 8:32) and Hammurabi.

Although metal was less often used than stone as a writing material, cuneiform inscriptions are found in Akkadian, old Persian, and Sumerian on objects made of bronze, copper, silver, and gold, and sometimes on plaques of such metals. References to bronze plaques are found in 1 Maccabees 8:22, 14:18, 27, 48, and Exodus 28:36 refers to gold as a writing surface.

The alluvial soil of the Tigris-Euphrates Valley made clay the easiest and cheapest writing material available. In Mesopotamia this led to the rise of the Sumero-Akkadian pictographic signs in the odd cuneiform shapes. First, the moist clay was kneaded into shape and the surface smoothed with one end of the stylus. The tablets were usually flat on one side and convex on the other. The writer would impress his signs on the clay with his stylus first on the flat side and then, if he needed more space, on the convex side. The clay tablets soon hardened, but, to make them last longer, they would be baked in the sun. If it was necessary to make them permanent, they would be baked in a fire.

Legal documents were generally signed with cylinder seal impressions. They might be encased in a clay envelope on which either a copy or summary of its contents were written. Longer literary works consisted of a series of tablets, each labeled and numbered.

Potsherds

The use of pieces of broken and discarded pottery as writing materials was widely known in the ancient world. Since they were abundant and readily available, they took the place of the rather expensive papyrus. A message could be written on the potsherds (ostraca) and dispatched. It could be re-used by simply washing off the original written material. In Egypt, these were used from about 2664 to 2155 B.C. for school exercises, for literary and nonliterary texts, and for such daily purposes as letters, accounts, and receipts.

Wood and Bark

In ancient Egypt wooden tablets were coated with stucco so that children and others might have writing materials. The Bible offers evidence of wood as a writing material—for example, the wooden rods or staves in Numbers 17:2–3 and Ezekiel 37:16–17. *Luah* in Isaiah 30:8 and Habakkuk 2:2 are believed to refer to a wooden tablet, although Isaiah may refer to a metal case.

Papyrus

Plants grew abundantly in Egypt from which was manufactured the excellent material papyrus. Although it is not known when it was first found in Egypt, a blank roll was found dating back to 3000 B.C. and the earliest inscribed roll dates to about 2470 B.C. Scriptural references to paper are found in Isaiah 19:7 and 2 John 12.

Leather

Because of the climate of Mesopotamia, there are no leather examples of the period extant. Hides were tanned early by the Hebrews (Num. 31:20; 2 Ki. 1:8) but there is no reference in the Old Testament to writing on leather. Most of the Dead Sea Scrolls found, however, were written on leather. The Talmud prescribes that copies of the Hebrew Torah to be read publicly in synagogues must be inscribed on leather (parchment). About the third century B.C., parchment began to replace papyrus. Sheepskins and goatskins were now prepared by removing their hair and rubbing them smooth.

Writing Instruments; the Stylus

A chisel was used to inscribe on hard surfaces such as stone or metal; to inscribe on a softer material such as clay or wax, a stylus would do. In Mesopotamia, the stylus was of reed, hardwood, bone, or metal. The tip of the stylus used to write cuneiform was either square or triangular. The Bible speaks of an iron stylus (Job 19:24; Jer. 17:1) for use on stone. Jeremiah 17:1 may refer to a stylus of diamond or flint. In Isaiah 8:1, the *heret* used for carving may have been a stylus for use on a wooden tablet.

It is plausible that specialists manufactured the pens used for writing with ink on papyrus, leather, wooden tablets, or ostraca. Both the Egyptians and the Hebrews used a rush cut obliquely and then frayed at the end to form a brush (Ps. 45:1; Jer. 8:8). The Mesopotamian scribes carried their styli in a case, which may have been made of leather, worn in their waistband.

Ink

The manufacture of ink required a certain skill that seemed to have been known by the Egyptians from the earliest times. Black ink was made from carbon in the form of soot mixed with a thin solution of gum. This was dried into cakes, then moistened with water. Red ink was also used, particularly for headings from which the word "rubric" derives. For carbon, red ocher or red iron oxide was substituted. The Hebrews called ink which could be washed off *dyo* (Jer. 36:18; Ex. 32:33; Num. 5:23; Ps. 69:28).

Early Egyptian scribes used a hollow reed case for their brushes, to which they added a wooden palette containing two cavities for the cakes of black and red ink, which were tied by a cord to a small pot built to contain the water necessary to moisten the ink. Later, the case and the palette were combined. These wooden or ivory palettes had grooves for the ink and a slot for the brushes, and they could be tucked into the belt. These were used by the Hebrews and others throughout the Near East (Ezek. 9:2–3).

See *Letter Writer, Scribe, Seal Maker, Tanner.*

Appendix I

COMMERCE AND TRADE

Early in his history man learned to exchange his surplus products for items he lacked. Many centuries later he developed money, which enabled him to acquire more convenient, easily transportable wealth. A major source of wealth and income was commerce and trade. How advanced commercial life was in Biblical times is discernible from the earliest business documents written on clay tablets and filed in town office vaults. Many clay tablets reveal extensive business activities. We know that three thousand years before the Christian era, Mesopotamian merchants were widely experienced businessmen who drew up contracts and often resorted to litigation. By 2500 B.C. they had formed trading companies and had extended their activities to remote areas. They traded in such varied items as wool, spices, soda, silver, and fair-skinned slaves. They rented shop sites, offered credit to their customers, and exchanged threats of court action when vexed by their competitors. From time to time, these business pioneers produced new or improved products. One dig revealed four thousand standardized hatchets neatly bound with wire. In the nineteenth century B.C. Abraham and his clan led caravans of as many as six hundred donkeys within Syria and Palestine.

The Tell el-Amarna letters (1500–1200 B.C.) reveal that in 1400 B.C. there was lively trading between Babylonia and other states of the farther east and Assyria and Egypt. There are many references to the trips of caravans and to trade in many products.

In trading, the basic standard of value was a head of cattle. In time, currency such as objects of metal—brass or rings, ingots of gold and silver—replaced crude bartering. Precious metals were used as a measure of commodities, for example, bars stamped with the guarantee of some temple or its deity.

Transportation for Trade Purposes

Ancient Palestine, which was a bridge between the Mesopotamian and Syrian cultures, also had many dealings with Cyprus, the Aegean Islands, and the coasts of the Red Sea. Its land routes and harbors along the eastern Mediterranean shore made Palestine important in international commercial relations. Since it controlled the commercial routes from western Asia to Egypt, it was the key to commerce between the Mediterranean and the Red Sea. At various periods, Palestine's wide variation in terrain, soil, and climate profoundly influenced its economic development.

Since Palestine had no internal waterways, imported goods had to reach it by sea or by overland route. A system of roads leading from Egypt, Arabia, and Mesopotamia seems to have converged at Sela or Petra, then spread northward to Gaza and to the eastern shore of the Dead Sea, continuing north on the left bank of the Jordan. When Jerusalem became the capital, goods were probably brought there by the same route, which was used until the railroads were built. Elath served as a port of Jerusalem on the Sea of Reeds.

Methods of Transportation

Transportation was by slaves (2 Ki. 5:23), by asses (Gen. 42:27), by mules (2 Ki. 5:17), by oxen (1 Chr. 12:40), by camels (Gen. 37:25), and by sea. For long overland trips, asses were not useful. Horses were used mainly for drawing chariots, and only kings and the very rich used chariots for other than military purposes. Caravans were usually escorted by armed men (Ez. 8:22). Because travel was often unsafe, kings and the rich who could afford to send guards as protection dominated foreign commerce. For protection against brigands, they formed groups for hazardous business journeys. During peacetime, merchants traveled either alone or in small groups, carrying their merchandise to the markets or to customers (Neh. 13:16). They bought farm products or clothing, produced by the housewife and her maids (Pro. 31:24).

As for sea travel and transport, this had always been controlled by the Phoenicians, who succeeded in maintaining their hold on traffic in ore, so important for the bronze industry. Through Phoenician sailors, there was a lively exchange of culture, arts and crafts, and ideas. The ships of Tarshish continued to sail the Mediterranean and east Atlantic lanes. Until Roman times, the chief seaports of Syria were Tyre, Sidon, other Phoenician cities, and Joppa.

Products

Since Palestine was basically an agrarian economy, farm products and cattle were its main items of commerce. Oil, wine, and honey were its most stable crops, since olive trees and vines grow almost anywhere. Next in importance were herds of cattle, especially sheep and goats. Livestock was sold mainly by nomads and seminomads and by peasants who owned large farms. Trading in sheep, oxen, and goats was strong while trade in saddle or pack animals was light. The third main commercial product was the winter grains: barley and wheat. Next came fruits and vegetables (except citrus fruits, bananas, peaches, and apricots). Figs, grapes, almonds, apples, and sycamore figs also were common. Among the vegetables were onions and garlic, vegetable marrows, and cucumbers (potatoes and tomatoes were unknown). Dairy products such as sweet and sour milk, butter, fat, and cheese were sold to city people all year round. Metal utensils such as tools and weapons, kettles, and silver and gold ornaments were sold by traveling merchants or manufactured in the local area.

The Tell el-Amarna letters reveal that the main exports from Canaan were oil, wine, various fruits, perfumes, copper, iron, and timber, especially the cedars of Lebanon. Exports from Egypt to Canaan were mainly manufactured goods since Egypt was then the leading manufacturing nation along the Mediterranean. Egypt exported art objects and, during periods of drought, it also exported grain to Canaan. The list of articles sent by a king of Egypt to a king of Babylon, and of the wedding presents or dowry of an eastern princess, fill fourteen large octavo pages in small type. These commercial documents found in early Babylonia and Assyria suggest substantial internal as well as foreign trade.

Markets

There are a number of references to markets or market places in the Bible (Ezek. 27:14, 17, 19, 25; Isa. 23:3; Matt. 20:3; Mk. 12:38). Generally, they were located at the city gate where the peasants assembled with their products (2 Ki. 7:1). Sometimes, however, the market was a bare, open space (1 Esd. 2:18). The foreign merchants also brought their merchandise to the market place (Neh. 13:16). Merchants who specialized in one product assembled at a designated gate, for example for the sale of fish, while livestock and other merchandise were sold at other gates. The town's artisans provided the local residents with pottery and textiles; the latter were mainly wool and woolens, much of which was homespun.

Although the primary function of the market was that of a trading center, it also served a number of other purposes. It was an employment center where the unemployed waited to be hired (Matt. 20:3). In gentile towns, preliminary trial hearings were held in the market place (Acts 16:19), and justice was administered there. Because many persons gathered there, prophets and preachers found it a convenient location to address their audiences (Mk. 6:56). It also served as a place for amusement where children played games (Zec. 8:5) as well as a gathering place in times of calamity (Eccl. 12:5).

Fairs

Fairs arose in ancient times because they offered special facilities for trading, which could be carried on more effectively when sufficient goods accumulated. Annual fairs as well as more frequent markets were held at neutral sites in or near temples during religious feasts and under the control of priests, chiefs, or officials, to guarantee security of exchange. Many of the religious festivals in the Near East were visited by caravans of Phoenician merchants. The safety of the merchants against robbers was considered guaranteed while they traveled to, and participated in, the fair.

In ancient Palestine, fairs were held in three cities: Gaza, Tyre, and Botna. The latter was denounced as an idolatrous place (Yer. Ab. Zar. 4; Gen. R. 47). Ezekiel 27:12–27 refers to fairs. Contrary to the custom in Ezekiel's time, however, when Jews conducted all kinds of business at the fairs of Tyre (22:17), the Talmudic authorities permitted only the purchase of slaves at fairs so that the slaves might be removed from idolatry (Yer. Ab. Zar. 1.1.4).

Talmudic authorities opposed the attendance of contemporary Jews at pagan fairs because the fairs had evolved from, and were related to, pagan festivals. The Talmudic word for fair, *yarid,* still employed by European Jews, is believed to be akin to the Arabic *warad,* "to go down to the water," and stemmed from the religious processions made to the ponds near temples.

Exports

The Hebrews exported from Palestine to Transjordan and the Negev (the south of Palestine) mainly olive oil and cereals (1 Ki. 5:11; Ezek. 27:17). Also in demand in foreign markets were expensive balms, fragrant resins, gum, myrrh, honey, dried nuts, pistachios, almonds (Gen. 43:11; Ezek. 27:17), wine, dates, pressed figs, and raisins. Industrial exports included raw wool, woolen cloth, and embroidered or woven multicolored woolen garments.

Imports

Imports were mainly industrial materials: tin, lead, and silver from Khurasan, Italy, Spain, Brittany, Great Britain; iron from Asia Minor; copper from Asia Minor and Cyprus; gold from South Arabia (Gen. 2:11; 1 Ki. 9:14, 10:10–11). Some white linen may have been imported from Egypt and Syria (1 Ki. 10:28; Ezek. 27:7). Purple-dyed wool and cloth came from Phoenicia, which virtually monopolized this industry. Pottery was imported from Cyprus, the Aegean Islands, and continental Greece. It was also very popular in Palestine during the latter part of the Bronze Age (1300–1200 B.C.). During Solomon's reign and spasmodically during the reign of his successors, such products as precious woods, drugs, gums, ivory, and spices were popular (1 Ki. 10:2, 10–11; 2 Chr. 9:9–10, 21).

In time, Jerusalem became the commercial center of the entire country. The Talmud (Er. 10:9) mentions it as a center for horses and wool. Elsewhere, there are references to its importance as a market for ironware, clothing, and lumber (Josephus, B.J. 2.1.9), and for fruit (Bik. 5:8). Other towns, such as Tiberias, Scythopolis, and Botna, were known as cereal markets exporting to Tyre (Yer. Dem. 1.31). Olives were sent to Italy (Shab. 26a), and olive oil, to Syria and Egypt.

Royal Merchants

Kings in ancient times played dominant roles in the trade and commerce of their countries. The priest king was also a merchant prince who let contracts to the trader or *damkar*. Some merchants became rich and important (Isa. 23:8; Rev. 18:3). They were often so busy that they formed partnerships (Job 41:6). There were great Babylonian business families such as Egibi. Nahum (3:16) declared that in Sennacherib's Assyrian capital, merchants were more abundant than the stars of heaven. Zephaniah (1:11) viewed their possible disappearance with alarm.

The Canaanite kings and, subsequently, their Jewish successors, were heavy traders in olive oil and grain, which they stored in the basements of their palaces or in special warehouses. The kings of Israel had almost a monopoly of oil and wine. Uzziah, king of Judah, promoted agricultural and economic interests in these products.

Solomon had highly diversified and extensive business interests. He built ships and developed sea transportation and trading (1 Ki. 10:22). With his naval base at Ezion-geber (1 Ki. 9:26), he developed it into one of the most active industrial centers of the ancient world for copper mining and smelting. His merchant fleet brought cargoes of copper ingots to Ophir, southwest Arabia and perhaps to the African coast. The round trip took three years. On its return voyage, it brought back gold, silver, ivory, apes, peacocks, sandalwood, and precious stones (1 Ki. 10:22). Solomon also enjoyed a monopoly on horses and chariots, importing the former from Egypt (1 Ki. 10:28). The rate of exchange was four horses for one chariot. He established a trade alliance with Hiram of Tyre who controlled Mediterranean commerce. In exchange for skilled labor, timber, and gold, he exported oil and wheat to Phoenicia. The twenty-seventh chapter of Ezekiel gives a vivid picture of the exports and imports of Tyre. The high lands of Palestine exported to Phoenicia honey, balsam, wheat, and oil (1 Ki. 5:11; Ezek. 27:17).

The domestication of the camel made caravan travel through deserts feasible. Solomon controlled the entire caravan trade between Arabia and the north, and apparently imposed levies on the traffic of surrounding nations, which came through Palestine. He had commercial agents who represented his interests in foreign countries (1 Ki. 10:28, 29).

Solomon's vast construction projects such as his palaces and the Temple alone employed numerous persons in its construction and subsequently drew thousands of pilgrims thrice yearly who spent money for sacrifices and made purchases during their stay in Jerusalem.

After Solomon, Jehoshaphat attempted to continue Solomon's shipping activities to Ophir (1 Ki. 22:48) but his ships foundered. Ahab (1 Ki. 20:34) and other kings also attempted to promote foreign trade. Prophetic utterances during the eighth century

B.C. suggest that there was lively commercial activity (Isa. 2:7; Hos. 2:8; Am. 6:3–6). The only competitors to the kings were the seminomads who traversed the great international trade routes between Egypt, Syria, Arabia, and Mesopotamia with their long travel trains. When they passed through Hebrew territory, they were required to pay tolls.

Military defeats and the capture of many of its people in Judah and Israel between 740 and 587 B.C. undoubtedly stifled commerce, much of which was conducted by Phoenicians and other foreigners. Ezekiel's description of Mediterranean commerce in chapter twenty-seven cites the nationalities and products that led to Tyre's economic strength. The passage summarizes ancient Mediterranean commerce: silver, iron, tin, and lead . . . slaves, bronze . . . horses . . . ivory tusks and ebony, precious stones, embroidery . . . wine, wool, lambs . . . goats . . . spices, carpets . . . gold . . . while Judah and the land of Israel . . . exchanged for merchandise wheat, olives and early figs, honey, oil and balm (27:5–25). During the Persian period, the restored Jewish community was weak and poor (Hag. 1:11; 2 Ki. 17; Zec. 8:4–5, 10; Neh. 1:3) and there was little commerce except at Jerusalem.

Commerce in Later Biblical Times

By the time of the Greek period, the restoration of the Temple, the reforms of Nehemiah, and the natural increase of the community undoubtedly promoted trade, which was further increased by the Greek colonization of western Asia.

Sirach (Ecclus. 42:1–8) suggests an acquaintance with commerce, while Ecclesiastes' silence on the subject might indicate the Palestinian Jews' relative indifference to commerce.

When the Jews regained their autonomy and expanded their territory under the Maccabees, trade must have expanded, especially with the acquisition by Simon of Joppa as a Jewish port (1 Mac. 14:5). During the Persian and Greek periods, the increasing commerce of the Jewish diaspora probably also stimulated Palestinian trade, especially during the regular pilgrimages to Jerusalem. Herod built Caesarea as a port to encourage business. The dispersed Jews settled throughout the Mediterranean lands. Within these areas lie the great commercial cities—Antioch, Corinth, Rome, Thessalonica—and their close ties with their coreligionists enabled the Jews to trade.

During Hellenistic and Roman Palestine, there was little change in the structure of the economy save for three developments. These were in the production of chickens and eggs, an expansion of fisheries on Lake Tiberius, and increased cultivation of flax in the valley of the Jordan area near Beth-shan. During this period, slave trading of males seems to have been an important economic activity. Impoverished persons under Greek and Roman rule were sold like livestock or other merchandise. Palestine now began to export high-grade linen and to import condiments and spices from Greece.

Merchants in the Talmud

The Talmud alludes to cloth dealers, horse dealers, and cattle dealers (Kel. 9:5; M.K. 2.5; B.M. 51b). Market days were every Friday, except in Jerusalem, where the days were Monday and Thursday. At the fairs, slaves and horses were sold (Yer. Ab. Zar. 1.4). Goods were sold by contract (Shab. 120b) and paid by bills which in turn were sold for cash before maturing (B.M. 4.9). Merchants communicated by post (Shab. 10:4, 9a), and there was some form of delivery service (R.H. 9b).

Although local authorities tried to fix prices, speculators in corn, wine, and oil, who tried to corner the market, artificially raised the prices on these commodities. There seems to be more reference in the Bible to the corn and olive oil trade than to any other business. The activities of these big operators were condemned by both the prophets and by the rabbis (B.B. 90b) because of the hardships they caused the poor.

During the early centuries, Jews continued to be rather disinterested in commercial activities. Josephus summarized this attitude: "We do not dwell in a land by the sea and do not therefore indulge in commerce either by sea or otherwise" (Contra Apion 1.12). There are, however, a number of references to commerce in the Apocrypha; (Ecclesiasticus 26:29) refers to wholesale and retail trade. In Tobit 4:9, there is reference to a deposit of money repaid upon the supplying of a receipt. In the New Testament, Paul sails on trading vessels, meets with Lydia, "the dealer in purple" (Acts 16:14) and the manufacturer of silver shrines for Diana (Acts 19:24).

Roman Commerce

The commerce of Rome under the name of Babylon is mentioned in the eighteenth chapter of Revelation, adapted from the twenty-seventh chapter of Ezekiel. Throughout New Testament times, the main activities in trade and commerce were in the hands of the Romans and Italians. The foreign trade of the Empire was diversified and intensive. In the second century B.C., there was a Roman city at Delos, a center of slave trade, where many of the inhabitants were merchants. The eighteenth chapter of Revelation describes the wealth and extent of Roman trade and the economic debacle destined to follow the loss of this rich market. From archaeology, we learn of Roman trade with India during the first century. Roman merchants traveled almost everywhere selling amulets, souvenirs, and other luxury items. Oysters came from Britain to Rome in barrels of sea water. Cornish tin came along the same sea route and large cargoes of wine were carried by boat.

Commercial Centers

Important commercial centers were Tyre, Corinth, and Damascus. Corinthian bronze ornaments and mirrors were sold (1 Cor. 13:12). Goat's-hair cloth was probably distributed by individuals. There was a Laodicean trade in valuable black woolen garments (Rev. 3:14–18) as well as in eye salve. There is archaeological evidence that in Thyatira, a trading center, wool and linen workers, dyers, leather workers, tanners, potters, slave traders, and bronzesmiths flourished. There were dyers who dealt in a purple dye made from the madder root, which was cheaper than the sea dye from the murex shell. There were trade guilds or collegia (Acts 19) under the patronage of pagan deities. Regularly, at their guild dinners, they offered a sacrifice to the pagan deity, thereby discomfiting the Christians. Ephesus, for example, manufactured silver souvenirs and other pagan cult objects of Artemis.

Business Regulations

The Torah and rabbinical law forbid dishonest practices and impose sanctions for such malpractices. It is forbidden to use false measures of length, false weights, hollow measures, and false scales (Lev. 19:35, 36). Two kinds of weights and measures, one great and one small, are termed an abomination of the Lord (Dt. 25:13–16). The Talmud adds that this law holds for dealings with non-Jews as well as with Jews (B.K. 113b). In rabbinical law, when one of the parties in a dispute suffers a loss through misrepresentation or the suppression of the truth, he may cancel the contract and is to be awarded damages for his loss. A sale may be nullified because the price was too high or too low or the product sold failed to measure up to its declared quantity or quality (Mish. B.B. 56).

When anyone is given more money than he is entitled to, he must return it even if not asked (B.M. 63b). If land, slaves, or chattels were sold and the item purchased were found defective, if the purchaser was ignorant of this, he might return the purchase at any time and be refunded.

In the Bible, when a penalty is cited for embezzlement (Lev. 5:15–19), offenders were required to make full restitution and add a fifth of its value to the principal. Moreover, they were to bring a ram without blemish as a guilt offering to the priest so that their sin would be forgiven. Among references to honesty in the New Testament are: "Let us walk honestly as in the day" (Rom. 13:13); "in all things willing to live honestly" (Heb. 13:18).

Summary

In summary, Abraham and his clan appear to have been active traders but Israelite participation in trade was slow until after the conquest (1300 B.C.) when the economy of the country and the cities passed into Jewish control. The subsequent growth of cities created an expanding market for the exchange of commodities. At first, substantial foreign commerce was concentrated in the hands of Jewish monarchs such as Solomon and Jehoshaphat. From about the sixth century B.C. on, however, some individuals became traders and businessmen serving either as middlemen or wholesalers.

From the tenth century B.C. on, closer international relations between the Jews and other countries, periods of peace, and the opening of international trade routes throughout the Near East stimulated commerce. Jews became merchants on a significant scale during and after the Babylonian exile (587 B.C.) when many Jews were compelled to abandon their traditional occupations and turn to trade. Even then, the great majority of the population did not engage in trade.

Appendix II

FINANCES

MONEY

Our understanding of the references to money in the Bible may deepen if we bear in mind the different stages of the use of money: (1) barter, (2) exchange of metals for objects or duties, and (3) the use of minted metals. In simple societies, barter was usually practiced since the differences in geography and the specialization of handicrafts made mutual exchange of products necessary. Man's most important movable possession was his cattle, which soon became the accepted means of evaluation. Smaller objects such as sheep, goats, oil, corn, and wine also served as means of barter. Since cattle was also the most important offering to the gods, it automatically became the most popular form of currency. Because of the accumulation at the holy places of herds which couldn't be consumed by the priests, they traded them for other commodities. Thus, the temples became the oldest places for commerce and the first sites for fairs.

There are many examples of barter in the Bible. In exchange for Hiram's help in building the Temple, Solomon gave him wheat and olive oil (1 Ki. 5:11). King Mesha paid tribute in camels and rams (2 Ki. 3:4). The Israelites paid taxes to the king in grain and wine (1 Sam. 8:15), wheat, barley, oil, and sheep (Ezek. 45:13–16).

Eventually, the fluctuating value and the awkward size of cattle and wheat as media of exchange led to the use of more convenient items such as metals, which were easier to handle and possessed far more stable value than the earlier media of barter. Moreover, copper was essential to the production of agricultural equipment as well as to that of implements of war. Persons who had copper could trade it for anything. For larger transactions, silver and gold were used. Abimelech gave Abraham one thousand pieces of silver (Gen. 20:16). The Midianites paid Joseph "twenty shekels of silver" (Gen. 37:28). Micah gave his mother eleven hundred pieces of silver (Jg. 17:2).

When the visual appraisal of value proved imprecise, uniform pieces of metal were shaped in the form of bars, ingots, bracelets, heads of animals, and tongues. Achan informed Joshua that the spoils of Jericho included "a bar of gold" (Jos. 7:21). Eliezer gave Rebekah a gold ring weighing a half-shekel and, for her arm, two bracelets weighing ten gold shekels (Gen. 24:22).

Since even these molded forms of metal lacked precise value, the next step was to determine their exact weight. In the Bible, the weight was adopted from the Sumero-Babylonian method based on the shekel, which originally meant "thing to be weighed," but which later signified balance or weight. The weight of the shekel was about eleven and one-half grams of silver or about four ounces. Since silver was more plentiful than gold, it became the medium of valuation. Consequently, the Hebrew word for silver, *keseph,* came to mean money. The essential amount of silver was weighed in front of the dealer. When Abraham purchased the cave of Machpelah, he weighed out for Ephron the silver—four hundred shekels of silver, according to the weights current among the merchants (Gen. 23:16). When Jeremiah bought his cousin's field in Anathoth, he weighed out the purchase price, seventeen shekels of silver (Jer. 32:9).

Because of differences in purchasing power, we cannot know the exact value of the ancient shekel, but we can calculate its purchasing power in Biblical times. It was then possible to buy a ram for two shekels (Lev. 5:15); a homer of barley (about eleven bushels), or one and one-half pecks of fine meal, for a shekel; or two measures of barley, about three pecks, for a shekel (2 Ki. 7:16).

The next step in the development of money was to produce a piece of metal whose weight and purity were determined by a stamp, that is, a coin, thus eliminating the need to examine its weight and purity. Nevertheless, tricksters also found a loophole in this improvement by counterfeiting inferior metal and coating the coins with silver. Many ancient coins bear deep cuts revealing attempts to determine the authenticity of the coins. These activities necessitated again weighing coins to be sure of their value.

The invention of coins appears to have occurred during the seventh century B.C., possibly simultaneously in Aegina, Greece, and Lydia, Asia Minor. The Israelites probably became familiar with the first coins about the time of the Babylonian exile (587 B.C.). Prior to this period, references to money in the Bible denote bars, ingots, and bracelets.

Money is first mentioned in the Bible in Ezra 2:69. When the Jews returned from the Exile, they donated sixty-one thousand darics of gold and five thousand minas of silver for the erection of the Temple. The coins were of pure gold and represented an early phase of coinage.

Following Alexander's conquest of the Persian Empire, the unified coinage of the new empire was valid for Palestine. Coins used were minted in Acre and Sidon. Although they are not mentioned in the Bible, archaeological finds indicate that this currency was widespread. The Ptolemies who followed Alexander added mints at Gaza, Joppa, and Tyre, but made only slight changes in the currency. In 132 B.C. in Jerusalem, Antiochus struck his own coins which carried his name and confirmed his rule. When John Hyrcanus declared his independence from the Seleucidae about 111 B.C., he minted his own coins with the inscription "Johann the high priest and the community of the Jews." These are considered to be the first real Jewish coins, while those attributed to Simon the Maccabee are considered erroneous. Because of the lack of experience in minting, these first Jewish coins were very modest, and because of the second commandment (Ex. 20:4), they did not bear the head of the king. The obverse of the coin bore a wreath and inscription and the lettering was in the ancient Jewish script; the reverse bore a double horn of abundance and a poppy head, selected because they symbolized plenty and fertility and were common on Seleucid coins. They probably also represented the prosperity of the reign of John Hyrcanus I. This coin was the second smallest unit known as the *peruta.* The Seleucidae minted silver coins. If the Maccabees had minted their own currency, it would have been deemed an insurrectionary act. Judah Aristobulus, son and successor of John Hyrcanus, left few coins since he reigned only a short time. His brother, Alexander Jannaeus (105–78 B.C.), succeeded him and also became high priest. It was he who used the title *King* for the first time on the coinage. The last of the Maccabees, Antigonus (40–37 B.C.) also struck his own coins, but in great haste, with the result that they were poorly done and barely preserved. His most unusual coin was the seven-branched lampstand which is the first representation of the sacred lampstand from the Temple known to us from its famous representation on the Arch of Titus in Rome. Most of his other coins repeat the issues of his predecessors.

During the New Testament period, Herod I (36–4 B.C.) was appointed king of Judea by the Romans. By temperament strongly Hellenistic, he established Greek-type towns and fostered the building of Greek temples and prize fights in the Roman manner. Herod's coins are the first Jewish coins bearing dates. The inscriptions are in Greek and bear the old Jewish symbols such as cornucopias.

Archelaus (4 B.C.–6 A.D.), Herod's son, carried on the tradition of refraining from striking representations which might offend the traditionally minded Jews. Herod Antipas (4 B.C.–39 A.D.) was the king who founded Tiberias in honor of Emperor Tiberius and selected it as his mint. Philip (4 B.C.–34 A.D.) defied Jewish tradition when he had engraved the head of the Roman emperor on the coins he struck (Lk. 3:1). Herod Agrippa I (37–44 A.D.) called himself on his coins "a great king, friend of Caesar," and was the first to place his own portrait on his coins.

Herod Agrippa II (50–100 A.D.), the last ruling descendant of the house of Herod, struck coins, but they lacked any Biblical reference. The Roman procurators minted copper coins, which served as the small currency of the country till 58 A.D. and are found in great quantities in Palestine. All of them depict palms, vine leaves, or cornucopias, symbolizing wealth and prosperity. They bore the name and title of Caesar and the year of his reign. Pontius Pilate had struck two coins, one of which shows a ladle and the other a curved staff or wand, both well-known emblems of Roman priests.

In the New Testament there are many coin names, but because coins were minted from so many different sources, it is difficult to identify their denominations. The most commonly mentioned coin is the denarius or penny which was minted mainly in Rome under the supervision of the emperor. It was the most common silver coin in the first century and the troops were paid with it. One denarius was the daily pay of the laborer (Matt. 20:9–10, 13), and it was also used to pay tribute to the emperor. After the destruction of the Temple by Vespasian, all Jews were required to pay two drachmas per head to the temple of Jupiter Capitolinus. This sum equaled the amount which the Jews had paid as annual sacred tribute to their own Temple (Matt. 17:24). Mark 12:42 refers to a widow's mite. Two mites equaled a farthing. In the Jerusalem Temple, only Jewish coins were allowed, in harmony with Jewish tradition. All were of copper. When pilgrims brought unacceptable coins, the money-changers probably changed them.

During their war of independence against the Romans, as one sign of their independence, the Jews struck a variety of their own coins, first silver then bronze coins. There are half-, quarter-, and eighth-shekels, all in bronze. All of the coins bear religious symbols such as Temple offerings and celebrations, or they stress the liberation theme.

Similarly, during their second war of independence, Jews again began to mint silver and bronze coins as a sign of their new status. However, now they used the current coinage and stamped their own symbols on top of it, obliterating the despised portraits of their persecutors. Because some were done hastily, evidence of the former mintage is detectable, which enables experts to date the coins more precisely. On these restruck coins, we find the designs of the first war of independence: palm, grape vine, and vine leaf. There are dated coins only in the first and second years. The name of Eleazar the priest often appears. Some coins bear the inscription "Redemption of Jerusalem." The rebellion of Bar Cocheba (132 A.D.) against the Romans produced the last and best of Jewish numismatics, whose symbols were drawn from Temple worship.

INCOME

FEES

Fees were paid in Biblical times for professional and other services rendered. The duties performed by the Levites in connection with the Tabernacle and later in the Temple were rewarded by the tithes of Israel. The priests received a tithe of the income of the Levites and other gratuities known as the "twenty-four gifts of the priesthood" (Tos. Hallah 2).

Samuel, however, refused gratuities (1 Sam. 12:4). Similarly, Elisha rejected Naaman's offer of gifts for curing him from his leprosy and denounced Gehazi for his duplicity in accepting a gift (2 Ki. 5:16–27). Elisha, however, accepted the hospitality of the Shunamite. The Talmud, commenting on this, states that it is permitted to accept a gratuity. Samuel, however, in order to be wholly independent, even carried his household with him on his trips (Ber. 10b).

A scholar was allowed to accept favors or benefits but was forbidden to demand payment for teaching the Torah. A primary school teacher, however, was allowed to charge a fee for taking care of children or for teaching the Biblical accents and the division of the verse (B.B. 37a). Maimonides allows the customary fee for teaching the Bible, but not for the common law (Yad Talmud Torah 1.7). A student unable to obtain free tuition was required to hire a teacher. In the words of Proverbs, "Buy the truth and sell it not" (23:23). Rabbi Zadok, however, declared, "Make not the Law thy hoe, for whoever derives a benefit of the Law loses life in the world to come" (Ab. 2).

In Temple times, teachers were assigned to teach the priests procedures of the service, for which they received a stipulated sum from the Temple treasury (Ket. 106a).

As for the physician, he was often considered a communal worker but does not seem to have received a fixed salary. He apparently supported himself through casual fees. Scribes of the court of justice or of the Temple received an annual salary (Ket. 106a; Shab. 56a). There were also private notaries who drew up deeds of sale, bills of marriage and divorce, promissory notes, and other legal documents, who received a special fee for each service rendered. The scribe's fee was usually paid by the party who gained most from the transaction.

When the documents were prepared for litigation in court, the litigants shared the costs (B.B. 167b). Judges, however, were forbidden to accept fees for their service. They were allowed to accept payment for the time or loss of income they sustained because of absence from normal occupation. This sum was shared equally by both litigants.

Judges who had no other source of income were permitted to be compensated by the communal treasury (Yad Sanhedrin 23:5; Hoshen Mishpat 9:3). In Temple times, magistrates of Jerusalem who guarded the public safety also received an annual salary from the communal treasury (Ket. 105a).

See *Judge*.

WAGES

One of the earliest examples of wages, the code of Hammurabi (*ca.* 1800 B.C.), informs us of the wages of different occupations in Babylonia ranging from doctors to tailors. Field laborers earned about a shekel a month. A silver shekel ranged from thirty-two to sixty-four cents, a gold shekel from about five to ten dollars. More typical salaries were six shekels a year plus food and clothing. Frequently an advance payment of a shekel was paid and the remainder given at stipulated intervals. Bricklayers and tailors received five *she* a day or from about ten to twenty cents a day. Herdsmen earned about eight *gur* or about eight shekels a year. Other services were paid for in grain.

The Bible gives us little explicit information about wages. For much of Biblical times, farm work was performed by the Hebrew farmer and his family. If he was rather affluent, he was aided by a few slaves. Hired servants were few and were mainly aliens. There is no precise data as to the wages of the field hands. Jacob, who worked for Laban, complained that his wages were changed ten times (Gen. 31:41) but mentions no specific amount. Workers were expected to be paid a fair wage and to be paid daily (Dt. 24:15; Lev. 19:13). Some persons were engaged by the year (Lev. 25:53). Unspecified wages were paid by the princess to Moses' mother (Ex. 2:9).

The first clear-cut example of definite wages in the Bible was the case of the Levite whom Micah hired as his domestic chaplain for ten shekels a year with a suit of apparel and victuals (Jg. 17:10). Neighbors who helped to build barns and to harvest crops were paid in unspecified wages (Jer. 22:13).

In the Book of Tobit (Apocrypha), Tobit hires the angel Raphael as his son's traveling companion for a drachma a day (nearly fifteen cents) and all that he finds (Tob. 5:14). The laborer in the vineyard received a denarius (about fifteen cents) for a day's work, from sunrise to sunset, exclusive of meals (Matt. 21:1). We do not know the purchasing power of these wages. During periods of inflation, wages were referred to as a bag full of holes (Hag. 1:6).

In many sections of the New Testament (Matt. 10:24; Lk. 17:7; Jn. 13:16), a just relationship between employer and employee is urged. The worker earns his pay (Lk. 10:7) and "to him that worketh is the reward [wages] not reckoned of grace but of debt" (Rom. 4:4) are famous expressions.

In Talmudic times, the following regulations obtained: a worker was paid the amount stipulated when he was hired; he was to be paid in cash and not in kind; the community was allowed to set wage scales; the worker was paid for travel time coming to work but not for time spent returning home; the law that canceled debts during the Sabbatical year did not apply to the unpaid salary of a worker; he was to be paid within twenty-four hours of the end of his work; a dayworker had to be paid before the following dawn, and a nightworker before the following sunset (B.M. 9:10–11); and finally, persons paid by the week, month, or year were to be paid before sundown of the day or before sunrise following the night after his period of work ended.

The employer was expected to supply lunch during working days unless this was not customary in the community (B.M. 7:1). Typically, the worker could retain objects he found while working. Harvesters, threshers, vintagers, and olive pickers were permitted to eat more than their salary's worth of produce and even select from the best part of the crop.

The employee had to be paid the promised salary even if he were assigned to another type of work (B.M. 76a). If he finished his task sooner than expected, the employer might assign him at the same pay to either an equal or lighter post but not to a harder one. If such were unavailable, he was to be paid for his time.

An employer who breached a contract had to pay the full, stipulated wage besides whatever saving he effected by hiring at lower salary (B.M. 6:2). Other than certain emergencies, the employee might cease work at any time without forfeiting any wage earned up to the moment of the stoppage.

Full pay had to be given to an employee when, for reasons beyond his control, he was unable to work. Examples were messengers who could not locate the intended receiver or carriers who came to designated locations and failed to find the merchandise. A similar policy prevailed with "acts of God" such as floods. A drafted worker was paid for the work which he had already completed (Tos. B.M. 7:8). A worker who was made idle because he was not supplied with materials or because of other factors beyond his control was also paid (B.M. 76b). The above regulations as well as the earlier Biblical rules reflect a deep concern for the welfare of the wage earner.

Wealth

For much of the approximately twelve hundred years that is spanned by the Bible, wealth was concentrated in the hands of the relatively few rich, who often exploited the poor. Sometimes, kings (1 Ki. 21:1–16) expropriated property by violent means, which actions the prophets excoriated. When it suited their fancy, rulers acquired land through forced purchases (1 Sam. 8:14). Similarly, avaricious landowners seized the heavily mortgaged lands of their neighbors (Isa. 5:8).

The Bible speaks of the dangers of wealth, declares that the rich often failed to acknowledge that God is the source of their blessings (Dt. 8:17–18; Hos. 2:8) and that they were prone to lean on their wealth and to abandon their trust in God (Ps. 52:7). An awareness of the materialism, greed, and other evils that often characterize the wealthy is discernible throughout the Bible. "He who loves silver will not be content with silver" (Eccl. 5:10). "The love of money is the root of all evil" (1 Tim. 6:9–10). Rich persons as a class are also denounced in several passages of the New Testament (Lk. 6:24; Jas. 5), while blessings are offered for the poor (Lk. 6:20).

The Bible, however, is not opposed to the acquisition of wealth if its possessors are upright and considerate of the needs of the poor. "God . . . giveth us richly all things to enjoy" (1 Tim. 6:17). Abraham is considered an example of such a man (Gen. 13:2). The Psalms, too, praise material well-being; "wealth and riches are in the house of the man that feareth the Lord" (Ps. 112:1, 3). Among the wealthy persons mentioned in the Bible were Abraham (Gen. 13:2), Nabal (1 Sam. 25:2–3), Barzillai (2 Sam. 19:32), Zaccheus (Lk. 19:8), and Joseph of Arimathea (Matt. 27:57).

The Bible emphasizes that wealth is transient (Ps. 49; Job 21) and urges that generosity be shown the poor (1 Tim. 6:18; 2 Cor. 8:9). Such action was promised spiritual reward (Lk. 16:11) because true wealth is deemed the spiritual blessings which God bestows rather than material things (Lk. 12:33).

Appendix III

ATTITUDES TOWARD THE WORKER

As in all societies, in Biblical times, there were special occupational groups that presented unique problems and characteristics. The attitudes in the Bible toward women, the aged, children, the handicapped, and other groups give an unusually interesting sociological picture.

Female Workers

Women played an essential role in the economic life of early societies. In the basically agricultural economy of Biblical times, they were pre-eminently housewives (Pro. 31:13–27) and mothers. They helped to draw water for the family and the animals and were busy grinding corn, baking, cooking, spinning, and weaving. At the appropriate season, they helped to tread the grapes and the olives for wine and oil. They also engaged in gleaning (Ruth) and sheep tending (Rachel and the daughters of Jethro). Proverbs 31:16 refers to their real-estate activities. Ananias and his wife, Sapphira, sold property (Acts 5:1). Others engaged in the manufacture and sale of linen garments. Lydia sold purple dyed cloth for which Thyatira was famous (Acts 16:14). Priscilla, wife of Paul's colleague Aquila, produced and sold cloth and was a tentmaker (Acts 18:2, 3).

There were also women prophetesses, professional mourners, soothsayers, and harlots.

See *Mourner, Prophet, Prostitute.*

Low-Ranking Occupations

During Biblical times, as well as in all periods, some occupations were highly esteemed while others were disdained. Highly esteemed were priests, prophets, scribes, and musicians. In Egypt, during the time of Joseph, shepherds were held in contempt (Gen. 46:34), and later the merchant was viewed with suspicion (Hos. 12:8) because he was prone to be deceitful, give short weight, and be generally dishonest.

In the Talmud, too, there are a number of occupations held in low esteem and called "of evil character" because of the alleged dishonesty or the illicit behavior of their practitioners. Among these occupations were the smelter, potter, chiseler, grease worker, and bathing attendant. All of these were barred from the kingship and the high priesthood.

Other occupations also viewed unfavorably were the barber or bloodletter, to whom the Talmud attributed ten objectionable traits; the goldsmith, because his trade brought him into close contact with women and presumably into illicit relationships; and the shepherd, because he grazed his flocks on other persons' property.

Also viewed with disdain were ass-drivers, butchers, sailors, cameleers, and transport workers. Shopkeepers, too, were stigmatized because they were prone to adulterate products and to overcharge. Peddlers were looked down upon for similar reasons (Kid. 82a; Yeb. 63b). Even physicians were not exempt from disapproval: "the best of physicians are hell bound" (Kid. 82a). This view was based on the belief that physicians were disinterested in their poor patients and careless in treating them.

The Aged

The problem of the aged who is considered superfluous and is often rejected in most of the industrialized countries of the world did not exist in Biblical times. The basic economy was agricultural, and in such societies there is usually work for all hands. Consequently, the older person who was able to function could retain a sense of usefulness. Moreover, wars, disease, and famine usually conspired to keep the number of older persons relatively low. It is likely that the elderly could function into old age as priests, judges, physicians, and as other professionals who did not require great physical strength.

Those who managed to survive to old age and were able to maintain their health, probably occupied themselves with their normal activities on a reduced scale. Unlike the Greeks and Romans, who were known to dismiss aged and infirm slaves who were unable to perform their duties, the Hebrews retained their aged workers when they were unable to function properly.

A quaint story is told in rabbinical literature regarding Emperor Hadrian. On his way to war, he rode past a garden where he observed a very old man planting a fig tree. The king halted his horse and inquired, "Why in your old age do you work so zealously? Do you expect to eat the fruit of the tree you are planting?"

The old man answered, "If it be God's will, I shall eat of it; if not, my sons will enjoy it." (Vay. Rab. 25).

It is likely that with relatively few opportunities for recreation, the older person pursued as many activities as his age and health permitted. As for his probable productivity, we know (Lev. 27: 1–9) that while persons from twenty to sixty were valued at fifty shekels, a male over sixty was valued at fifteen shekels and females at ten shekels.

The Bible does not specify when a person was considered aged. It avers, "The days of our years are three score and ten, and if by reason of strength they be four score years, yet is their strength labor and sorrow" (Ps. 90:10). Later the Talmud declared, "If one dies at eighty, he has reached old age" (M.K. 28a; B.B. 75a). Ben Sirach, however, called one hundred a ripe old age (Ecclus. 18:9).

With the exception of the Chinese, few, if any, people exhibited as great a reverence for the aged as the Hebrews. The young were bidden, "Thou shalt rise up before the hoary head and honor the face of the old man" (Lev. 19:32). "The hoary head is a crown of glory" (Pro. 16:31). "The beauty of old men is the gray head" (Pro. 20:29).

There were, however, periods of upheaval and moral chaos when the aged were scorned. This attitude was deplored as a sign of the times (2 Chr. 36:18; Isa. 3:5; Lam. 5:12). The Talmud declares that a sign of the troubled times preceding the arrival of the Messiah will be the disrespect and discourtesy shown by the young toward the aged (Sot. 49b).

Generally, however, the prevailing attitude toward the older person was reverent. He was considered more experienced and hence wiser in the ways of life. He was, therefore, looked to for counsel. He represented discretion and knowledge (Job 12:12; 15:10). Solomon's son, Rehoboam, spurned the counsel of his mature advisers in favor of his young cronies, an act which led to the division of the kingdom (1 Ki. 12:13–14).

A famous passage in Ecclesiasticus 25:4–6 asserts, "How comely a thing is judgment for gray hairs and for elders to know counsel. How comely is the wisdom of old men and understanding and counsel to men that are in honor."

There were varying opinions in rabbinical literature about the learning ability of the aged. One held that "when the old receives instruction, it is like writing a palimpsest" (Ab. 4:20), while another declared about those who had studied in their early youth and continued throughout their life, "the older the scholar grows, the greater his wisdom becomes" (Shab. 152a).

While the aged were generally praised, the Biblical authors were fully aware of the infirmities that come with age. The most impressive and best-known Biblical description of the aging process is in Ecclesiastes 12:1–7. The Psalmist (Ps. 71:9–18) also refers to the melancholy aspects of aging, such as the cessation of childbearing (Gen. 18:11–14) and the blindness of Isaac (Gen. 27:1) and Eli (1 Sam. 3:2, 4:15). Barzillai deplored his loss of taste and hearing (2 Sam. 19:35), and David suffered chills in his old age (1 Ki. 1:1–4).

It was considered the duty of the young to aid the aged person (Ruth 4:15). The famous Essene brotherhood made it its task to honor the old and to provide for them. "Just as children honored and provided for their parents, so they offered the aged all possible comfort by personal care and wise forethought" (Philo. ed. Mangery, 2, 459).

As realists, the ancient Hebrews perceived that not all aged were wise and worthy of being followed (Job 32:6–9). The preacher declared, "Better is a poor and wise child than an old and foolish king" (Eccl. 4:13). The author of the *Wisdom of Solomon* acutely observed, "Honorable old age is not represented by length of time, nor is it measured by the number of years, but understanding is gray hairs unto men and an unblemished life is ripe old age" (4:8–9).

Rabbi Judah ha-Nasi also affirmed, "Look not upon the vessel but at what is in it; for there are new vessels full of old wine and there are old vessels which do not contain even new wine" (Ab. 4:20). The Midrash also said, "There is an old age without the glory of long life, and there is long life without the ornament of age. Perfect is that old age which hath both" (Gen. R. 69).

The Handicapped

The number of blind, deaf, and other disabled persons must have been a heavy burden upon society's often meager resources in Biblical times. Congenital disabilities were commonly viewed as divine punishment for sin. It simply did not occur to early man that even persons with disability could be productive members of society. A comprehensive view of the Biblical attitude toward the handicapped follows.

In general, the Biblical view toward illness and the handicapped is that suffering is a human experience with varying causes, but that sin is a primary causative factor (Pro. 23:29–32; Ex. 15:26; Lev. 26:14–16). Other explanations offered for illness and disabilities are that they are the result of the sin of others (2 Sam. 2:15), or seduction by Satan (Matt. 9:34; Lk. 13:16; 2 Cor. 12:2). Job 1 and John 9:3 suggest that there is no definite explanation for some diseases or for man's plight. Whatever the explanation, it is a melancholy fact that, in general, the physically handicapped person was looked down upon in antiquity.

While human suffering from disease or from other conditions is generally viewed as punishment of the individual, the whole nation may also be chastised for its sins. One pervasive Biblical view holds that punishment or suffering is disciplinary and not malevolent: ". . . whom the Lord loveth He correcteth" (Pro. 3:12). Job presented the problem by expressing the thought that the human mind cannot encompass the full meaning of suffering, implying that man submit to his divinely appointed fate.

A survey of the Biblical attitudes toward various disabilities indicates that, in many ways, these attitudes still persist, especially in the less advanced areas of the world. For example, the blind, the crippled, and the lepers were social outcasts in Biblical times and were kept isolated outside the town limits. They were always paupers, neglected and disdained, who petitioned passers-by for alms. When David besieged the Jebusites at Jerusalem, the blind and crippled mendicants thronged about him in such numbers that he had to take forceful measures against them (2 Sam. 5:6).

The attitude toward the blind was that their condition was punishment for their sin or the sin of others. The Bible sought to soften this attitude by declaring that thou shalt not "put a stumblingblock before the blind" (Lev. 19:14). It also condemned those who mistreated them: "Cursed be he that maketh the blind to wander out of the way." (Dt. 27:18).

Among the nations of antiquity, however, blindness was the lowest status to which man could descend. Consequently, they did not shrink from gouging out the eyes of an enemy as a means of wreaking vengeance. Thus, the Philistines are recorded to have torn out the eyes of Samson. The king of Babylonia blinded Zedekiah, and Nahash the Ammonite requested as a condition of surrender that he blind the right eye of every man of Jabesh-Gilead as a punishment to all Israel (1 Sam. 11:2).

Both the physically handicapped and the blind were believed to possess dubious character. In the Talmud, the blind are lumped together with the leper, the childless, and the indigent in being compared to the dead (Ned. 64b) because of their pitiable status.

The Bible prohibits the blind priest from offering sacrifices on the altar (Lev. 21:18), and he was exempt from the thrice-yearly pilgrimage to Jerusalem incumbent upon normal male Jews. In modern times, however, there have been, and are, blind cantors and rabbis.

The Talmud, which employs the euphemistic term *Sagi Nahor* —"man of abundant light"—when referring to the blind, exempts the blind from all religious duties. There were, however, several blind rabbis mentioned in the Talmud who decried this attitude (Pes. 116b). Even the blind are permitted to perform any religious service for themselves but cannot serve as proxy for others.

The Talmud reveals a growing enlightened attitude toward the blind. Judah Ha-nasi, editor of the Mishnah, accompanied by another rabbi, visited a certain town. When they inquired whether there was any learned man whom they could honor by a visit, they were directed to a blind scholar. When Judah Ha-nasi's escort heard this, he volunteered to visit alone, regarding it demeaning for Judah to do so. The latter, however, insisted and went along. As they were about to leave, the blind scholar gratefully acknowledged their visit by saying, "You have honored by your visit one who is seen but sees not. You shall be blessed and acceptable before One who sees but is invisible" (Hag. 5b).

Another incident concerns Rabbi Hoshaiah the Great, who hired a blind teacher for his son and dined with him daily. Once visitors came and the teacher was not invited to the table. The rabbi later apologized, asserting that he had not wanted to embarrass or disgrace him before the group. The blind teacher retorted, "May your apology be acceptable before the Invisible" (Yer. Peah, chap. 8–end).

In the Mishnah, the ordination of a blind justice was frowned upon. However, there was a blind justice who apparently functioned to everyone's satisfaction (Sanh. 34b). A justice who is blind in only one eye may be appointed (Hoshen Mishpat 7, 21). There were cases of totally blind justices who rendered decisions which were held binding.

The following types of blindness are mentioned in the Bible: the highly infectious ophthalmia aggravated by dirt, dust, and glare; and blindness that accompanies old age such as Isaac's (Gen. 27:1), Eli's (1 Sam. 3:2), and Ahijah's (1 Ki. 14:4). Leviticus 26:16 refers to blindness resulting from malaria. Paul, who became temporarily blind along the Damascus way, may have suffered from amaurosis affecting the optic nerve (Acts 9:8). Jesus is described as having ministered to the blind (Lk. 4:18–22; Jn. 9:1–41; Mk. 8:24; Matt. 12:22, 20:30–34; Lk. 7:21). Those described as being directly punished with blindness for their sins were the men of Sodom (Gen. 19:11), the Syrian army (2 Ki. 6:18), and Elymas at Paphos (Acts 13:11).

Leprosy was another disease that was viewed as divine punishment for transgressions as well as for evil thoughts and utterances. The rabbis believed that Miriam was smitten with leprosy because she spoke disrespectfully of her brother Moses (Num. 12). Joab, his family, and his descendants were cursed by David for his treacherous murder of his rival, Abner. Gehazi aroused the ire of Elisha by his cupidity. King Uzziah was smitten with incurable leprosy for his alleged usurpation of priestly duties by burning incense on the golden altar of the temple.

Scholars maintain that the symptoms describing the so-called leprosy in the Bible indicate that the disease was not leprosy but a variation of a skin disease, psoriasis. A close description is given in Leviticus 13. Its characteristics were bright white spots or patches of skin on which the hair was white; the depression of the patches below the level of the surrounding skin; the quick, raw flesh; the spreading of the scab or scale. All this is believed to represent psoriasis.

Because the Biblical description fails to mention the typical form of leprosy, which manifests itself in a revulsive facial deformity, loss of feeling, and rotting of organs, Biblical leprosy was not really leprosy. Authentic leprosy is a slowly developing disease so that a fortnight of waiting, mentioned in Leviticus, would not have revealed any significant changes.

However, whatever the exact diagnosis of their skin malady, the following were cured of what the Bible calls leprosy: Moses cured his sister, Miriam (Num. 12:10). Naaman was cured by bathing in the waters of the Jordan River (2 Ki. 5). There is an interesting tale regarding "lepers" recorded in the Elisha stories (2 Ki. 7:3–10).

The Talmud, curiously, did not consider leprosy contagious (Neg. 3.1, 11.1). The Bible had required that those pronounced as suffering from leprosy be quarantined (Lev. 13) until the priests considered them sufficiently cured to mingle with others.

Lameness prevented a man from becoming a priest. The denial was based on the belief that his blemish would defile the altar and the holiest part of the sanctuary (Lev. 21:18, 23). It was forbidden to offer a lame animal as a sacrifice (Dt. 15:21; Mal. 1:8, 13). Malnutrition probably contributed to many spinal abnormalities. There seem to have been many orthopedically disabled persons in ancient Jerusalem (2 Sam. 5:6–8). Saul's grandson, Mephibosheth, became lame on both feet following an accident in early childhood (2 Sam. 4:4, 9:3, 13). Jesus and his followers are reported in the New Testament to have cured the lame (Matt. 11:5, 15:30; Acts 3:2–13, 8:7).

Paralysis or palsy, which involves the loss of muscular power, is also recorded to have been cured by Jesus (Mk. 2:1–17; Lk. 5:18, 7:1–10; Jn. 5:1). The case cited in Matthew 8:6 may have been acute spinal meningitis or another form of painful paralysis. The withering hand in Matthew 12:10; Luke 6:6 was probably due to a complete atrophy of the bones and muscles. There is an orthopedic disability, probably withered limbs, suffered by the man in John 5:5–9.

There were emotionally disturbed persons in antiquity as in all times. The disturbed person, however, was believed to have been invaded by some superhuman or demonic force which sometimes enabled him to be privy to extraordinary information or to possess arcane power. In the Pentateuch, however, madness was considered as divine punishment to be meted out to those who disobeyed God's laws (Dt. 28:28). There are examples of emotional frenzy in Numbers 24:3–4, 2 Kings 9:11, and Isaiah 8:19. Saul seemed to suffer from recurring bouts of depression (1 Sam. 16:14). A form of monomania appears to be described in Daniel 4–the lycanthropy of Nebuchadnezzar. There are also various emotional manifestations implicit in the cases of demoniac possession cited in Luke 11:14 and Matthew 12:22. Temporary aphasia seems indicated in Luke 1:22 and Acts 9:7. Unlike most other disabilities, it was possible for the emotionally disturbed to function and even to enjoy prestige as seers or oracles and to be paid for their services. Socially and economically, emotional instability was not always a handicap.

The Bible exhorts that "thou shalt not curse the deaf" (Lev. 19:14). In rabbinical law, the *heresh,* deaf-mute, the *shoteh,* idiot or insane, and the *katan,* minor, were grouped together for legal purposes. The ancient rabbis considered the maniac, idiot, and others who persist in needlessly exposing themselves to danger and who destroy their garments for no good reason, as irresponsible. If the deviant behavior is temporary or periodic, the sufferer is not deemed totally irresponsible but is held accountable for actions committed during his lucid period (Hag. 3b). The insane person is not regarded as responsible; "he has action but no thought" (Maksh. 3:8). Consequently, he is not able to enter into situations that require consent (Yeb. 31a) and he is considered incompetent. He cannot bear testimony, and the court can ignore claims he institutes or those instituted against him. In all civil and ritual matters, he is placed in the same category as the deaf-mute. The court must act for him and appoint a trustee for the emotionally incompetent and for minors (Ket. 48a). In Biblical times, as throughout history, the disabled person usually was unable to support himself.

Child Labor

The exploitation of child labor such as followed the Industrial Revolution is unknown in the Bible. Although children learned to aid their parents in performing chores on the farm or in the home, there is reason to believe that for most children during normal times life was reasonably pleasant.

When children were orphaned or their parents were unable to pay their debts, they were sometimes sold into slavery (Ex. 21:7; 2 Ki. 4:1; Neh. 5:5, 8; Isa. 50:1), but generally the treatment of the Jewish child even when enslaved appears to have been humane. The child probably worked along with his master in performing his assigned duties. A girl slave above the age of puberty performed both menial tasks (1 Sam. 25:41) and field labor (Ru. 2:8) and was generally also a concubine (Lev. 19:20). Her mistress considered her as her special property (Gen. 16:6, 25:12, 30:3).

While the child slave was considered chattel, he nevertheless possessed certain religious and civil rights and privileges. As a part of the master's household (Ex. 20:17), he was allowed to rest on the Sabbath (Ex. 20:10) and to share in the religious festivals (Dt. 12:12, 18). If he were maimed by his master, he was to be freed (Ex. 21:26).

See *Slave.*

Appendix IV

LABOR ORGANIZATION

Guilds

Social groupings for various purposes is a phenomenon which reaches far back in history. The formation of guilds is one example. C. H. Gordon in his *Ugaritic Literature* (page 124) declares that during the fourteenth century B.C., there was a widespread organization of guilds that included the following: herdsmen, fowlers, butchers, bakers; bronze-, copper-, and silversmiths; potters and sculptors; houseboat and chariot builders; local and long-distance traders; priests, musicians, and special classes of warriors. The Babylonian authorities recognized the guilds and negotiated tax problems with them.

With the rise of urban civilization, especially after Solomon's rule, new economic and social developments occurred that generated new trades and vocations. As a result of this specialization of labor, a new class of artisans arose. Some of them who also lived in the same community eventually grouped together for common needs and benefits. In Jerusalem there was a baker's street (Jer. 37:21), a fuller's field (Isa. 7:3), a fish gate (Neh. 3:3), a valley of craftsmen (1 Chr. 4:14), and according to Josephus, bazaars of the wool and clothing merchants and of brassworkers (B.J. 5.8.1).

Among the ancient Hebrews, the father taught the son his

skills so that as the boy matured he followed the same occupation. Later, he in turn taught his son the occupation. Consequently, in its earliest stages, the guild organization was patterned after family groupings (Neh. 3:8, 31–32; 1 Chr. 4:14). Certain Biblical expressions regarding family relations have been found to denote guild membership. Thus *Hananiyah ben Harakahim,* "son of a perfumer," signifies a member of the Perfumers' Guild; similarly, with the goldsmiths (Neh. 3:18) and craftsmen (1 Chr. 4:14), the clan of weavers of byssus (1 Chr. 4:21), scribes (1 Chr. 2:25), and the sons of the prophets (2 Ki. 2:5), who were members of the Prophets' Guild (Mendelssohn, "Guilds in Ancient Palestine," *Basor,* vol. 80, December, 1940). There is no indication, however, that these Biblical associations were as rigidly exclusive as the medieval craft guilds.

Family or dynastic occupational choices continued during the period of the Second Temple, according to the Talmud (Kid. 29a, 30b). Thus, the family of Garmu monopolized the baking of the shewbread, while that of Abtinas prepared the holy incense of the Temple (Yoma 3:11). An effort made by the Temple to break this monopoly by importing artisans failed, and the original workers had to be rehired at double their former salary (Yoma 38a).

During Talmudic times, the craftsmen of the same trade continued to inhabit individual neighborhoods and markets. The professional organization took on more of the distinctive nature of guilds. Thus, the coppersmiths and embossers had their own synagogue (Meg. 26a) and burial place (Nazir 52a) in Jerusalem. The weavers had a chief known as *rabban shel tarsayim* (Ab. Zar. 12b). Mule drivers and shipowners even carried a form of mutual insurance (B.K. 116b).

Members of different vocations would wear something representative of their occupations, such as the scribe who carried his quill in his ear (Shab. 11b; Hul. 57b); the carpenter, his rulers; the leatherworker, his apron; the carder, a woolen thread.

With the increase in the number of craftsmen, competition sometimes became bitter, giving rise to the common adage, "Every artisan hates his fellow practitioner." Nevertheless, the rabbis did not permit usurping of trade or unfair competition (Sanh. 81a). Thus, to avoid destructive competition, two butchers agreed to slaughter on alternate days (B.B. 9a, 89a).

Following the destruction of the Second Temple (70 A.D.), Jews generally lived in urban communities, and many pursued skilled vocations. In Alexandria, they followed mechanical trades. In Rome, they worked as butchers, weavers, tentmakers, and dealers in purple. In Alexandria, Jewish craftsmen lived in special sections of the city and every trade occupied a special section of the basilica there. A newly arrived craftsman would repair to the section of his fellow craftsmen to find work (Suk. 51b). In Rome, there was a synagogue of lime burners, and, in Tarsus, one of linen dealers.

Strikes

Even in Biblical times workers who felt aggrieved sought redress for their grievances by abstaining from work. When workers found their conditions intolerable, they resorted to the only weapon at their disposal—the strike. However, the strike in ancient times appears to have been a spontaneous act, unlike the planned strategy of contemporary trade unions. Probably the first known strike in history is recorded on a clay tablet by Babylonian stonecutters who struck because the king, their employer, had failed to pay them for several months.

Strikes occurred among miners, quarrymen, boatmen, workers of all sorts, royal peasants, retailers, police, and even among officials. Curiously, the strikers did not make any demands for better wages or improved working conditions; they simply stopped working out of despair over their desperate plight. One strike notice reads: "We are worn out, we will run away"—which they usually did, taking refuge in some temple offering asylum (W. W. Tarn, *Hellenistic Civilization,* page 199).

The Talmud also records a strike by two families who exercised a monopoly in the Temple. When these families struck for an increase in salary, strike breakers were brought in, but the strategy failed, and the families had to be reinstated at double their former salary (Yoma 38a).

Selected Bibliography

Albright, W. F., *Archaeology and the Religion of Israel,* Johns Hopkins Press, Baltimore, 1942.

———, *From the Stone Age to Christianity,* Johns Hopkins Press, Baltimore, 1940.

———, *The Archaeology of Palestine and the Bible,* Fleming H. Revell, New York and Chicago, 1932.

Analytical Concordance to the Bible, Wm. B. Eerdmans, Grand Rapids, Mich., 22nd edition.

Anchor Bible, Old and New Testaments, Doubleday, Garden City, New York, 1964.

Babylonian Talmud, Soncino Press, London, 1935–1952, 35 vols.

Baron, Salo W., *Social and Religious History of the Jews,* Columbia University Press, New York, 1952–1965, 10 vols., revised.

Beard, Mary, *A History of Business,* University of Michigan Press, Ann Arbor, Mich., 1962, Vol. 1.

Cambridge Ancient History, Cambridge University Press, New York, 1923–1951, 12 vols.

Douglas, J. D., *The New Bible Dictionary,* Wm. B. Eerdmans, Grand Rapids, Mich., 1962.

Encyclopedia Biblica, A. and C. Black, London, 1899–1903, 4 vols.

Encyclopaedia Brittanica, 1963 edition.

Finkelstein, L., *The Jews,* Harper, New York, 1960, 2 vols., revised.

Forbes, R. J., *Studies in Ancient Technology*, E. J. Brill, Leiden, 1955–1964, 9 vols.

Frank, T., *Economic Survey of Ancient Rome*, Johns Hopkins Press, Baltimore, 1933.

Friedlander, L., *Roman Life and Manners under the Roman Empire*, G. Routledge, London, 1910–1913, 4 vols., 7th revised ed.

Glotz, G., *Ancient Greece at Work*, Barnes and Noble, New York, 1965.

Glueck, N., *Rivers in the Desert*, Jewish Publication Society, Philadelphia, 1959.

——, *The Other Side of the Jordan*, American School of Oriental Research, New Haven, Conn., 1940.

Gordon, C. H., *Ugaritic Literature*, Pontificium Institutem Biblicum, Rome, 1949.

Hastings, J. (ed.), *Dictionary of the Bible*, T. and T. Clark, Edinburgh, 1898–1904, 5 vols.

——, *Encyclopedia of Religion and Ethics*, Scribners, New York, 1955.

——, *International Standard Bible Encyclopedia*, Wm. B. Eerdmans, Grand Rapids, Mich., 1960, 5 vols.

Interpreter's Bible, Abingdon Press, New York, 1952–1957, 12 vols.

Interpreter's Dictionary of the Bible, Abingdon Press, New York, 1962, 4 vols.

Jewish Encyclopedia, Funk and Wagnalls, New York, 1901–1906, 12 vols.

Josephus, F., *Collected Works*, Putnam, New York, 1926–1965.

Louis, Paul, *Ancient Rome at Work*, Barnes and Noble, New York, 1965.

Moore, G. F., *Judaism*, Harvard University Press, Cambridge, Mass., 1930, 3 vols.

Moscati, S., *The Face of the Ancient Orient*, Doubleday, Garden City, N.Y., 1962.

Pfeiffer, Charles F., *The Biblical World*, Baker Book House, Grand Rapids, Mich., 1966.

Pfeiffer, R. H., *Introduction to the Old Testament*, Harper, New York, 1948, revised.

Pritchard, J. B. (ed.), *Ancient Near East Texts,* Princeton University Press, Princeton, N.J., 1950.

———, *The Ancient Near East in Pictures,* Princeton University Press, Princeton, N.J., 1954.

Reifenberg, A., *Ancient Hebrew Arts,* Schocken Books, New York, 1950.

Rostovtzeff, M., *A History of the Ancient World,* Oxford University Press, New York, 1930.

———, *Social and Economic History of the Roman Empire,* Oxford University Press, New York, 1926, Vol. 2.

Singer, C. (ed.), *A History of Technology,* Clarendon Press, Oxford, 1958.

Strack, H. L., *Introduction to the Talmud and Midrash,* Jewish Publication Society, Meridian Books, New York, 1959.

Tarn, W. W., *Hellenistic Civilization,* World Publishing Co., Cleveland, 1965.

Vaux, Roland de, *Ancient Israel,* McGraw-Hill, New York, 1961.

———, *Universal Jewish Encyclopedia,* New York, 1939–1943, 12 vols.

Wischnitzer, M., *History of Jewish Crafts and Guilds,* Jonathan David, New York, 1965.

Wright, G. F., *Biblical Archaeology,* Westminster Press, Philadelphia, 1962, revised.

Zimmern, A., *The Greek Commonwealth,* Oxford University Press, Oxford Paperbacks, Great Britain, 1961.

Holy Bible, King James Version, New York Bible Society, New York.

Holy Scriptures According to the Masoretic Text, 2 vols. Jewish Publication Society, Philadelphia, 1955.